Fourth edition
THE AUSTRALIAN POLICY HANDBOOK

Catherine Althaus, Peter Bridgman & Glyn Davis

This edition published in 2007
First published in 1998

Copyright © Catherine Althaus, Peter Bridgman and Glyn Davis,
1998, 2000, 2004, 2007

All rights reserved. No part of this book may be reproduced or transmitted in any form or by any means, electronic or mechanical, including photocopying, recording or by any information storage and retrieval system, without prior permission in writing from the publisher. The *Australian Copyright Act 1968* (the Act) allows a maximum of one chapter or 10 per cent of this book, whichever is the greater, to be photocopied by any educational institution for its educational purposes provided that the educational institution (or body that administers it) has given a remuneration notice to Copyright Agency Limited (CAL) under the Act.

Allen & Unwin
83 Alexander Street
Crows Nest NSW 2065
Phone: (61 2) 8425 0100
Fax: (61 2) 9906 2218
Email: info@allenandunwin.com
Web: www.allenandunwin.com

National Library of Australia
Cataloguing-in-Publication entry:

Althaus, Catherine.
 The Australian policy handbook.

 4th ed.
 Bibliography.
 Includes index.
 ISBN 978 1 74175 331 8 (pbk.).

 1. Policy sciences. 2. Public administration - Australia.
 3. Political planning - Australia. 4. Australia - Politics
 and government. I. Bridgman, Peter, 1956– . II. Davis,
 Glyn. III. Title.

320.60994

Text design by Lisa White
Index by Russell Brooks
Set in 11/14 pt Granjon by Midland Typesetters, Australia
Printed by ANL Printers, Singapore

8 7 6 5 4 3

CONTENTS

List of figures and tables	vii
Acknowledgments	ix
Introduction: Why *The Australian Policy Handbook*?	1
1 Why policy matters	**5**
Policy as authoritative choice	6
Policy as hypothesis	7
Policy as objective	8
The policy making environment	10
Understanding policy making	11
2 The institutions of public policy	**12**
The Australian system of government	12
The executive	13
Cabinet	14
Public servants	16
Ministerial advisers	16
A map of government	17
The third sector	18
The fourth estate—the media	19
A functional map of government	20
Government as politics	21
Government as policy	21
Government as administration	23
Bringing the players together	26
Coordination through routines	28

3 A policy cycle — 32
Alternatives to the policy cycle — 34
Policy making vacuums — 36
An Australian policy cycle — 37
The policy cycle and institutions — 40
Good process and good policy — 41
Utilising the policy cycle approach — 42

4 Identifying issues — 43
The policy agenda — 43
The agenda metaphor — 44
Issue drivers — 44
What issues make the agenda? — 48
Issue attention cycle — 50
Identifying issues — 50
Defining problems — 52
Wicked and intractable problems — 53
Non-decisions — 54
Issue identification skills — 55

5 Policy analysis — 57
The purpose of policy analysis — 58
Rationality — 59
A sequence for policy analysis — 60
Evidence-based policy — 67
The analyst's toolkit — 72
Agreement: An analytic tool — 82
Why analysis? — 83

6 Policy instruments — 86
Classifying policy instruments — 87
Australian policy instruments — 88
Policy through advocacy — 89
Policy through network — 91
Policy through money — 91
Policy through government action — 92
Policy through law — 94
Choosing a policy instrument — 95

7 Consultation — 97
- The role of consultation — 97
- Deliberative democracy — 100
- Deliberative polling — 103
- Pluses and problems of consultation — 104
- Different types of consultation — 106
- Consultation instruments — 107
- Social capital and community engagement — 113
- E-consultation — 116
- Designing a consultation process — 119
- Consultation as participation — 122

8 Coordination — 124
- Network governance — 125
- Coherence — 125
- Consistency — 128
- Consultation and efficiency — 128
- Central agencies — 130
- Policy alignment — 138
- The centre versus the periphery — 142

9 Decision — 144
- Cabinet routines — 146
- What goes to cabinet? — 150
- Briefing ministers — 152
- Recording cabinet decisions — 154
- Executive council — 155
- Cabinet — 156
- Sample cover page for a cabinet submission — 157

10 Implementation — 159
- Policy design includes implementation — 160
- Policy learning and policy feedback loops — 160
- Cabinet implementation units — 163
- Political dimensions to policy implementation — 164
- Conditions for successful implementation — 166
- Implementation instruments — 167
- Implementation traps — 168
- Designing an implementation strategy — 174

Opinion polling	176
Checklists	177

11 Evaluation — 179

Evaluation and the policy cycle	180
Types of evaluation	182
Evaluation measures	183
Method	184
Findings	189
Evaluation	190

12 Managing the policy process — 191

Policy process management	192
Procedural integrity	193
Roles and ethics	194
Politicisation, professionalisation and democratisation	197
Planning projects	200
Timing	202
Management and the policy process	204
Organising for public policy: machinery of government	206
Constraints	208
Organisational choices	212
Some principles for well-organised public policy	213
Measuring policy advice performance	215
Policy capacity	217
Managing the policy process	219

Appendix 1: Checklists for policy development — 220

Policy objectives checklist	223
Policy advice objectives checklist	224
Managing the policy cycle checklist	224
Policy cycle objectives checklist	224

Appendix 2: Internet research tools for public policy — 229

Glossary	239
References	251
Index	263

FIGURES AND TABLES

FIGURES

Figure 2.1	Coordinating the three spheres of government	27
Figure 3.1	A 'policy process' approach	35
Figure 3.2	The Australian policy cycle	37
Figure 4.1	The agenda-setting process	49
Figure 5.1	The rational comprehensive approach to decision making	60
Figure 5.2	Policy analysis iteration	61
Figure 5.3	Developing policy advice	66
Figure 7.1	The consultation diamond	105
Figure 7.2	A consultation continuum	106
Figure 8.1	Best practice: whole of government	126
Figure 11.1	Opportunities for evaluation in policy formulation and implementation	181
Figure 11.2	Evaluation types	183
Figure 11.3	'Conventional' approach to evaluation	185
Figure 11.4	'Alternative' approach to evaluation (conducted within a comparative framework)	185
Figure 12.1	A sample Gantt chart	201
Figure 12.2	A sample critical path chart	202
Figure 12.3	World Bank criteria for machinery of government decisions	207

TABLES

Table 4.1	Gaining attention for an issue	56
Table 5.1	Economic analysis tools	73
Table 5.2	Australian public sector initiatives based on economic objectives	75
Table 5.3	Fundamental legislative principles	81
Table 5.4	Two models of policy analysis	83
Table 6.1	Policy through advocacy	90
Table 6.2	Policy community and policy networks: the Rhodes typology	92
Table 6.3	Policy through money	93
Table 6.4	Policy through government action	94
Table 6.5	Policy through law	95
Table 7.1	Consultation objectives and instruments	108
Table 7.2	Advantages of citizen participation in government decision making	116
Table 7.3	Disadvantages of citizen participation in government decision making	117
Table 8.1	Factors determining choice of a governance model	142
Table 9.1	Cabinet conventions and procedures	149
Table 10.1	Implementation instruments	169
Table 10.2	Implementation choices: program delivery	170
Table 11.1	Evaluation methods	187
Table 12.1	Indicative timetable for a policy cycle	203
Table 12.2	Management skills for policy officers	206
Table 12.3	Quality standards for policy advice	216
Table 13.1	Summary of the policy process	222
Table 13.2	Designing a new program	227

ACKNOWLEDGMENTS

Why write a handbook on public policy? As the original authors told readers of the *Australian Journal of Public Administration* back in 2003, they drafted *The Australian Policy Handbook* from a decidedly pragmatic perspective: to help make sense of policy processes for the puzzled (Bridgman and Davis, 2003).

In 1993 Glyn Davis took a call at Griffith University from a somewhat-panicked graduate trainee in Queensland Health. Though she had never studied politics, policy or administration, the trainee had been instructed to 'write a food nutrition strategy for Queensland quickly', in order to meet an overdue intergovernmental obligation. The most junior, inexperienced person had just been handed this daunting task, and she could find no departmental or academic publication to help. She did stumble on a public policy textbook (Davis et al., 1993), but found its emphasis on the complex and political nature of decision making unhelpful. So she turned to one of its authors hoping for some practical hints.

Independently, Peter Bridgman was also contemplating the problems facing novices to public policy. His experiences were informed by working with professional staff in a large government department. They too were often required to design significant public policy programs armed only with their disciplinary training and some bureaucratic experience. Even basic civics sometimes proved unfamiliar to those trained as engineers or lawyers. They needed a bridge from technical expertise to the policy domain.

These are commonplace experiences; most public servants do not have degrees in public policy, yet they are expected to manufacture policy products. So Glyn and Peter's thoughts turned to the usefulness of a 'primer' in the American sense, a practical, how-to guide for those encountering public policy anew. They decided to create a policy manual, a user-friendly text for public servants, something beyond the formal advice presented in cabinet handbooks. They believed such a manual should combine description with prescription, since effective action requires both. Weaved into that mixture they wanted some context about the institutions of government and an introduction to concepts informing the policy literature, so readers could pursue more critical knowledge.

In 1995 Peter led a team preparing the *Queensland Policy Handbook* (Office of the Cabinet, 1996). The *Queensland Policy Handbook* was proudly 'hands-on', even listing the phone numbers of officers who could advise on particular aspects of a cabinet submission. Launched in early 1996, the book quickly found an audience inside the local public service. Government Bookshop stocks sold out in days. However a change of government soon after publication rendered the text out of date, and though much photocopied it was not reprinted.

If this experience was any guide, Glyn and Peter suspected other public servants might welcome simple advice on writing policy. So they took the underlying concept but started writing again from scratch, producing an entirely new volume aimed at a national audience. There was no text in common across the two books but writing the first version provided a wealth of ideas for rethinking the approach. The intention remained to provide a practical grounding for public servants who might (sadly) never read another book on policy or ever engage with critical material about their practice.

A key educational challenge was how to describe the policy process in a simple, accessible way. It had to be precise, setting down in sequence the actions required to turn an aspiration for, say, a nutrition strategy into concrete, fully-costed recommendations a minister might take to cabinet. Glyn and Peter wanted this description to be memorable as it conveyed three key features:

- the dynamic, provisional, unending nature of policy effort
- a match with the familiar institutions of Australian government
- a pathway of actions to help public servants start the long journey from inchoate demand ('we need a policy') to something that could inform a cabinet decision.

They knew this path to be well trod but hoped to improve on existing schema. Many frustrating hours later, they were not so sure. They produced various two- and three-dimensional policy cycles, complex triangular designs, cycles in which each stage had its own spinning wheel, loops both open and closed. These versions succeeded in conveying complexity but not the desired intuitive step-by-step approach.

Finally they returned to classic writing in the field, in particular the writing of Harold Lasswell (1951), who characterised policy making as a sequence of intelligence; recommendation; prescription; invocation; application; appraisal; and termination. In subsequent decades many writers offered different labels but essentially stayed with the schema of policy making as a sequence of actions. Such steps were presented as not rational but logical, a chain of steps with each informing the next.

As they noted in the accompanying text, a policy cycle approach views government as a process rather than a collection of venerable institutions. It disaggregates complex phenomena into manageable steps. A policy cycle suggests a particular sequence practitioners can use to comprehend and implement the policy task. The target audience for the *Handbook* was and remains narrow—public servants who must develop a policy and guide it through the institutions of government. Hence the policy cycle starts with an issue, seeks evidence, tests proposals and puts recommendations before cabinet. Its outcomes are subject to evaluation and the cycle begins again.

First published in 1998, *The Australian Policy Handbook* quickly found an audience, and we are gratified by its continuing popularity. For this fourth edition, we are delighted to welcome co-author Catherine Althaus. She brings the perspective of a younger generation to the text, challenging some of our original assumptions and providing new insights into familiar material.

We hope this policy cycle offers a modest and flexible framework for policy makers, a way to think about the how and why of policy development. If this volume serves as a pragmatic guide for the bewildered, it will have met our aspirations.

Through multiple editions, *The Australian Policy Handbook* has drawn not just readers but critics too. Indeed, Hal Colebatch (2006) has edited an entire volume dedicated to demonstrating that policy making is more complex than the policy cycle adopted in this book.

Just so—all three editions of this book have stressed the policy cycle as a starting point for understanding. Where we disagree with Hal and others is about how to teach policy to those for whom it is not second nature, a familiar companion from a lifetime of practice or study. We argue a simple model helps order reality and provide some sense of direction. With time, it may seem too simple—but by then the model has done its work, identifying patterns in apparent chaos, helping participants build understanding and their own critical judgment.

Thus a policy cycle is a first foray into complexity, organising observations into categories and providing a guide to action. No policy model can claim universal application since every policy process is grounded in particular governmental institutions. Practice varies from problem to problem, as Edwards (2001) confirmed when she applied the policy cycle model to a range of Australian national policy histories.

A policy cycle is just a heuristic, an ideal type from which every reality will curve away. It is designed to help answer the daunting question 'What do I do now?' Following a policy cycle might assist a public servant move from vague problem to authoritative government deliberation. *The Australian Policy Handbook* offers that first step, to open up a broader world of inquiry and interest. As readers move beyond the concepts in these pages, so they begin the journey to grasping and influencing complexity.

In preparing this fourth edition, we thank again all those who inspired, assisted and cajoled—this edition is better for the comments of those teaching, inquiries from students, feedback from consultants and those on the front line of contemporary public policy. In this regard, we would particularly like to acknowledge with thanks Marcia Dwonczyk, Lewis Hawke, Anne Tiernan and Patrick Weller and, from the University of Melbourne, Andrew Norton, Donald Speagle and Syeed Ahamed. We should note again the wonderful support from Allen & Unwin, especially from Elizabeth Weiss and Clara Finlay, and recall, with familiar sadness, the shade of John Iremonger, who commissioned the original book, and reaches out still to encourage the lively debate of ideas he so enjoyed. This book is dedicated to his memory.

Catherine Althaus
Peter Bridgman
Glyn Davis

INTRODUCTION
Why *The Australian Policy Handbook*?

We shape our world through public policy.

This public policy is made not only by politicians, but by thousands of public servants and the tens of thousands of women and men who petition parliaments and ministers, who join interest groups, comment through the media or represent unions, corporations and community movements. All have a stake in public policy. The entire community is affected by public policy.

Public policy draws people, institutions, markets and governments into the familiar patterns of decision making. This necessarily means that settling and administering policy is complex, because many players influence the choices made.

Preparing a viable policy proposal can be a daunting task, requiring intense activity and coordination with other government decisions to ensure consistency. The process is long and often convoluted, as decision makers weigh up expert evidence, political and bureaucratic advice, and the competing interests of those affected by the policy proposal. Finding a way through the policy maze can seem impossible.

There are clues to guide us and skills that can be practised; despite appearances, policy processes generally follow a logic, a system. That system seeks to structure the way problems are understood and presented, so that decision makers can:

- hear about issues
- understand options
- learn of informed opinion

SNAPSHOT

The Australian Policy Handbook is designed for those embroiled in the sometimes turbulent world of public policy, that terrain between politics and public administration.

They range from senior advisers and executives to technical advisers and support staff.

Standing outside the process looking in are the students of politics and policy, and interest groups keen to influence policy choices. They too might find something of interest in these pages.

The Australian Policy Handbook offers one view of the policy process and suggestions about each step. It is designed to be pragmatic and accessible, of immediate use to practitioners, clients and those who observe. We aspire to best practice in public policy, but recognise the constraints on all who enter the maze. The cycle identified in these pages is by no means the only way to make sense of policy making. It is a systematic approach that can bring a consistent set of actions to each policy issue, thereby assisting our understanding of how the process can work and what might be possible.

- make choices
- test their decisions
- evaluate their actions.

In *The Australian Policy Handbook* we suggest a model to describe this system, a *cycle* depicting the rhythms and patterns of the policy world. This is a tool to illustrate the regular sequence of steps involved in decision making. The policy cycle is used to identify a need, explore possible responses, apply the resources and expertise of government and, finally, to test whether the desired outcome has been achieved.

The Handbook is unashamedly written from the perspective of practitioners working from within the formal government machine. Governments more than ever are feeling the limits of power. They increasingly rely on the proactive participation and involvement of the community in developing, negotiating and arbitrating policy. Of course policies bubble and coalesce within complex, iterative processes and communities. Policy making occurs in all manner of ways, emerging from all manner of sources and settling in all manner of forms. Nonetheless it is the politician, adviser and public official who are called upon—on a daily basis—to make legitimating or authoritative decisions, to provide some semblance of policy shape. It is their viewpoint and task—assigned to look out at the external world and 'make policy'—that we seek to capture here.

To some, the idea of a policy handbook might seem misguided; if policy is the artistic pinnacle of political enterprise, a policy handbook is painting by numbers.

We recognise the complexity and discretionary nature of policy decision making, but we know from experience that good process can help create better policy. By process we do not mean something mechanical or standardised; policy is too much shaped by the particular problem it addresses and by a rich constellation of laws, budgets and political circumstance to be reduced to immutable rules.

However, there *are* constants in good policy making—an intellectual rigour about issues, a commitment to procedural integrity and a willingness to experiment and learn through implementation and adaptation.

Policies are theories about the world; some flourish while others wither. The better designed the theory, the more tested its assumptions, the greater the chances for success. Process helps with design and more rigorous testing, but does not substitute for substance.

We discuss policy making in an Australian context, since local institutions and traditions help order how choices regarding policy making are reached. Because national and state governments in Australia rely on similar policy structures and routines, it should be possible to describe a process that holds across this country. Variations across jurisdictions seem less important than shared Australian assumptions about how to make public policy. Readers can substitute their particular for our general.

A policy cycle is something of an ideal—worth striving for, if not always attainable. Good process is a foundation for good policy, even though the world does not always allow for, or covet, the careful, sequential policy cycle discussed in these pages. It is important to be realistic yet strive for the best possible policy outcomes. *The Australian Policy Handbook* is a contribution to that endeavour.

1 Why policy matters

Public policy is how politicians make a difference. Politicians are the elected decision makers with formal responsibility for complex, intricate subsystems of participants and players. Policy is the instrument of governance, the decisions that direct public resources in one direction but not another. It is the outcome of the competition between ideas, interests and ideologies that impels our political system.

There have been many attempts to define 'public policy', but its meaning and boundaries remain ambiguous. Some policy documents and pronouncements are clearly expressions of public policy. Others are of uncertain status. For example:

- A bill states policy but may not pass parliament.
- A white paper states government policy intentions but these may not be realised.
- A ministerial statement might be policy, or it might just be one view on the way to the government forming a position.
- Election platforms describe a political party's intentions, but do they state the policy of the resulting government?
- Is it 'policy' when departmental activities proceed without explicit statement of intent, continuing from government to government, never exciting public interest or political scrutiny?

Hal Colebatch (1998, 2006) has explored the many definitions offered for 'public policy'. Often, policy is no more than 'whatever governments choose to do or not to do'. Sometimes we use the term to describe very specific choices, but the notion also embraces

SNAPSHOT

We can agree public policy is important without being certain of the definition. However, we can describe some important characteristics of public policy. It:

- is intentional, designed to achieve a stated or understood purpose
- involves decisions, and their consequences
- is structured and orderly
- is political in nature
- is dynamic.

This chapter describes public policy as an authoritative statement by a government about its intentions. It also views public policy as relying on hypotheses about cause and effect, and as structured around objectives.

Policy implies:

- authority
- expertise
- order.

Colebatch (1998:7)

general directions and philosophies. There are also times when 'policy' becomes clear only in retrospect; we look back and discern the patterns and continuities of a set of choices, and call these 'policy'.

This multitude of meanings is inevitable, since policy is a shorthand description for everything from an analysis of past decisions to the imposition of current political thinking.

This chapter describes policy in three different but compatible ways. First, policy can be the *authoritative choice* of a government. Second, policy is an *hypothesis*, an expression of theories about cause and effect. Finally, policy is explored as the *objective* of governmental action.

POLICY AS AUTHORITATIVE CHOICE

Public policy emerges from the world of politics. This can be a chaotic place in which ideas must find a path between the intentions of politicians, the interests of various government institutions, the interpretations of bureaucrats and the intervention of pressure groups, media and citizens.

> Public policy is 'deciding at any time and place what objectives and substantive measures should be chosen in order to deal with a particular problem, issue or innovation'.
> *Dimock et al. in Colebatch (1993:33)*

Central to this political world is the executive, that group of ministers around the leader, who exercise the authority of government on behalf of the parliament. Ministers understand the political nature of their work, but also appreciate that other players need authoritative statements of policy direction. Power is exercised through the ability to issue directives and decisions expressing intention. Through policies, governments make their mark. From the chaos of politics must emerge the certainty of action.

> Public policy is about what governments do, why, and with what consequences.
> *Fenna (2004:3)*

Policy, then, can be seen as an authoritative response to a public issue or problem. This suggests that public policy:

> Politics is about who gets what, when and how.
> *Lasswell (1951)*

- is *intentional*; public policy means pursuing specific government goals through the application of identified public or private resources
- is about *making decisions* and testing their consequences
- is *structured*, with identifiable players and a recognisable sequence of steps
- is *political* in nature, expressing the electoral and program priorities of the executive.

Policies reached through a decision making framework:

- express a considered response to a policy issue
- help shape a government's philosophy
- are an authoritative framework of the government's beliefs and intentions in the policy area.

Policy decisions are authoritative because they are made by people with legitimate power in our system of government. These decisions might bind public servants to act in a particular way, or direct future action (such as preparing legislation for parliament's consideration) or allocate money to a program.

But realistically, even authoritative decisions may not be realised with the slip between hope and outcome all too familiar. Nor does the authoritative nature of public policy mean that government has deliberated on every issue. Each government must work from the legacy of its predecessors, and comfortable bureaucratic routines often reflect an ancient policy decision. It is all the more important, then, for a well developed policy process to ensure that intentions are regularly considered and examined against results.

POLICY AS HYPOTHESIS

Policies are built on theories of the world, models of cause and effect. Policies must make assumptions about behaviour. They contain incentives that encourage one behaviour over another, or disincentives to discourage particular actions. Policies must incorporate guesses about take-up and commitment, and mechanisms to deal with shirking and encourage compliance.

But public policy is not a laboratory experiment, and it is difficult to test behavioural assumptions before a policy is implemented. Cabinet might, for example, judge that a package of taxation measures will elicit a desired response from the citizens. Until the government announces the tax and measures its effects, ministers remain unsure whether they have correctly identified cause and effect in the tax system.

Policy is created amid uncertainty, and tested in the most demanding of circumstances. Policy makers learn by finding and correcting errors in policy assumptions and design. They

PUBLIC POLICY VERSUS PRIVATE POLICY

Public policy is a course of action by government designed to attain specific results. Non-government organisations have policies too, but they cannot call on public resources or legal coercion in the same way.

Policy can be seen as:

- a label for a field of activity
- an expression of general purpose or desired state of affairs
- specific proposals
- decisions of government arising from crucial moments of choice
- formal authorisation—a specific act or statute
- a program—a particular package of legislation, organisations and resources
- output—what government actually delivers, as opposed to what it has promised or has authorised through legislation
- the product of a particular activity
- theory—if we do X, then Y will follow
- a process unfolding over a long period of time.

Adapted from Hogwood and Gunn (1990:13–19)

improve policy by recognising changes in the environment as well as associated shifts in the needs and desires of the community and elected officials. Time can completely transform the policy making environment and this must be accommodated. Opportunities should be exploited, risks managed. Appreciation for policy environment is as important as shifts in government priorities, resources and contexts.

Good policy processes will make behavioural assumptions explicit, so that decision makers understand the model of the world that supports a recommendation. To think of policy as hypothesis puts into words the mental calculations that guide all policy advisers and makers.

Understanding policy as hypothesis also stresses the importance of learning from policy implementation and evaluation. Good policy making assumes an ability to draw lessons from policy experience and to apply those lessons in the next turn through the policy cycle. Given the multiple players in policy making, and the often drawn-out processes involved, incorporating policy learning can be difficult. As Levi-Faur and Vigoda-Gadot (2006:254) point out, policy learning is not an uncritical transfer of policy such that governments become 'rule takers rather than rule makers'. Hence the need for a structured policy process, so that learning is documented and passed on with an eye for extracting useful lessons and general principles that might be applied locally to particular demands. Only then can opportunities be exploited and risks managed.

American policy analyst Aaron Wildavsky (1987:393) observed, 'we hope that new hypotheses expand into theories that better explain the world'. These better theories, guided by the results of evaluation, become the basis for improved public policies.

POLICY AS OBJECTIVE

Public policy is ultimately about achieving objectives. It is a means to an end. Policy is a course of action by government designed to attain certain results.

The policy process must help decision makers clarify their objectives. A policy without purpose may do a great deal of harm. When policies that lack point or coordination take effect, programs begin to draw in different directions, the overall strategy disappears, and commentators soon speak of a government 'losing its way'.

Good policy advice avoids this trap by making explicit:

- the form of authoritative statement required
- the model of cause and effect underpinning the policy
- the goals to be achieved.

As later chapters illustrate, an effective policy cycle checks a particular policy proposal against the broader objectives of government. Through consultation and interaction, the policy cycle encourages consistency, so a new policy will fit into the wider picture of government activity. Public policy is made by many people, in a chain of processes that includes analysis, implementation, evaluation and reconsideration.

This coordination is only possible, though, if policy objectives are stated clearly and honestly. When intentions are uncertain or contradictory, a policy has little chance of success. Setting an objective is the first step in a long process. It is also the most important since only an objective can give point and reason to a public policy choice.

It is easy to lose sight of policy objectives. The 'solution' may become more important than the problem. Policy activity is very fast moving; once a decision is made, work gathers momentum. Time and authority to reflect on the chosen direction are limited, allowing a poor decision to cascade into a policy far removed from the original intention.

Objectives may be overtaken by unintended consequences—side effects discovered only after the policy is implemented, and which undermine the policy's effect or create new, complex problems. A scheme to license a particular activity can create a powerful elite, strongly wedded to the policy and so politically influential that later modification becomes costly and difficult. Taxation relief may distort the market for goods or services other than those originally targeted.

To keep policies focused on objectives, policy makers rely on a policy cycle that includes project planning and evaluation. Along the way they are likely to ask:

- What is the purpose of the policy?
- How will it affect:
  — overall government direction
  — the department
  — client groups
  — interest groups
  — society?
- What is the relationship between the means of implementation and the policy objectives?
- Are there other means of implementation that are simpler?
- How will this policy relate to other government objectives?
- Can it make a difference in the ways intended?

Through a systematic policy cycle, decision makers seek an authoritative choice, based on a plausible hypothesis, that can deliver required outcomes. This deceptively simple formula sums up the challenge of good public policy.

THE POLICY MAKING ENVIRONMENT

Viewing policy as an authoritative choice, based on plausible hypotheses that can deliver required objectives, compels us to consider the environment within which policy making occurs. Attention to the policy making environment raises new questions as well as demanding consistent tackling of enduring issues. Society continues to grapple with how to allocate scarce resources and provide basic services such as health, education, community order and transport. Governments continue to tax and spend, to regulate and reform, to legislate and monitor, to engage in conflict as much as to seek peace. The political landscape is familiar in its constraints and opportunities.

But today there are overlays that lend new parameters to the policy making arena. The demands of globalisation and localisation promote new ways of looking at the world and fresh calls for innovative cultural practices that deliver global solidarity at the same time as renewed local identity. Changed technologies have also created an invasive media presence and a communications focus based on emotional persuasion, marketing and promotion. It has been said that policy making is nine-tenths press release and one-tenth substance. In the contemporary

> We have two types of politicians—the incapable and those capable of anything.
> *Slogan written on a wall in Paraguay,* The Economist *(2001)*

policy making environment, good policy ideas are assessed for their emotive fit as much as—and often rather than—against criteria of logic, consistency, intellectual rigour or political coherence. Timing imperatives, too, have shifted to accommodate the pressures of continual media scrutiny resulting in policy makers being forced to account for their actions, respond to disasters and present solutions on hand with breathtaking immediacy. Disenchantment and institutional breakdown are propelling shifts towards greater participation and trust-building activities. Governments are moving to engage in networked governance and more fluid interaction between different sectors of society in the policy process.

These are just some of the overarching factors characterising the contemporary policy making milieu. Their detail will be canvassed in later chapters of this handbook as we progress around the policy cycle. The point for now is that policy makers are expected to be attentive to the policy making environment, no matter how subtle or dramatic the shifts in terrain or how familiar the landscape might appear.

UNDERSTANDING POLICY MAKING

Policy making matters in the academic literature as much as in political practice. The literature is home to a range of models and debates, sparking critique and stimulating reappraisal of mindsets and approaches. These contending texts are encouraging evidence of a concerted pursuit of improved policy making processes and understandings. Policy makers should always glean the value of original or improved frameworks for appreciating the policy process in an effort to secure improved practical outcomes.

DIFFERENT WAYS OF CONCEPTUALISING THE POLICY MAKING PROCESS

A wide array of debates and theories exist in the literature as theoreticians aim to assist practitioners understand and appreciate the policy making process. Some latest edition texts to consider include:

Bardach, E. 2000. *A Practical Guide for Policy Analysis*, New York: Chatham House.

Birkland, T.A. 2005. *An Introduction to the Policy Process: Theories, Concepts and Models of Public Policy Making*, Armonk: ME Sharpe.

Colebatch, H.K. (ed.) 2006. *Beyond the Policy Cycle: The Policy Process in Australia*, Sydney: Allen & Unwin.

Considine, M. 2005. *Making Public Policy: Institutions, Actors, Strategies*, Cambridge: Polity Press.

Fischer, F. 2003. *Reframing Public Policy: Discursive Politics and Deliberative Practices*, Oxford: Oxford University Press.

Geva-May, I. (ed.) 2005. *Thinking Like a Policy Analyst: Policy Analysis as a Clinical Profession*, New York, Palgrave Macmillan.

Kay, A. 2006. *The Dynamics of Public Policy: Theory and Evidence*, Cheltenham UK: Edward Elgar.

Kjaer, A. 2004. *Governance*, Malden MA: Policy Press.

Pal, L.A. 2006. *Beyond Policy Analysis: Public Issue Management in Turbulent Times*, 3rd edn, Toronto: Thomson Nelson.

Radin, B. 2000. *Beyond Machiavelli, Policy Analysis Comes of Age*, Washington DC: Georgetown University Press.

Weimer, D.L. and Vining, A.R. 2005. *Policy Analysis: Concepts and Practice*, 4th edn, Upper Saddle River NJ: Pearson Prentice Hall.

2 The institutions of public policy

SNAPSHOT

Public policy cannot be separated from its institutional context. Policy is essentially an expression of the political will of a government.

So for policy professionals and for partisan participants alike, an understanding of the nature of government and the political dynamic is crucial.

In this chapter, the traditional hierarchical theory of responsible government is complemented by a functional division of government into political, policy and administrative roles to explain the reality of the institutions and operations of government.

Governments pursue their objectives by implementing policy. A statement of public policy is therefore a statement of political priorities. In the Australian system of government, though, not all actors involved in policy formulation are political. Indeed, much policy advice is prepared by public servants committed to notions of professional neutrality. The system must find ways to mesh such impartial expert advice with a political perspective.

This chapter sketches the institutional context of policy making. It offers both the formal model of the Australian political system—usually described as 'responsible government'—and a more dynamic representation of the interaction between politicians, advisers and the public service.

THE AUSTRALIAN SYSTEM OF GOVERNMENT

Australia is a liberal democracy. Emy and Hughes (1991:226–63) broadly define a liberal democracy as referring to a political system heavily influenced by liberal concepts of politics characterised by belief in the individual, a consensual theory of society, belief in reason and progress, and suspicion of concentrated forms of power. It is hybrid polity organised according to particular views of power, legitimacy, justice and freedom.

The Australian system of government melds notions of ministerial responsibility, drawn from the House of Commons in the Palace of Westminster in London, with a federal Senate modelled on US practice. It includes a governor-general, as the representative of the Queen, and a powerful executive that reflects party domination of the parliament. This unique system, given national expression in the Commonwealth Constitution of 1900, combines parliamentary government with federal institutions.

Australian governments gain their authority and legitimacy through the electoral process. A compulsory universal franchise makes voting both a civic privilege and a duty for all adults. The people elect representatives to serve in the parliament and to exercise power on their behalf. In Australia, the national and state political scenes are characterised by two strong, major party blocs that typically 'make the formation of governments manageable' (Lovell et al., 1998:256) by creating a system of disciplined support that provides electoral advantage and contributes to policy formulation. These political parties are a link between voters and governments that, from federation, has shaped Australian voting sentiments, thereby helping to structure political representation as well as the authority chain between institutions (Lucy, 1993).

Responsible government is traditionally described through its three main activities:

1. *legislative*, or the making of laws, exercised by parliament
2. *executive*, or the administration and enforcement of the law, and the management of the resources of government. This function is carried out by ministers and the administrative agencies of government such as departments and statutory authorities
3. *judicial*, the application and interpretation of the law to particular cases. This is the function of the courts.

The responsible government system allows for some overlap between these roles. Ministers are also members of parliament. Parliament delegates some law-making power to the executive. The judiciary, though, comprises independent judges who value highly their separation from political decision making.

THE EXECUTIVE

The principal focus of *The Australian Policy Handbook* is the executive arm of government. The various Australian, state and

Hugh Emy and Owen Hughes (1991:338–9) identify five key components of Australian responsible government:

- Formal constitutional authority is vested in the governor-general, as the Queen's representative.
- In practice, executive authority is exercised by ministers individually and collectively. They meet as a cabinet to make choices on policy issues.
- The executive can be dismissed from office by losing an election, or by losing a confidence vote in the House of Representatives. The Senate may block supply, depriving the government of sufficient money to continue its programs.
- The executive is advised by a career public service, committed to serving 'without fear or favour'. The public service advises but does not govern; final decisions are the prerogative of ministers.
- The system is kept honest and open by a direct accountability link 'running from officials to a minister and so to cabinet; then from ministers and cabinet to parliament, and from parliament and the cabinet to the electorate'.

In practice, of course, 'things are a good deal more complicated'.

> ... the most intense hatreds are not between political parties but within them ...
> *Phillip Adams*

The Australian form of government is an innovation, drawing on Australian colonial traditions, British concepts of responsible government and American models of federalism. The result is captured in a written constitution and the surrounding constitutional conventions, the major features of which are a federal division of powers, a strong parliament, a separate Australian judiciary which reviews the constitutional validity of legislation, and an Australian representative of the monarch who exercises nearly all his or her functions on the advice of the executive and who performs the national ceremonial role normally associated with a head of state.
Republican Advisory Committee (1993:38)

Due process is ... an important safeguard against overloading decision makers. The processes involved in getting issues to the cabinet table are designed to assist cabinet to focus on broad strategic matters rather than petty detail. As far as possible details and questions of fact are settled outside cabinet by ministers and their advisers and, if necessary, by the appropriate cabinet committee.
Keating (1996:64)

territory constitutions vest formal authority in the executive council. However, the governor-general, governor or administrator is only a symbolic repository of power. The real authority of government is exercised by cabinet.

The principles of responsible government make parliament paramount. The executive must comply with parliament's wishes, expressed as legislation. Parliament can and does amend proposals made by the government, and monitors executive activity through an extensive committee system. Yet in practical terms, the executive controls the legislative program of the parliament. The executive will fall if it loses the confidence of the lower house. Ministers hold office because they are part of a majority in the lower house.

The executive arm of government comprises the ministers, who are responsible for the policy directions of government departments and agencies under their supervision. Ministers must account to parliament for their stewardship of public service functions. Short of personal impropriety, though, resignations for poor administration are exceedingly rare in Australia (Thompson and Tillotsen, 1999).

CABINET

The cabinet is a meeting of ministers, chaired by the prime minister, premier or chief minister, at which political and policy decisions are made. Not all ministers necessarily sit in cabinet; the Commonwealth cabinet comprises only the most senior ministers although junior ministers may be present when cabinet considers issues affecting their portfolios. State and territory cabinets usually include all ministers.

Cabinet is the apex of government, the institution that must consider political, policy and administrative implications of any proposition, and settle a government position. Though a body without formal legal standing, it is the source for an authoritative allocation of government resources.

> Despite the power and significance of cabinet, it is essentially an informal body governed largely by convention. There is no reference to cabinet, or to the other key office of prime minister, in the Constitution ... This informality

has generally been seen as an advantage, providing much needed flexibility that has allowed cabinet to evolve with changing political patterns. (Keating and Weller, 2000:46)

Patrick Weller (1990:33) argues that cabinet performs at least six major roles:

- Cabinet as a *clearing house*—across government, committees meet and choices are reached that require ratification. Cabinet acts as a clearing house for this activity. Including a matter on the cabinet agenda makes all ministers aware of issues that may have been handled by a small committee, and provides an authoritative decision on an issue.
- Cabinet as an *information exchange*—government is so complex ministers can find it difficult to see beyond their own portfolio role. Weekly meetings of cabinet ensure ministers see the broader picture, and know what their colleagues are doing.
- Cabinet as *arbiter*—when government agencies disagree, cabinet provides a forum for resolution. More generally, cabinet arbitrates the inevitable tensions over resources and priorities that every government must address. This role is particularly important in the annual budget process, when agencies and programs compete for limited resources.
- Cabinet as *political decision maker*—though signed by ministers, most submissions put before cabinet are written by public servants. Cabinet must cast a political eye over policy proposals, asking about the electoral consequences of a course of action.
- Cabinet as *coordinator*—since agency responsibilities often overlap, policies that contradict initiatives elsewhere in government may arise. Cabinet is the only institution that can impose a coherent overall direction for government, by ensuring coordination of policies.
- Cabinet as *guardian of the strategy*—a government needs to set overall themes and objectives for its term in office, yet ministers can quickly become locked into a departmental perspective, seeing all issues from the narrow view of their own policy concerns. Cabinet is the forum that balances the

---

CABINET COMPOSITION

It is the prime minister who decides on the size of the cabinet and who determines which ministers are to be included in the cabinet.
John Howard (1998:4)

PORTFOLIO MINISTERS

The prime minister sets out his priorities and strategic direction for each portfolio in a letter sent to respective ministers shortly after they are appointed. This letter may also indicate in broad terms how the prime minister sees functions being shared by ministers in the portfolio.
John Howard (1998:3)

Prime ministers must work with their ministerial colleagues and through the institution of cabinet. In Australia, executive government is collective in its form and its expectations. The influence of the prime ministers and their impact on policy will depend on their capacity to cajole, persuade or bully cabinet colleagues—either individually or collectively—into accepting their approach or their solutions.
Patrick Weller (1992:5)

particular with the general, so encouraging ministers to see issues from a 'whole of government' viewpoint.

In performing these multiple roles, cabinet often relies on the chair. It is the prime minister who must look to the overall strategy, and weigh the benefits of a proposal against the goals of the government. There is no rational calculus guiding cabinet in many of its choices, only a willingness to think through all the implications of a submission and judge which course of action is best for the government and for the polity.

Ministers are assigned responsibility for certain organisational structures of government, the departments and agencies, and for administration of various laws and programs. The acts, organisations and programs listed in the administrative arrangements order make up the minister's portfolio. Each minister at the cabinet table represents portfolio concerns, and presents the portfolio's proposals for consideration.

PUBLIC SERVANTS

Public servants are part of the executive arm of government. Not all public service work is directly concerned with policy development, but all public service endeavour is affected by public policy. The work of public servants is driven by the policy priorities of the government of the day.

Thus service delivery, administration and policy advice are integrated into the work of government and its political direction. In the ideal responsible government system, public servants advise governments on policy but do not become involved in direct political questions. These are the prerogative of the cabinet and of parliament. According to this simplistic model, ministers make decisions, while public servants offer advice and then implement government choices.

MINISTERIAL ADVISERS

There is a third significant group within the Australian executive who, since the 1970s, have played a critical role in policy making. Ministerial staff are appointed as partisan activists to 'provide a firewall around ministers' (Walter, 2006:26). Their role has expanded greatly due to spiralling pressures placed on ministers

---

The centre of government must constantly provide some cohesion and coherence in the development of policy, while maintaining political support for its actions. These are the great challenges for cabinet government.
Keating and Weller (2000:45)

to respond to media demands, as well as the ever-increasing expectations associated with the ministers' departmental and parliamentary roles.

Ministerial advisers are anomalies in the Westminster chain. While the *Members of Parliament (Staff) Act 1984* governs the employment framework of such staff, the accountability processes surrounding their role and activities are substantially outdated (Tiernan, 2007). Ministerial staff variously serve 'to mediate between the political and administrative domains; to drive, sieve and skew advice; and to insist upon what the minister wants as opposed to the public interest or the integrity of the policy process' (Walter, 2006:24).

Ministerial advisers are useful helpers for ministers in the policy making process. They can also assist public servants by being significant contributors in the endeavour of achieving ministerial attention and approval of policies. Their inclusion in the system as an authoritative force, interposed between political decision makers and neutral officials, however, muddies any neat model of responsible government.

> The growth of ministers' personal staff was originally thought to create a rival source of policy advice, added means of interfering in the work of the public service and more opportunity for ministers to exercise influence without responsibility. Like public servants, ministerial staff are accountable through ministers to the parliament and to the people... Working well, staff are an extension of busy ministers enabling them to cover a much wider range of policy issues and to scrutinise a wider range of program administration.
> *Tony Abbott, May 2002*

A MAP OF GOVERNMENT

This standard picture of responsible government offers a chain of accountability: public servants answer to ministers, ministers to parliament, parliament to the people. Some institutions, though, do not fit into this simple scheme. The courts can override the executive in some issues but are not accountable to the people. Further complications arise from administrative law, with its accountability measures outside the standard chain. Still, the familiar institutions of parliament, the executive, the public service and the courts are usefully defined and linked by the responsible government model.

Of course, theoretical niceties do not always explain or allow for the vagaries of reality and policy makers ignore complexities and additional actors at their peril. The modern policy sphere is influenced by input from key players who are traditionally seen outside the formal political system. One of the most influential of these is the business sector, but there is also the third sector and the fourth estate. Recognition of these players is essential to building alternative perspectives on how Australian governments actually operate.

> Peter Shergold, Secretary of the Department of Prime Minister and Cabinet... admitted to having about 250 meetings a year with business or community groups... A parliamentary secretary today no longer enjoys a monopoly on the advice going to the minister. Different government agencies, political advisers, advocacy and lobby organisations and public and private think tanks now vie for the attention of government.
> *Fitzgerald (2006:16)*

THE THIRD SECTOR

Lyons (2001:5) defines the third sector as 'organisations that are not part of the public or business sectors'. It is often referred to as the non-profit sector, the social economy, civic or civil society, the non-government organisation (NGO) sector, the community sector, or the voluntary sector. Third sector organisations are:

- private
- formally organised
- the product of collective action that generates common value and benefit
- voluntary in nature
- not seeking personal profit
- usually democratically controlled (Lyons, 2001:6–9).

The sector is diverse and includes lobby and interest groups as well as community groups and think tanks that span a huge array of activities, sizes, structures and objectives.

Australian culture and history has seen the third sector play a significant role in society. Approximately 65 per cent of Australians belong to at least one third sector organisation with some 40 per cent describing themselves as active members (Lyons, 2001:xi). While Australians only donate to third sector organisations at about half the rate found in the United States, Australians have a high record of voluntary activity in comparable international terms (Commonwealth Department of Family and Community Services, 2005:ix).

There is a two-way interaction between the third sector and government (Fitzgerald, 2006). The third sector can often be involved in the delivery of government services as well as playing a role in lobbying government on particular issues. They can act as an alert mechanism for government but primarily act to secure certain goals on behalf of their constituents or representative interests. Third sector organisations can provide a useful source of information for politicians who can also use them to influence certain voting blocs or community opinion. Either way, the third sector contributes in significant ways to the development, implementation and evaluation of policies (even

---

Governments can provide financial support to the third sector under five different models:

- Philanthropy (e.g. gambling, arts and sports funding)
- Submission (e.g. matching grant capital/infrastructure funding)
- Planning (e.g. consumer organisations)
- Quasi-voucher (e.g. childcare and nursing home funding)
- Competitive tender (e.g. employment services).

Lyons (2001:183–90)

The most comprehensive research on philanthropy in Australia has found that Australians and businesses are giving and volunteering more than ever before, contributing more than $11 billion in 2004 ... Comparing giving in Australia with the USA in 2004 we find that giving as a proportion of GDP in the USA is 1.6% and for Australia it is 0.68% ... When difference in the size of economies is taken into account, the USA generates more than twice the level of giving than Australia, and Australians give about one and a half times as much as Canadians on average.

Giving Australia: Research on Philanthropy in Australia, *(2005, www.partnerships.gov.au/philanthropy/philanthropy_research.shtml)*

if Lyons and Passey (2006) suggest that Australia, comparatively, is slow institutionally and intellectually in encouraging third sector involvement). Along with the business sector, the contribution of the third sector cannot be ignored.

THE FOURTH ESTATE—THE MEDIA

Another prominent actor in the policy process is the media, sometimes referred to as the fourth estate (Schultz, 1998; Young, 2007). The term derives from the early 19th century, during the age of revolutions, and refers to the rise of press influence alongside that wielded by the traditional three estates of parliament—the king and church, the lords and nobility, and the common people.

The position of the media changed dramatically following the inception of the printed press. Television and digital technology marked further advances. The modern advent of internet, virtual reality communications, and citizen journalism through minute-by-minute blogging and international reporting practices are also contributing to new ways of communicating. It is these changes that help shape political life.

Today, the media is more than a scrutineer, watchdogging on behalf of the public interest. It can become a de facto opposition in which democratic institutions or practices are thin. Most certainly it is a player, a powerful framer of political action. The mass media promotes politics as an entertainment medium (Schwartzenberg, 1980) and has elevated communication as a dominant currency to be traded in the political sphere. The media is not a passive player in the communication game. It is an influential contributor, structuring the game as well as being the subject of political activity on the part of governments and all the other players in society seeking particular ends.

Focus on the third sector and the fourth estate brings attention to social movements: widescale social change or transformation that emerges not from any particular group but from shifts in society concerning particular values or ideals. An example of a social movement is the global environmental concern which cuts across classes, national borders and traditional groups to span the entire community.

> In all my life I have treated the press with marked contempt and remarkable success.
> *Sir Robert Menzies to American president Richard Nixon*

> The debate has taken on a hopeful Zen-like quality for besieged politicians: If a crime occurs and no one is around to reveal it or to report it, does it really exist?
> *Jonathan Turley on domestic surveillance by the National Security Agency,* USA Today, *2006*

> Many of our commentators are polarised between their genitals and their minds; they seem to have suffered a complete heart bypass.
> *Caroline Jones, Australian television and radio journalist*

A FUNCTIONAL MAP OF GOVERNMENT

Policy makers act within the confluence of all these players and ideas. How we view our Australian system of government will shape our perception of who and what is important and guide attention to what is possible in moulding the policy process.

There are yet other ways to look at the players within Australian government.

A functional approach sets hierarchical notions aside and considers government from the perspective of three key coordination tasks (Davis, 1996:19):

- *Politics*. In a parliamentary system, governments must be seen to be united and coherent, to speak with one voice. Such consistency is an important political virtue, portraying a shared philosophy and shared goals. Politics is not only about implementing party platform; it also involves attaining and keeping government through policies that attract voters. While philosophy and ideology are important, pragmatic politics will pervade every government's judgments about the consequences of its decisions.
- *Policy*. A government stands or falls on its policy choices. These choices must be well considered and sufficiently coordinated so that one policy does not undermine another. Governments need to develop and monitor policy, and to achieve consistency across the many agencies which make up a modern public sector. The formulation of public policy is thus a key government task.
- *Administration*. Policies mean nothing if not implemented. Typically this means relying on the public servants or contractors who work for government. Ministers are accountable for efficient, effective and honest administration, and answer for the programs in their portfolios.

Some overlap is inevitable between these functions. Ministers perform political roles, but are also involved in policy development and administration. Public servants are principally focused on policy advice and administration, but must also be sensitive to the political circumstances of their ministers. Viewing the

---

A politically impartial public service is one which can act with equal efficiency for either side of politics—not one which picks and chooses which government policies to implement. The provision of 'frank and fearless' advice should not be confused with becoming an in-house opposition.
Tony Abbott, May 2002

... when it comes to the crunch, outcomes are decided in the practical world of political conflict, compromise and consensus-building rather than according to some ideal of rational choice informed by objective analysis.
Painter (1998:125)

political system in terms of political, policy and administrative tasks helps separate roles while providing some sense of the interplay between governmental players. The following sections outline each of these roles, and its characteristic participants, in more detail.

GOVERNMENT AS POLITICS

Walk around Parliament House in Canberra and the intense activity is hard to miss. Parliament is the centre of the political world, the place where ministers put in long hours governing while their opposition numbers plot and scheme to bring them down. Around the politicians are their advisers, partisan figures hired to assist with political strategy and media presentation. Many also develop significant policy expertise in their own right, and offer ministers alternative political views about appropriate courses of action. While the public service tradition endures from one government to the next, advisers hold office only while their patron prospers. Their terms may be very influential but short lived.

At the centre of the political world is the office of the leader—the prime minister in Canberra, the premier or chief minister in the states and territories. In a parliamentary setting, prime ministers are powerful but not presidential; they are still subject to the party in power, and can be removed from office by their own side at any time. Prime ministers must offer effective and strong leadership, while maintaining party room support. The standard test is electability—leaders who seem likely to win the next election can usually carry their colleagues in any challenge.

Leaders matter because they provide a public identity for a government, and a sense of coherence and direction. Leaders play a political role, but they are also the point at which politics must be married with policy and administration. While advisers are largely confined to the political world, prime ministers must reach beyond the confines of Parliament House to engage the broader agenda of public policy.

GOVERNMENT AS POLICY

When politicians become ministers, they assume responsibility for public policy outcomes. This requires ministers to work

> It is expecting too much for a politician to be sincerely interested in the free flow of information.
> Graham Perkin—Editor of the Age, Melbourne

> The sheer complexity of government makes it hard for decision makers, especially ministers, to do their job effectively. There is so much to be read and understood. This does not just include the paperwork associated with the portfolio and cabinet. It includes newspapers, journals and the wide world of books. It has been observed that men and women who do not read are not fit to govern, yet ministers and chief executives rarely have time to do so.
> David Newman, public servant

together as a cabinet in setting goals for the government. Policy duties also bring ministers into regular contact with the public service, and so into a world wider than politics.

At the centre of the policy system is cabinet, with its multiple roles and never-ending workload. To manage cabinet business, including the huge paper flow involved in circulating submissions and decisions, governments rely on a central policy agency and/or cabinet secretariats (sometimes located outside of the department). In Canberra this is the Department of Prime Minister and Cabinet (PM&C) working with the now partisan-appointed Cabinet Secretary, and in many states a department of the premier and cabinet or an office of the cabinet. As well as partially handling the logistics of cabinet meetings, PM&C provides the prime minister, as chair of cabinet, with a detailed briefing on all submissions (Walter, 1992; Weller, 2007). This ensures the prime minister has a comprehensive set of briefing notes on all government business and can interrogate any minister about the detail of a submission. Officials from PM&C also sit in on cabinet meetings and take detailed notes, though they never speak unless asked a direct question by the chair; in some states all public servants are banned from the cabinet room unless required to make a technical presentation on some matter.

> The primary role of PM&C is to coordinate government policy in total by ensuring that decisions taken across government are consistent with each other and with the policy decided by cabinet. What this effectively amounts to is an attempt to resolve conflicts between departments before they get to cabinet and to ensure that departments actually implement cabinet decisions.
> *Matheson (2000:44)*

Whereas the political domain draws primarily on parliamentarians, their political advisers, the party political machines and the organised lobbies, the policy domain inevitably draws on the wider public sector. Much of the substantive policy development takes place in government agencies, at interdepartmental committees, and on consultative bodies. It relies on expert and impartial bureaucratic advisers as well as the input of interested parties and specialist experts. Policy might be finalised in the political forum of cabinet, but this is frequently done on the basis of advice from professional public servants complemented with information and perspectives from other policy process participants.

This policy world is in one sense a rule-bound place, in which submissions and decisions follow strict formats, with clear roles ascribed to central agencies, keen to maintain the quality and accuracy of cabinet material. In the 'ideal' version of this model the authoritative nature of cabinet decisions demands that choices be reached on the basis of full and relevant information, succinctly stated options, and clear articulation of the advantages and problems of any proposal.

GOVERNMENT AS ADMINISTRATION

To be effective, policies rely on the resources and power of government. Once choices are made, activity must be directed to achieving the intended objective. This is the domain of administration, in which services are delivered, taxes collected, laws enforced.

The public service, that collection of departments and agencies, staff and resources making up the machinery of government, resides in this domain. Here ministers preside, responsible to the parliament for the administrative detail of how staff, money and other resources are deployed, how policies are implemented and whether they realise the objectives set by government. However, it is departmental and street-level staff (Lipsky, 1983) rather than the ministers who do most of the day-to-day policy work.

The division of labour between minister and public servant becomes crucial in the administrative domain. Ministers rely on chief executives to understand and pursue their political priorities, and on public servants to act in the interests of the government of the day. Ministers have little time or capacity for close involvement in the work of their portfolio: their interest is captured by endless consultation with interest groups, electoral matters, parliament and media activities. Ministerial staff often keep a watching brief, and may be a source of friction as they seek to intervene in departmental matters, to drive administrative activity in the direction required by the government. Most policy implementation, though, takes place deep within the public service, far from political eyes. Ministers must find ways to assert control while allowing the professional public service to get on with its tasks.

Three instruments assist cabinet to maintain authority over the public service: the architecture of government, an annual budget and rules setting out personnel policies.

Traditionally, *the architecture of government* is the responsibility of the prime minister, chief minister or premier. Departments can be created or abolished through administrative order, though changes to a statutory body usually require

> At the end of the day power resides in the parliament, influence resides in the public service. Power and influence are complementary, they're not competitive and it works if they're complementary, it doesn't work if they're competitive.
> Max Moore-Wilton, 2002

> I don't think ministers are as powerful as outside opinion would have them appear to be. The terrible thing that isn't acknowledged in Australia is that things are expected of government that government can't deliver.
> A federal minister, quoted in Weller and Grattan (1981:180)

consideration by parliament. Incoming leaders often rearrange departmental titles and responsibilities to reflect their own priorities. One Canadian study tracked in detail how successive prime ministers restructured central agencies to match their 'personal philosophies of leadership, management styles, and political objectives' (Aucoin, 1986:90).

Reorganisation allows leaders to provide a sense of direction and purpose for their governments. In 1987, Bob Hawke restructured the entire federal bureaucracy around a 'micro-economic reform' agenda. Nearly a decade later, incoming prime minister John Howard signalled a shift in federal policy by downgrading some functions inherited from Labor, while providing extra positions and offices for those policy concerns of particular interest to the coalition. State and territory leaders such as Jeff Kennett and Claire Martin imposed radically different structures on their governments, collapsing many agencies into just a handful of 'mega-departments'.

Smaller changes to the architecture of government may reflect a desire to capitalise on a strength or minimise a weakness, such as the merger of finance with administrative services after the politically embarrassing 'travel rorts' affair in 1997.

If the architecture of government symbolises the grand design, an *annual budget* is an opportunity for ministers to get into the detail of departmental operations. Recent decades have seen significant improvements in financial control technology (Wanna et al., 2000). Computers, new accounting systems and program structures allow central agencies, especially treasury and finance departments, to track financial performance with improved precision and empower senior managers to monitor detailed daily flows (O'Faircheallaigh et al., 1999:134). Such information in turn allows greater political scrutiny of public sector activity.

Budget processes provide an annual review and statement of policy in every area of government operation. Commonwealth and state governments rely on an Expenditure Review Committee (ERC), or its equivalent, to work through portfolio plans. The ERC is chaired by the prime minister or treasurer, but includes senior ministers and is assisted by officials from central agencies. It first sets broad financial parameters for the year ahead and then makes allocations across portfolios and programs. Ministers appear before the committee to argue a case. Optimists seek an additional allocation for new programs; realists hope to leave with their budget intact or cut by no more than the average. Across-the-board reductions in administrative expenditure, usually termed 'efficiency dividends', have become a standard part of the budget process.

Rules governing public service employment and operations are less dramatic and public than budget cycles, but can also be important in shaping agency activity. Public services across the nation are governed by legislation describing a permanent, merit-selected, equitable, impartial public sector outside the direct control of ministers. Some of these attributes no longer pertain in practice. Permanence has little effective meaning, since large-scale redundancies are now a common feature of public service life. Indeed, even the principle of tenure is no longer available to senior officers, who must sign five-year contracts and are subject to removal at any time by the government.

The issue of merit selection has been even more contentious. The ideal of a non-partisan public service clashes with the desire of many ministers for political appointments to senior positions. The emerging resolution has seen limited term political appointments, particularly in central agencies. Prime Minister John Howard, for example, established a Cabinet Policy Unit (CPU) within his department, soon after gaining office, with a small number of staff appointed on the same terms as those in ministerial offices. At the time, the CPU was 'involved in preparatory work that addresses the political and other aspects of Cabinet business where public servants could not appropriately do so. The CPU has not taken over any of the administrative and policy support functions for the Prime Minister and the Cabinet that can be provided from the department' (Department of Prime Minister and Cabinet, 2001:84). Some states have amended public sector legislation to allow a number of partisan appointments within the senior executive service, and all pay particular attention to the selection of chief executive officers. Australia has not entirely embraced the US 'spoils' system, where each new administration replaces the entire senior ranks of government with its own supporters, but

---

The Commonwealth and most states have a cabinet handbook which regulates what issues come to cabinet, and how submissions must be structured.

The Commonwealth *Cabinet Handbook* imposes a maximum of seven pages for any cabinet submission. It requires submissions to be lodged five days prior to consideration, and to include details of consultation within and beyond government.

Matters required to come before cabinet include:

- new policy proposals and proposed significant variations to existing policies
- proposals likely to have a significant effect on employment in either the public or private sector
- expenditure proposals (normally only considered in a budget context)
- proposals requiring legislation
- proposals likely to have a considerable impact upon relations between the Commonwealth and foreign, state or local governments.

Cabinet rules establish and give shape to the policy cycle, since cabinet submissions must include detail about issue identification, policy analysis, appropriate policy instruments, consultation, coordination, implementation and evaluation.

the line between politics and the public sector fluctuates in some jurisdictions.

In 1999 this was highlighted by the removal of the secretary of the defence department at the behest of the minister on the grounds of a loss of faith (Kimber and Maddox, 2003). The displaced chief executive embarrassed the government by challenging his removal in the courts. In the end, the political domain's dominance over the public service was affirmed, with the notional separation exposed as, at best, an ideal.

BRINGING THE PLAYERS TOGETHER

Government requires coordination across each of the political, policy and administrative domains. Some players cross more than one domain, but all look to the centre for coherence. Each domain is represented at the centre of government through figures who can speak with authority for their area of responsibility. In Canberra, the political world is represented by ministers and by the prime minister's chief of staff. The policy domain speaks through the heads of central agencies such as PM&C, the department of finance and administration (Finance) and treasury, though policy itself is typically developed within the relevant policy department. The central agencies also speak for the final domain, administration. Similar configurations are found in most states. Figure 2.1 sketches the centre of Commonwealth government, the core executive, to show how the domains cluster around the prime minister.

A key leadership task is to bring the three domains into alignment, so all aspects of government work in concert toward shared goals, taking into account the role of players external to government such as the media and the third sector and community more generally. An effective prime minister uses proximity to each of the domains as a basis for coordinating government. From the leader's point of view, the intersection of political, policy and administrative domains organises information and advice around a small group at the centre of government. With just a few people in the room, the prime minister can discuss strategic issues from different angles, and judge how a particular proposal might sit within the government's overall program.

When things haven't gone well for you, call in a secretary or a staff man and chew him out. You will sleep better and they will appreciate the attention.
Lyndon Johnson

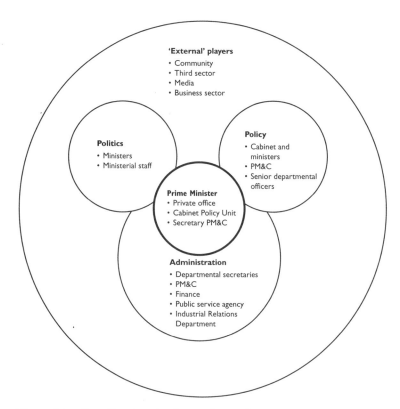

Figure 2.1 Coordinating the three spheres of government
(Based on Davis, 1996:28)

Those who work in each domain understand they must play a specific role. If they are politicians or ministerial advisers, they worry about politics and the media. Policy staff focus on cabinet procedures and documents. Administrators ensure programs are implemented, run effectively and evaluated. Making the system work requires the division of tasks into manageable pieces. Nonetheless, politicians and officers often talk across the boundaries, recognising the common enterprise of government and the blurring of expectations that makes for the magic and messiness of politics. All know, though, their place in a wider scheme, the duties and the limits of their assigned roles.

Different time dimensions operate within the domains. In the political world, all issues are urgent. Time is measured in days or even hours, as controversies flare and are addressed or dissipate. The media demand immediate responses, making long-term planning a rare luxury. When British Prime Minister Harold Wilson said 'a week is a long time in politics' he conveyed the rapid turnover in people and ideas marking his experience.

Policy advisers also face the weekly cycle of cabinet. They too must comprehend the political issues of the moment, being aware, informed and able to accommodate political needs while advising neutrally and without presumption. Nonetheless, they operate in a more orderly and rule-bound world, in which every issue before government is subjected to a standardised form of analysis and consideration. The policy–political demarcation is often chaotic, messy and unclear. Preferably, the system should encourage careful analysis and thoughtful research, even if some policy decisions are made on the run. The *Cabinet Handbook* usually requires agencies to prepare submissions weeks before they are brought to cabinet, allowing time for consultation and modification. While occasional urgent items disrupt the routines of decision making, the policy domain is less subject to the roar and tumult of political life.

Administration, too, follows a pattern, often using an annual cycle of budgets, strategic plans, program evaluations and staff appraisal. Accountability and management requirements are served through a predictable, repetitive sequence of tasks. For those busy delivering services, the political world can seem remote and even irrelevant.

These different temporal cycles encourage each domain to develop its own characteristic routines and language. Political advisers speak in ways that may seem brutal and blunt to a policy adviser or program manager, yet they express no more than the imperatives of their world, and the inevitably short time frame available to solve pressing problems. Public servants, in turn, can seem too concerned with process and propriety for ministers and their advisers. The task of those at the centre is to ensure communication remains open, so the domains can function together around shared objectives and time frames.

COORDINATION THROUGH ROUTINES

To achieve coherence across the domains of politics, policy and administration, governments rely on routines—those standardised procedures that structure decision making. Cabinet processes are the most visible routine. They organise information, pass proposals through a single channel for consideration, and record decisions made by government. Each domain has its own set of routines—standard operating procedures that remind players who can make decisions, what information is required, and what steps must be taken in particular circumstances. Routines are the standard repertoire of any institution, and exist as 'rules and codes which guide action and give effect to values' (Davis, 1995:25).

As James March and Johan Olsen (1989:24) suggest, the ubiquity of routines often makes political institutions appear to be bureaucratic, rigid, insensitive or stupid. The simplification provided by rules is clearly imperfect, and the imperfection is often manifest, especially after the fact. But some of the major capabilities of modern institutions come from their effectiveness in substituting rule-bound behaviour for individually autonomous behaviour. Routines make it possible to coordinate many simultaneous activities in a way that makes them mutually consistent. Routines help avoid conflicts; they provide codes of meaning that facilitate interpretation of ambiguous worlds; they constrain bargaining within comprehensible terms and enforce agreements.

The policy cycle presented in *The Australian Policy Handbook* is a routine for decision making. Each step carries its own sequence of procedures and processes, rules and conventions. The overall routine aims to gather information about a problem, assemble evidence and opinion, secure a decision, implement a course of action, and then begin the cycle again by requiring evaluation and rethinking. Yet the routines do not just structure actions within government. Routines legitimise power. If cabinet alone can make a particular decision, and if cabinet will only consider a submission prepared according to particular rules, then all players along the way understand their tasks and the lines of authority established by the routine. In this way routines guide action, but also tell us who is authorised to make a choice, and how that choice will be reached. The routines required for a policy cycle are the essential mechanisms of government, a

> A *routine* is a rule used in making decisions that has the following traits: it is employed widely among people who make certain types of decisions; it focuses their attention on a limited number of the considerations that are potentially relevant to their decision, and thereby simplifies decisions that might have been complex; at the same time, it excludes certain considerations from the decisions, and contributes to political stability by making the decisions predictable under most conditions.
> Sharkansky (1970:3)

> ❝ I like that horse Divide and Rule. I've done that for nearly twenty years.
> *Sir Henry Bolte, Premier and Treasurer of Victoria, 1955–1973*

CHANGING ROLES OF THE STATE

Public sector work can be characterised in a number of ways from traditional conceptualisations (often the product of historical functions) to more innovative contemporary roles. At any one time, the state can be viewed as any or all of:

- Developer
- Service deliverer
- Policy adviser
- Standard setter
- Regulator
- Enforcer
- Enabler
- Innovator
- Catalyst
- Protector.

THE RISE OF GOVERNMENT BY NETWORK

Network governance has emerged from a confluence of four international trends:

- Third-party government—recognising horizontal cooperation and competition in service delivery and achieving policy goals
- Joined-up government—recognising vertical cooperation and need for coordination to provide integrated service across multiple governments and layers of government
- The digital revolution—recognising technological advances that enable collaboration and partnerships not previously possible
- Consumer demand—recognising increased citizen demand for control, choice, input and variety in government services to provide customised provision.

Adapted from Goldsmith and Eggers (2004:10)

continual reminder of who governs within the Australian political system.

The map of government provided in this chapter complements the more traditional responsible government model and accommodates the existence and significance of players other than just politicians. From both perspectives, 'ministers are on top, public servants on tap'. Yet seeing government as three interacting tasks—as a meeting of political, policy and administrative routines—provides a sense of the close working relationships found at the centre of government. This model reinforces the notion that effective policy making requires people not only to understand their roles, but to learn to accommodate the differing needs of other players. As Sir Paul Hasluck (1968:1), a former Australian foreign minister and later governor-general, once noted, 'the public service cannot avoid politics any more than fish can avoid the water in which they swim'. Likewise, ministers and their advisers cannot avoid the public service, and none can ignore the political machinations and abilities of business, the third sector, the media or the wider citizenry. All players maximise their influence by learning from, and accommodating, the others.

The policy cycle approach also accommodates the contemporary environment of the policy process that features new levels and types of competition and cooperation. The emergence of alternative sources of policy advice (Tiernan, 2007), as well as the fluid interchange and interaction between sectors of the community (both in terms of labour and ideas), are creating new pathways in how policy comes to be. Traditional hierarchical notions of public service have given way to new forms of governance such as networks (Goldsmith and Eggers, 2004). Policy is not just about decisions, it is about relationships (Saunders, 2005). In the policy making environment, this means government has come to understand and describe itself in any number of new ways.

Using a policy cycle highlights the coordination of various routines that are inherently dependent on a range of relationships that extend horizontally across sectors as well as vertically within government. These relationships cover a spectrum from one-off interactions (a speeding ticket) to long-standing partnerships (the provision of healthcare facilities by charitable organisations). Policy making is not just about following rules or procedures but demands applied skills and nous. Policy makers must move beyond facts and figures and build legitimacy and trust.

A policy cycle

SNAPSHOT

A policy cycle brings a system and a rhythm to a world that might otherwise appear chaotic and unordered.

This chapter describes a policy cycle that starts with identifying issues, then moves through analysis and implementation to evaluation of the policy's effects. The cycle is a guide designed to inject rigour but not to limit potential and creativity.

Almost every description of policy routines moves through three main stages, where an idea is developed, acted on, and the result checked. These stages could be described formally as:

- ideation
- realisation
- evaluation

or less formally as:

- thinking
- doing
- testing.

If our system of government is to produce viable public policies, some order must arise from the endless interaction of political, policy and administrative worlds. That order is achieved through routines that help define the roles of each player and their respective responsibilities and channel policy ideas along a recognised sequence on their way to cabinet consideration, and then to realisation.

This chapter describes how a policy cycle can be used to understand and structure policy development. The most influential ways of describing policy making are those that break the policy process into clear and identifiable steps. As early as 1951, Harold Lasswell was characterising policy making as a sequence of intelligence, recommendation, prescription, invocation, application, appraisal and termination. Later writers stayed with the idea of steps, but offered variations on the labels, usually suggesting that policy making is a sequence of problem identification, agenda setting, adoption, implementation and policy evaluation (Sabatier and Jenkins-Smith, 1993:2).

For example, Anderson (2005:4) suggests that choices follow a 'commonsense' sequence:

- getting the government to consider action on the problem
- deciding what is proposed to be done about the problem
- getting the government to accept a particular solution to the problem
- applying the government's policy to the problem
- asking 'did the policy work?'

The Australian Policy Handbook works within that tradition by adopting a policy cycle approach. It suggests policy develops through a sequence of tasks that can be framed as activities or questions. The policy cycle presented here has been developed because it is a useful organising device, with a range of strengths:

- The policy cycle approach stresses that government is a *process*, and not just a collection of venerable institutions. A cycle conveys movement of ideas and resources, the iteration of policy making, and a routine that does not finish with a decision but carries through to implementation and evaluation.
- It *disaggregates* complex phenomena into manageable steps, allowing us to focus on the different issues and needs of each phase in the cycle.
- A policy cycle allows some *synthesis* of existing knowledge about public policy. We incorporate appropriate literature at the relevant step in the cycle, thus locking key lessons from policy making studies into the overall sequence.
- The cyclical approach acknowledges that policy making is *non-linear*, again facilitating recognition of the fluidity of the process. A winding or zig-zag path, even a recursive one, can be as valuable for policy outcomes as more direct routes.
- It serves as a *description* of policy making, to assist in making sense of policy development, past and present.

The normative values in a policy cycle are deliberate and explicit. Policy making is not a strictly logical pursuit, but a complex and fascinating matrix of politics, policy and administration. When electoral considerations, budget constraints and implementation problems pull in different directions, problems might be open to multiple solutions, or no solution at all. No single procedure guarantees a successful result; governments can make howling errors even using the most rigorous and exact policy processes.

A policy cycle, even as an explanatory tool, has its critics. The world is messy and complex. Even to those involved, policy making can appear rather like history—just one damn thing after another, with each event tied to earlier actions until it becomes impossible to separate cause from effect, problem from

> . . . it is *logically* impossible to understand any reasonably complicated situation—including almost any policy process—without some theoretical lens ('theory', 'paradigm', or 'conceptual framework') distinguishing between the set of potentially important variables and causal relationships and those that can safely be ignored.
> Sabatier and Jenkins-Smith (1993:xi)

ALTERNATIVE POLICY MODELS

Some other ways of looking at policy making include:

Systems approach
(e.g. Colebatch, 2006)

Views the policy world as a complex system and an 'intersection of ... diverse agendas, not a collective attempt to accomplish some known goal'. Policy development is 'an exercise in social construction' with policy work 'concerned with the construction of meaning'. Policy emerges 'from a differentiated world, in which a range of participants with different agendas and concerns, inside and outside government, interact in a variety of ways' with the perspective looking for 'determinants of continuing practice'.

Value-adding approach
(e.g. Moore, 1997)

The policy world is organised according to the concept of public value, with players encouraged to pursue and propose new ideas that aim to improve the working of the organisation and its services according to the value-adding idea. The culture and contribution of value creation is rewarded analogously to the growth of shareholder value in profitable companies. It is recognised, however, that public value has unique dimensions that distinguish it from simple private sector concepts of value.

Risk-uncertainty management approach (e.g. Perrow, 1984 and Boin et al., 2005)

Views policy making as the ongoing management of risk, uncertainty and crisis where there is incomplete information, disorder, urgency and either threats or opportunities (depending on what perspective is being taken and by whom).

continued over page ...

solution. To impose a policy cycle creates artificial expectations of a reliable, predictable policy world. It also presupposes the political will to follow due process in policy making when determination is not always present or possible.

There is merit in such concerns. Life is less than neat—but not necessarily inexplicable. Faced with 'history' we can look for the common elements to policy making, seeking some pattern amid otherwise chaotic events. A policy cycle provides the analytical tools, even if each example of policy making is unique, and often a narrative with the steps in all the wrong order and moving in dissociated directions.

We make a second, more contentious claim in presenting a policy cycle: that good policy should include the basic elements of the cycle (even if not in sequence). That is, a policy process that does not include everything from problem identification to implementation to evaluation has less chance of success. This will not hold true for every example—some policy issues are so simple that investment in process is redundant. But on balance, and across cumulated experience of policy making, a more thorough policy process is less likely to produce an obvious policy mistake. A policy cycle assists systematic thinking, even if many different types of policy cycle are conceivable.

ALTERNATIVES TO THE POLICY CYCLE

Many other models have been developed to bring order to the political-policy-administrative maelstrom. Some of note include Burch and Wood's (1989) analogy that portrays government as a firm, taking public and private resources on the supply side of the manufacturing process, producing goods and services, rules and regulations and transfer payments as policy outputs. Feedback to government through the citizenry influences future supply side choices. This model is illustrated in Figure 3.1.

Richard Simeon (1976:556) describes a 'funnel of causality' that allows policy to be understood at different levels. At the funnel's widest point, policies are responses to social and economic settings, attempting to steer people and institutions towards goals. The narrower the funnel, the more immediate the factors that come into play, until at its narrowest we see only those matters relevant to the policy under examination.

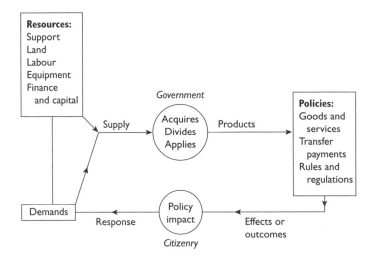

Figure 3.1 A 'policy process' approach
(From Burch and Wood, 1989:15)

Policy makers must act strategically and with leadership in order to make sense of the problem and what to do about it, provide or re-establish a sense of order, and undertake learning and contingency practices for the future. It is expected that systems complexity makes occasional failures or crises inevitable. Typical precautions often help create new categories of 'normal accidents', with crisis and risk being a never-ending cycle that impinges upon, as well as generates, policy activity. The policy world becomes broadly charged with either of two reactions to crisis and risk: resilience/management or prevention/eradication, and crisis becomes a source of innovation.

Simeon's model is a powerful reminder that policy is context dependent, and reflects the dominant thinking of the day. Consider the practice of removing Aboriginal children from their families that occurred from the 1930s until the 1970s. The complex raft of state policy instruments that facilitated the Stolen Generations was based on the assumption—now outrageous but widely held during the period—that Aboriginal children needed to be protected from their parents by being placed in the custody of the church or state. Which contemporary policies, apparently now so natural and logical, will in the future prove to be just as obviously a product of their times, unacceptable to future generations?

Other models focus on the many participants in the policy process. Sabatier and Jenkins-Smith (1993) offer an 'advocacy coalition framework' that describes policy making in areas subject to long-term negotiation between government and interest groups. They argue that the interaction between coalitions of interests, policy brokers and political institutions produces a policy community that discusses ideas and develops a shared understanding of the problem, even while disagreeing about the solution. Environmental policy is one area ripe for analysis using this model, given the strong interactions between

In a sense everything in the policy world is really just process, the movement of people and programs around common problems such as education, transport and employment. None of the initiatives in these fields stays fixed for very long because the problems themselves keep moving and changing. We cannot afford, therefore, to view policy as just a study of decisions or programs. The specific decisions which often interest us are merely important punctuation marks within this flow—not the thing itself.
Considine (1994:3–4)

GARBAGE CAN APPROACH

'Organisations can be viewed for some purposes as collections of choices looking for problems, issues and feelings looking for decision situations in which they might be aired, solutions looking for issues to which they might be an answer, and decision makers looking for work.'
Cohen, March and Olsen (1972:1)

'green' groups and industry as they work with government through consultative committees. The Hawke government's accord model deliberately created a policy community in industrial relations. This model reminds us that policy making is an ongoing dynamic, rarely one-off, and involves powerful interests other than government.

Any approach has limitations. The policy cycle model is a valuable description and guide to action but it does not provide causal explanations for why a policy has developed in particular ways. As a normative model, there is a risk the policy cycle may impose too great a neatness on policy making, renowned for complexity and discontinuity rather than the relentlessly logical unfolding implied in the diagram. A policy cycle helps us pursue better practices, but it cannot entirely tame the human and political imbroglio of making public policy.

POLICY MAKING VACUUMS

What would policy making be like in the absence of models? Creative ad libbing and spontaneity in the policy process is something like the innovation that occurs in the creative arts—it comes only with great skill and experience. A jazz musician must have a deep knowledge of harmony and instrumental technique before apparently abandoning them to perform with the spirit and pizzazz of her craft.

The same can be said of policy making. A skilled player sees the various formal heuristics and available models not as constraints to be strictly applied in legalistic manner, but as basic principles to inform natural talents, invention, innovation, ingenuity and imagination in the pursuit of good policy processes. Models help policy makers follow through on the particular requirements of the problem at hand. It is not always expected that a standardised, ordered process will be appropriate, let alone followed. Be it mellow or heavy metal, the mood and tempo of the issue demands its own spotlight, care and harmony. Censoring policy cycles because they are 'not realistic' is unhelpful.

Many policy makers bemoan the 'irrationality' of politics with its power struggles and manoeuvrings, pork-barrelling, media hype and spin, and layers of awkward coalitions that constrain the purity of analysis. Policy makers feel frustrated when

> Not everyone appreciates the bureaucratic need for order. Honoré de Balzac said that 'bureaucracy is a giant machine operated by pygmies'.

politicians make snap decisions which have to be justified after the fact with material pulled together to support a predetermined position. If such an environment is present in the policy process, policy makers should not give up on good policy. The idea of good policy is worth holding onto, even if the process is hard to defend.

And policy makers cannot and should not presume the worst of politics. The very 'irrationality' of politics is its greatest asset and can result in imaginative, even brilliant outcomes in the face of the complex dilemmas faced by governments.

AN AUSTRALIAN POLICY CYCLE

While policy making can be represented in many ways, Australian experience suggests a policy cycle is likely to begin with issue identification, and then proceed through policy analysis, policy instruments, consultation, coordination, decision, implementation and evaluation (see Figure 3.2).

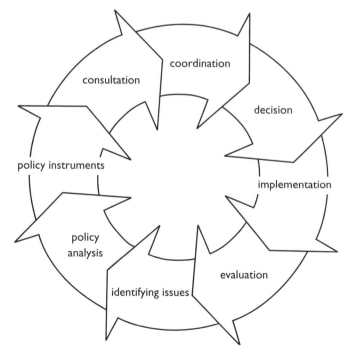

Figure 3.2 The Australian policy cycle

The important point about the policy cycle approach is that it usefully suggests that the policy process can be broken down into elements. But there are problems with the approach ... The emphasis upon phases suggests some kind of chronological sequence which is inevitably involved in policy making. We believe the process to be more fluid ...
Burch and Wood (1989:16)

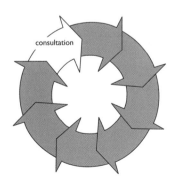

Much policy begins with *identifying issues*. A new problem emerges in private discussions with interest groups, or in the media, with demands for government action. Sometimes an existing policy ceases to be effective and requires an overhaul—there is never a shortage of people telling government what it should be doing. Issues have many sponsors, and proponents compete to attract attention for their cause. Indeed, much of politics is about defining an agenda for public policy.

Once an issue has caught the eye of government—and sometimes this can be through a knockout punch—*policy analysis* becomes important. For without information it will be difficult to frame options. With long-standing problems, governments may be guided by their overall party philosophy and program. New issues, though, demand research and reflection. Policy analysis is often—though not always—the work of the public service, drawing on broader debates among specialists and practitioners in a policy field. It is designed to provide decision makers with sufficient information about the policy problem to make an informed judgment, and typically takes the form of briefing papers for senior officials and ministers.

Should government intervention appear likely, policy analysis leads to identification of appropriate *policy instruments*. Some problems require legislation, others adjustment of the internal operations of government agencies or use of tools that promote the cooperation and motivation of players in the policy community. It is not sufficient to understand a problem, since little will be achieved if the likely policy response is not targeted and plausible; analysis must carry through to recommending policy responses.

One important method to develop ideas and test the strength of the analysis, and the feasibility of the proposed response, is *consultation*. The architecture of government tends to duplication and overlap, since many problems draw in a wide range of players. Assisting a major economic project, such as a new private power station, can variously be an issue for the treasury, the mines and energy department, the trade and industry portfolios, and the environmental protection authority. The proponent will need access to coal and water, and ability to supply the electricity grid as well as venture capital and commitment to purchase power in the future. All these agencies have something to contribute to the ultimate solutions, each will have its own interpretation and perspective regarding the issues, and each will be vitally interested in any proposed policy changes.

Any constructive policy initiative in a broad field such as economic development or social policy will inevitably involve more than one agency. Within government, therefore, it is essential to discuss and develop proposed policy initiatives with related agencies. Policy consultation will probably also include discussions and proactive interaction with non-government interests. In many complex areas, government relies heavily on the expertise of those working in the field (such as econometricians and financial analysts when making decisions about power stations). Through consultation, policy proposals are improved, ideas tested and, when appropriate, support gathered.

Once a policy proposal is ready for consideration by the government, issues of *coordination* arise. This typically requires discussions with treasury about available funding for a policy, and with other central agencies over the relation between a new proposal and overall government direction including coherence and consistency with other existing policies. Coordination may also be necessary to resolve issues between agencies sharing an interest in a field; mechanisms such as interdepartmental committees bring together related agencies and work toward agreement on a common policy strategy.

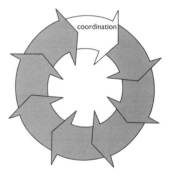

As the cycle proceeds, a policy issue is identified, analysed, matched with appropriate instruments, discussed with relevant interests, and tested against central policy and financial considerations. The time for a *decision* has arrived. In the Australian setting, this often means consideration by cabinet. Each week cabinet receives a range of submissions, and must make binding choices about each. If insufficient information is provided, cabinet may require the whole process of identification and analysis to begin again; too much information and cabinet may be unable to work through the detail and achieve a resolution. The art of good policy advice is to provide sufficient information in succinct form and in a format that carries the reader through a logical sequence of steps toward options or a recommendation. Good policy advice also recognises that the final

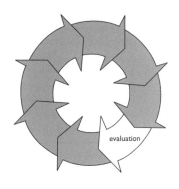

judgment properly belongs with ministers and not public servants.

The cycle does not conclude with a cabinet decision. *Implementation* must follow, in which the policy is given expression through legislation or a program, in pursuit of the goals agreed by ministers.

And, since policies in practice often drift from the objectives of the original submission or are imperfect in realising their goals, *evaluation* is essential so government can gauge the effects of a policy and adjust or rethink policy design as appropriate. Such evaluation, of course, starts the cycle afresh, with a new look at the problem, and a reconsideration of the recommended instruments. Policy is a wheel continually turning, a task never completed.

THE POLICY CYCLE AND INSTITUTIONS

Much of the work implied in the policy cycle is undertaken by public servants. However, the cycle ranges across all the institutions of the Australian political system and encompasses the contributions of all the sectors. Cabinet submissions have political, policy and administrative implications, and each of these domains will be involved throughout the cycle. Input varies, depending on the political prominence of the issue.

Policy can proceed in linear fashion through the policy cycle but this is rare. Political pressure can see a 'whole of government' approach emerge quickly. There is, however, also a tendency for 'parallel processing' within government. Even if politicians do not directly pick up the first signs of community and industry distress on an issue, routine bureaucratic processes would hopefully have collected and analysed appropriate data and advised the minister. The sequential steps in the policy cycle include internal cycles as issues are revisited and reanalysed. Political responses pre-empt later activity, as electoral considerations come to the fore. Ideas and problems do not come from just one source, but are traded across government. Some policy proposals emerge from political considerations, others are more administrative in character. All will journey through the policy cycle but the trajectory of each will be unique.

... practitioners do not simply seek to deal with uncertainty on a 'technical' basis using evidence, but rather seek to cope with ambiguity on a 'practical' basis, making wise judgements about the appropriateness of policy action in relation to a range of technical, political, moral and ethical concerns.
Sanderson (2006:126)

GOOD PROCESS AND GOOD POLICY

A policy cycle is a first foray into complexity. It organises observations into familiar patterns, and provides a guide for future action. It suggests a process that transcends particular institutions or policy designs, a process that can carry decision makers through a simple sequence. Yet the claims made for a policy cycle (or any other model of policy making) must be modest. In political life processes tend to be shaped by problems, with each issue facing government demanding attention in its own way. The dilemmas of making policy do not resemble a 'Gordian knot awaiting the cut of a single superior technique'. Policy is a 'discontinuous series of actions, played out simultaneously across multiple arenas, given unity only through the selection and synthesis of a narrator' (Davis and Weller, 1987:384). Used carefully, a policy cycle can go some way towards constructing a narrative. Like all good stories, it suggests ways we might behave in future, and so shapes the world it describes.

The policy cycle model begs the question: 'Does good process lead to good policy?' Experience shows that good process is integral to consistently good policy. While some very poor policies have grown out of the most rigorous process, rarely does good policy grow from a haphazard approach.

Consistently good policy will only be developed by combining rigour of both process and intellect. The best process in the world cannot substitute for high quality thinking and analysis. Likewise, the most creative and technically exacting thinking can fail to produce good policy if there is no process to integrate the complex web of activities that marks any public policy endeavour.

A policy cycle cannot capture the full ebb and flow of a sophisticated policy debate, nor does it accommodate fully the value-laden world of politics. Experience shows that the normative sequence is easily disrupted. The policy dance is sometimes seemingly random movements rather than choreographed order.

The interplay of politics, policy and administration is a hurly-burly, wrenching sometimes this way, sometimes that. Decisions can be pre-empted. Outcomes can be delayed or sacrificed by powerful forces. Reality impinges on the order of a

---

A good policy process is the vital underpinning of good policy development. Of course, good process does not necessarily guarantee a good policy outcome, but the risks of bad process leading to a bad outcome are very much higher.
Keating (1996:63)

Problems are not always clearly defined, values and goals conflict, time and information for analysis is limited and techniques for comparing options are often crude and unreliable. Policies are not required one at a time but are interconnected so that to ameliorate one problem may be to aggravate another. Causal links cannot always be established, so a technically rational option may have disastrous unanticipated consequences ...

This is not the counsel of despair, but a warning against simplistic prescriptions. When problems are intertwined, goals a moveable feast and resources limited, then only approximations are possible. Australian administrators, like their political masters, are pragmatic. If techniques which consistently improved policy were available, they would be used.
Davis and Weller (1987:384)

normative process resulting in apparently messy and accidental activity. Sometimes the end product is an essential creativity; sometimes, unruly disorder. Our system of government dictates that politics wins any contest of wills, and policy's role is to make sense of that victory. The policy cycle merely provides a framework for understanding.

Although good process and good policy are the ideal, they do not always occur together. In February 2001, John Howard made changes to fuel excise policy after repeatedly stating that to do so would be fiscally irresponsible. For the first seven months after the introduction of the GST, the prime minister had resisted intense pressure from rural and motoring lobby groups, as well as a restless backbench, to cut petrol excise and review automatic indexation. After big election wins to Labor in Queensland and Western Australia, and facing a federal election at the end of that year, the prime minister relented and cut excise by 1.5 cents per litre as well as abolishing automatic indexation. The decision was projected to cost $2.6 billion over three years. The prime minister apologised to the public for the government's handling of the matter, stating: 'I was plainly wrong in not understanding some of the concerns held by the Australian people about the price of petrol' (Miragliotta, 2002:122). Sometimes policy and politics go together. In this case, however, the prime minister judged a political need more pressing than policy consistency. A subsequent rise in the government's standing in opinion polls suggests the choice was right.

UTILISING THE POLICY CYCLE APPROACH

Policy makers use practical reason, a concept used to describe a form of reflection on the world using applied judgment. Practical reason involves assessment of the usefulness and applicability of the policy cycle, selecting the stage at which the policy might be and judging how an issue might be conceptualised and managed.

Deployment of the policy cycle does not demand a consistent, ordered, sequential process. Rather, the model provides a map of how things could be done and how, perhaps, they might be done better.

4 Identifying issues

Political life is contested around issues. Parties and interest groups, parliament and media, departments and private companies all compete to draw attention to their key issues. Contending voices use parliament, the media, public events and private lobbying to press their case. Information, uncertainty and prioritisation are the 'stuff' of issue development (Jones and Baumgartner, 2005). Politics becomes an argument about which topics, and which interpretation of any particular topic, have a legitimate right to government responses and public resources.

THE POLICY AGENDA

The outcome of this contest is a 'policy agenda'. A policy agenda represents the narrowing of an infinite array of possible policy problems to those few that command government interest.

When an issue is identified, it becomes part of the policy cycle, subject to analysis, policy instrument development and so on round the circle. There is a crucial moment in the policy cycle, a point at which a private concern is transformed into a policy issue. Suddenly it commands the resources of government while myriad other concerns languish as merely private matters. No wonder competition among issue advocates is so fierce.

This chapter examines how and why topics are accorded this privilege. It explores how an issue becomes important enough for government to commit resources, by looking first at the nature of the drivers of the policy agenda, and then at the nature of policy problems.

Policy officers must develop sensitivity to the nature of issues, to minimise surprise and anticipate problems. They must also

SNAPSHOT
This chapter looks at how issues are selected for attention from among the myriad of matters pressed on government. Many topics vie for attention but few are chosen.

Policy professionals need to understand how issues arise, and how key concerns may be overlooked if they do not attract political interest.

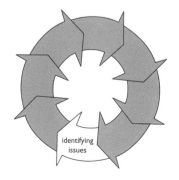

identifying issues

understand how lobbyists work to influence government agendas, and the self-interested nature of many proposals offered as public policy solutions. The battle to elevate issues to the attention of cabinet is, in microcosm, the struggle of interests and ideas that marks all politics.

THE AGENDA METAPHOR

To speak of a policy 'agenda' is to use a metaphor implying a vast committee with a single set of topics for discussion. Though cabinet is in one sense the commanding committee of government, neither politics nor the policy debate is particularly neat. At any moment there will be urgent issues demanding instant attention, while once pressing problems fade until they are almost forgotten. Some issues of narrow but strongly held concern attract no interest at all. Other important issues languish because influential forces seek to preserve the status quo.

When cabinet meets, ministers do have an agenda, a list of topics for discussion. But this list is only a small sample from the policy agenda, in turn a tiny selection from a universe of possible topics. The idea of a policy agenda is simply a useful reminder that, with limited time and resources, policy makers pay attention to only a few issues. So what drives some issues onto the agenda and confines others to also-ran status?

ISSUE DRIVERS

Much detailed policy advice arises from within government. The domains of politics, policy and administration interact to produce an agenda for government, assign responsibility for preparing options, and draw up a timetable for cabinet consideration and implementation. Yet much that government does is foisted on ministers from outside. Issues can emerge from clients, from advocacy groups, from disasters or crises, or from media scrutiny. A number of overarching patterns are discernible. The wheels of government keep churning, generating their own schedules and rotations of routine system maintenance. At other times a spurt of enthusiasm sees reform planned and plotted. The template of crisis management calls governments to attention, demanding a rearrangement of affairs and plans.

POLITICS IS NOT PERFECT
Defining a policy agenda through political competition risks some important but unattractive issues missing out. In the same way, endangered but photogenic species such as eagles and bilbies have a better chance of attracting funding and research than less glamorous but also threatened contributors to biodiversity.

Policy cannot ignore the 'issue drivers'—those external and internal factors that throw up topics for resolution. Governments have priorities, but they rarely set the broader policy agenda unilaterally. Examples of political issue drivers include:

- party political platforms
- key government achievements of the past
- ministerial and governmental changes.

In theory, ministers are masters of the policy cycle. They decide whether an issue receives attention, and how much. In reality, politicians are subject to an array of external influences—parliament and their colleagues, the party they represent, interest groups and political donors, the media and public opinion. The political agenda reflects a shifting mix of ministerial policy concerns and those external issues that cannot be ignored.

The political domain is volatile, to the point of fragility. The rise or fall of a prominent minister can dramatically shift priorities. When parliaments are finely balanced, as has been the case with the Australian Senate, an independent member can become a significant source of policy initiatives.

The ideology of the government party will dictate certain issues. This is clearest immediately after a change in government. For example, the Howard government, elected in 1996 after thirteen years of Labor administration, quickly introduced policy issues different in kind from those of its predecessor. Industrial relations change became a prominent issue, as did public service spending reductions. Later, tax reform dominated the government's agenda. What government decides to pursue will affect what people talk about.

On the other hand, after some years in office the fiery platform of opposition may be exhausted. Governments come to rely more on policy advice and issue identification from within the public sector as well as from alternative sources such as policy 'think tanks' (Stone, 1996). Still, politics never disappears entirely from the equation. Even long established governments find themselves overtaken by new issues requiring rapid responses (see Considine, 1998), or redefining their own agendas, exemplified by the need to focus on international relations and

---

A policy agenda is that 'list of subjects or problems to which government officials, and people outside of government closely associated with these officials, are paying some serious attention at any given time' (Kingdon 2003:3).

Kingdon suggests certain circumstances are more likely to gain government attention:

- Problems in existing programs are of more interest than new problems.
- Politicians are drawn to issues that challenge important values.
- Problems attracting unfavourable comparisons with other parts of the country or other nations have more chance of being noticed.
- Attaching a problem to an important legal principle may attract renewed interest. For example, providing public transport for people with disabilities became a whole new concern when redefined by interest groups as a civil rights issue.

counter-terrorism efforts after the September 11 and Bali attacks. Moreover, the information contest increasingly characterises contemporary issues on the agenda. Governments must often arbitrate on what information is heard and what is ignored or reinterpreted. Stem cell research and global warming are contemporary examples of contested science in need of moral ruling or evidence reprioritisation (see for example Jones and Baumgartner, 2005).

The political process includes periodic changes within government as a prime minister reshuffles cabinet, and ministers resign or fall from grace. Each change of minister brings the potential for a fresh policy agenda, and for new internal and external influences. Policy professionals learn that an individual minister's preferences are important and must be accommodated. They also observe that politicians often cannot set the agenda; responding to problems and complaints consumes much ministerial time.

Ministers cannot control the world that buffets government from outside. There are powerful external forces that shape the agenda and demand immediate attention. These same outside forces also limit the policy responses available to government.

Examples of external drivers include:

- economic forces (e.g. share market fluctuations, interest rate adjustments, employment rates, business fortunes)
- media attention
- opinion polls
- legal shifts (e.g. High Court judgments)
- international relations (e.g. refugee arrivals, diplomatic representations over human rights issues, wars between other nations)
- technological development (e.g. the internet as a vehicle for movement of currency outside the existing tax net)
- demographic shifts (e.g. population growth and movement will change patterns of demand for government services).

A sudden dip in the Tokyo stock market can have ripple effects on Australian economic policy. A High Court decision might force a reinterpretation of some policy fundamentals. A US decision to restrict commodity imports can shift industry policy

---

The celebrated High Court case, *Mabo v Queensland*, redefined legal understanding of land tenure by rejecting terra nullius, the notion that land belonged to no one when discovered by Europeans. The High Court drew on long-standing legal principles, yet governments took eighteen months to agree on a *Native Title Act*. John Uhr describes this response as 'an unusually open example of public policy making, involving extensive community consultation and many rounds of pre-legislative negotiations' (1998:127).

Mabo demonstrates how an apparently technical ruling by a court can have far-reaching political and social consequences.

priorities. An influential company or community group can exert great pressure for its particular interests to be brought into public policy. A war on another continent shifts resources from one policy activity to another. Drought, flood, fire and cyclone demand attention and money for displaced residents and financially stricken farms and businesses. A lone gunman can change a nation's approach to weapons policy.

Market forces are probably the most powerful, precisely because they are largely beyond the regulation of governments. One might control the rate of, say, industrial relations change, but no government can control the price an Australian commodity fetches in the international market, with its implications for income and employment. Naturally governments attempt to manipulate such matters (for example, with excises or orderly marketing schemes) but they cannot influence another nation's bumper crop.

The media too are an integral part of governance, though journalists escape the detailed controls imposed on other political institutions. As Julianne Schultz (1998:1) notes, the 'fourth estate' has retained its independence through a 'curious process of hype, self-promotion, definitional flexibility and being a good idea'. Although the media claim objectivity in raising and covering issues, various biases—commercial interests, the imperative to entertain, a focus on celebrity and a limited audience for detailed investigative journalism—inevitably influence content. For many ministers, nonetheless, the media remain an indispensable guide to the policy agenda.

Factors within government also contribute to the agenda:

- emerging issues monitored by government policy specialists, who structure information and so shape the political domain's view of the matter
- monitoring policy issues in other jurisdictions (e.g. overseas responses to particular problems, successes or failures of policies in other states)
- ongoing monitoring of wicked problems and intractable issues of perennial government concern
- coordination of policy issues across government and between government structures and agendas

One of the reasons I am completely in sympathy with the present government is that they are faced with a barrage of sneering that seems to me facile. The problems they face, and the way they are trying to deal with them, are much more interesting than what their critics have to say. It's easy to jeer, it's very hard to do anything.
Michael Frayn (referring to the Blair government in the United Kingdom, The Telegraph, 2002)

- regular, programmed reviews, built into the budget cycle
- statutory 'sunset' dates
- budget overruns
- unfavourable audit reports
- performance audits, and benchmark failures.

Policy professionals must develop sensitivity to these external factors, to prevent surprises that force a government into unplanned costs or worse. A depth of understanding of external policy drivers is a prerequisite to high quality service delivery, since that is the basis of an appropriate and rapid response to emerging issues.

While political and external drivers shape much that governments do, policy professionals also influence the policy agenda. After all, they craft the words considered by cabinet, develop policy models and policy options and control the inner workings of the policy dynamic. Such professionals work in a political context, but their role is not political. Rather, they must provide independent policy advice on the issues of the day—and on those issues which deserve attention, including those that might be unknown, or only just emerging, as well as those being ignored.

The responsible government model assumes a permanent, independent public service, bringing continuity and stability to the administration of government. The policy specialist dwells in a grey world that is neither politics nor public administration, but is public policy—that intersection of the political, policy and administrative domains.

WHAT ISSUES MAKE THE AGENDA?

Cobb and Elder (1972:161–2) suggest issues have the best prospect of attracting the attention of politicians when the topic has mass appeal. Interest groups should redefine an unsaleable issue 'as ambiguously as possible, with implications for as many people as possible, involving issues other than the dispute in question . . . and as simply as is feasible'.

According to Cobb and Elder, there are common steps in how problems develop. Interest groups, officials and politicians identify a particular problem, and strive to make it of concern to

---

An issue arises when a public with a problem seeks or demands governmental action, and there is public disagreement over the best solution to the problem.
Eyestone (1978:3)

the public. If they succeed, the issue becomes part of the policy agenda, with discussion in the media, the legislature and the political process. If government feels it must respond, the issue is assigned to a public institution and so is drawn into the policy cycle. Figure 4.1 illustrates the journey from private problem to bureaucratic concern.

These common steps suggest a typical policy agenda will have several key characteristics. The agenda arises from competition among voices seeking attention. It is determined politically, with no guarantee the most significant issues will break through the pack, nor that all significant issues will break free from the control of vested interests. The policy agenda is biased toward areas already receiving government attention or with capacity to attract political interest. The agenda is set often not by policy opinion or media attention but by influential elites either already in government or with access to decision makers.

Those who work in the policy process must recognise the potential for important issues to be lost in the crush. The policy agenda is whatever preoccupies government at a particular moment, but this may not be the most important set of problems around. If policy makers rely solely on a mixture of political process, bureaucratic convenience and media enthusiasm to

> ... politics is about collections of ill-informed opinions moving in one particular direction.
> *Alistair McAlpine (1993)*

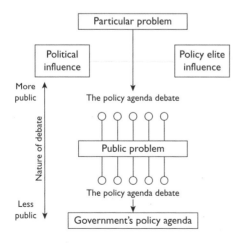

Figure 4.1   The agenda-setting process

compile an agenda, they will be reacting to a very limited set of interests. Most issues emerge through these familiar processes, but the government agenda can be expanded through regular scanning of economic and social conditions, extensive use of data and indicators, evaluations of policy effectiveness and a willingness to look beyond the easy subjects.

ISSUE ATTENTION CYCLE

Whatever the good intentions, government is susceptible to the media, with its capacity to present some issues as 'problems', even 'crises', demanding urgent government attention (Ward, 1995). Such topics travel through what Anthony Downs (1972) labels an 'issue attention cycle'. Pressure groups try to attract attention for some serious problem, but often must wait until a dramatic event and media coverage carries it onto the policy agenda. Then alarmed discovery and brave promises inspire a scramble by political, policy and administrative players for solutions, followed by growing realisation of the real costs of achieving change. By the time institutions and budgets have been established, the public has already lost interest and is chasing the next exciting problem. The issue may be largely forgotten, but at least there are now some programs, institutions and resources in place.

Not all issues attract even this cycle of attention. Those subjects lacking dramatic impact, that affect only minorities or do not lend themselves to simple analysis and presentation, are unlikely to find a broader audience. The policy agenda, always constrained, is further restricted when issues must also have entertainment value.

IDENTIFYING ISSUES

There are a number of stages in problem identification. To make the policy agenda and be taken up by government, an issue must meet at least four simple conditions:

- *Agreement on a problem*. A problem only exists when significant interests and individuals agree that present circumstances are unacceptable. Most issues presented to government fail to find a sponsor. It usually requires a coalition of voices within and outside government to raise

---

... each problem must compete for official attention because of limited time and resources. The demands that policy makers choose or feel compelled to act on at a given time, or at least appear to be acting on, constitute the policy agenda ...
Anderson (2005:87)

Issues arise from group conflict. These issues may eventually command a position on the agenda of governmental decision makers, who manage group conflict. An important way in which an issue may gain access to a governmental agenda is by expanding in scope, intensity and visibility. These processes are important determinants of where the conflicts will be resolved and how the issues will ultimately be defined, so groups attempt to control them to promote their own interests.
Cobb and Elder (1972:160)

an issue to the status of a problem requiring an authoritative response.
- *The prospect of a solution.* Even with agreement on the nature of a problem, policy makers prefer issues that offer plausible solutions. Some intractable problems cannot be avoided, but it is easier to sell a topic to cabinet where resolution seems possible. Few politicians are drawn to issues promising certain failure.
- *An appropriate issue.* Though policy makers might agree an issue exists and can be addressed, political considerations come into play. Each dollar spent on an issue is a dollar not available for some other program, and cabinet must be persuaded a problem is of sufficient consequence to warrant time and investment.
- *A problem for whom?* The ideological framework of the governing party or parties may influence whether ministers wish to deal with an issue at all.

Politicians and their advisers scan the political environment to identify potential political risks and run a risk filter over issues as they emerge to see if the topic is salient or even 'too hot to handle'. Whether a policy problem is *encountered* or a policy position is proactively *created* (maybe using sophisticated marketing and communication techniques), political risk identification delineates the initial issue, ascertains the political risk and dimensions, and drives the strategies and solutions available for use. Political risk calculation can elevate a matter to the top of the priorities or eliminate it from consideration.

In fact many problems do not get started in the policy cycle, but die at the issue identification stage. Kingdon (2003:116) uses a provocative biological metaphor: issue identification is like natural selection, in which external factors such as agreement on a problem, or technical feasibility, select out only a few issues for the next stage of the policy cycle. Kingdon stresses just how many problems, issues and ideas fall by the wayside early. Issues judged unacceptable—those 'that do not square with policy community values, that would cost more than the budget will allow, that run afoul of opposition in either the mass or specialised publics, or that would not find a receptive audience among

> In the United States the national obsession with celebrity is strategically exploited to attract political and media attention to an issue. Stars are increasingly appearing before congressional committees to raise the profile of an issue. 'Julia Roberts tearfully testified about a disease that strikes young girls. Meryl Streep was upset about insecticide sprayed on apples. Even Kermit the Frog lobbied for a bill regulating the breeding and sale of exotic animals. Expertise does not photograph well, Julia Roberts does,' said Eric Denzenhall (cited in Dart, 2002). 'Celebrity pays bigger dividends than knowledge in creating the buzz needed to push a cause.'

elected politicians—are less likely to survive than proposals that meet these standards'. Unseen, but systematic, biases can distort this judgment, a risk made all the greater when assumptions are not articulated.

Kingdon (2003:68–70) also distinguishes between visible and hidden participants—the very public politicians, political parties and media who champion particular issues, and the more shadowy world of specialist bureaucrats, policy advisers and ministerial staff. The chances of an issue attracting government interest are increased 'if that subject is pushed by participants in the visible cluster, and dampened if it is neglected by those participants'. To make the policy agenda, an issue benefits from recognition by visible players and meaningful commitment from those behind the scenes.

An innovative Victorian study, reported by Denis Muller and Bruce Headey (1996), found a range of players influencing agenda setting in an Australian case, in this instance a mix of political, economic and bureaucratic elites. Some issues emerge first in policy debate, but many enter the policy process through private interaction among those who have a direct interest in policy outcomes.

DEFINING PROBLEMS

Before a policy can tackle some pressing issue, the problem must be given shape and boundaries. Herbert Simon (1973) proposes a key distinction between *ill-structured* and *well-structured* problems.

We encounter ill-structured problems all the time: issues such as poverty or discrimination demand attention but are open to endless interpretations and potential solutions. To become the object of public policy, such problems must be tightly defined so they can be analysed. A well-structured problem is one open to solution. 'Much problem solving effort is directed at structuring problems, and only a fraction of it at solving problems once they are structured,' argues Simon (1973:187).

To address an ill-structured problem, suggests Simon, we should break it into smaller, well-structured issues. By solving each of these, we address the wider, and still ill-structured, issue.

To define a problem is to shape the options for a solution. How we perceive the problem will influence powerfully the range of potential policy solutions. Only some issues make the agenda, and these may be presented in ways that assist particular interests while ignoring others. The injunction for caution in accepting an agenda defined by others applies also to the way issues are structured.

WICKED AND INTRACTABLE PROBLEMS

To become subject to public policy, a problem must be given structure. This structure in turn comes from acquiring knowledge about the issue, so boundaries can be drawn and smaller component problems extracted from the larger issue. With structure come the first steps toward problem resolution.

But problems by their very nature are not simple. Some policy issues approach simplicity with identifiable causes and effects, enabling policy formulation skills to be applied to an easy resolution. More often, though, problems are complicated or complex, with cause and effect barely discernible, or discernible only after the event. No matter how much expertise is garnered, there is limited or no ability to define the issue and cause–effect relationships. The policy sphere is rife with such complexity. The types of issues confronting policy makers are not able to be sliced and dissected and tested, laboratory-like, against scientific criteria and experimentation is untenable for a host of technical and ethical reasons.

Some issues are simply not open to solution however well-structured the problem. Historical factors, competing interests or sunk costs can make all sides to a dispute unwilling to compromise. Government may have to balance priorities between interest rates and inflation levels or between encouraging rural exports and preventing further land degradation. These 'intractable problems' cannot be settled and will not go away.

For example, much of rural Australia faces the intractable problem of salinity. The clearing of land for agriculture or stock removes the large trees which once drew heavily from the underground watertable. As the watertable rises it carries salt closer to the surface. Land that was fertile becomes barren.

> The most terrifying words in the English language are: I'm from the government and I'm here to help.
> *Ronald Reagan*

Experts agree about the issue, but practical solutions to restore degraded land so far have proved limited. Until some way is found to reverse the trend, salinity will remain a policy problem without an effective response.

'Wicked problems' refer to those dilemmas that either cannot be defined or, at best, are not open to easy formulation. Rittel and Weber (1973) explain that wicked problems are unstable in that they are characterised by embedded interdependencies where a possible 'solution' can create yet another interlocking complex problem. Moreover, it is difficult to obtain clear or definitive expertise regarding possible solutions because the problem is either 'shifting' or there is no way of learning about the issue without trying potential 'answers' that come with unintended consequences. It is impossible to neatly isolate the problem, let alone work out what to do about it. How to combat violence and crime in a community might be an example of a wicked problem.

Much of social and economic policy is about managing (but not solving) wicked and intractable problems. They are a reminder that the capacity of government to impose its will on a recalcitrant world is always limited, and no policy can be permanent or final. Much policy making is not about solving policy problems but about managing policy conflicts. Policy makers who seek 'once and for all solutions' to wicked and intractable problems condemn themselves to frustration and failure.

NON-DECISIONS

One way to avoid wicked and intractable problems, and just plain difficult ones, is not to make a decision at all. Government may find it easier not to discuss a matter than to disappoint some supporters.

More fundamentally, though, non-decisions can be an expression of the same biases that keep issues from the agenda. They are an important exercise of power, an assertion that some matters do not warrant attention from government. Bachrach and Baratz (1963:641) believe non-decisions occur 'when the dominant values, the accepted rules of the game, the existing power relations among groups, and the instruments of force, singly or in combination, effectively prevent certain grievances from developing into full-fledged issues which call for decisions'.

In effect, non-decisions happen when government refuses to define a topic as a problem requiring a public policy.

It is also possible that policy makers suffer from risk aversion that prevents issues emerging onto the policy agenda in meaningful ways. The inherent red-tape inertia of bureaucracies coupled with 'straitjacket' accountability requirements and the careful calculations of political risk analysis often preclude bold action in issue identification. Of course this risk aversion is not all one-way. The community's willingness for government to experiment and take risks is rarely high. A certain conservatism arguably shapes the framework within which issues are identified and included on the political agenda.

Much of the political process is about promoting issues. Interest groups, policy advisers and politicians all spend time selling issues they believe do not get sufficient attention from government. There are manuals available for lobbying government, and groups for and against the status quo in many policy areas. A non-decision may not be allowed to close the argument.

Saul Alinsky's (1989) *Rules for Radicals: A Pragmatic Primer for the Realistic Radical* offers invaluable advice for those outside government seeking to draw attention to an issue and to manipulate policy process. Its provocative suggestions, and some implications for issue identification, are outlined in Table 4.1.

ISSUE IDENTIFICATION SKILLS

The question of how to identify and define problems has long troubled those seeking a rigorous approach to decision making. There is nothing necessarily rational or fair about the issues to which governments attend. So, though problem definition is essential to the policy cycle, there can be no reliable, prescribed way to proceed. Defining the policy agenda is the point at which creativity, chance and politics, rather than analytical method, are most likely to hold sway.

Public problems are not like games or puzzles, with neatly defined rules and ready solutions. They are mental constructs, abstractions from reality shaped by our values, perceptions and interests. Problems are 'not objective entities in their own right, "out there", to be detected as such, but are rather the product of imposing certain frames of reference' on reality (Dery, 1984:4).

Sundakov and Yeabsley (1999) argue that whereas private sector organisations diversify risk, the public sector concentrates it. A certain level of risk aversion thus characterises the public sector because:

- the political marketplace tends to punish failure without giving credit for success, leading to the encouragement of risk elimination even at the expense of lowering overall welfare
- the political marketplace does not tolerate diversified portfolios—a policy package that includes a failure and a success is usually treated as a failure and governments are often blamed for things they cannot control (e.g. global economic downturns)
- the failure of a single agency often reflects on the whole system of public sector management because citizens do not necessarily discriminate between agencies but treat them all as 'the government'
- equality of treatment limits governments' ability to experiment with institutional structure or processes
- citizens and the community do not like big change and this encourages incremental adjustments that discourage risk-taking.

ISSUE IDENTIFICATION SKILLS
- systematic monitoring
- networking
- intuitive issue monitoring ('political smarts')
- ongoing consultation with peak bodies
- media monitoring
- inter-agency information exchange
- issue recording

The imprecise and subjective nature of public problems requires a commitment to scanning by policy advisers. They must be prepared to look not just at those issues that make up the policy agenda, but at pressing needs that do not find articulate advocates.

Table 4.1 Gaining attention for an issue

Rule for radicals	Issues identification implications
Power is not only what you have, but what the enemy thinks you have.	Issues flow from those who are perceived to have influence in the political process.
Never go outside the expertise of your people. Feeling secure stiffens the backbone.	Policy issues arise where government has limited capacity to respond before issues become important.
Whenever possible, go outside the expertise of the enemy. Look for ways to increase insecurity, anxiety and uncertainty.	
Make the enemy live up to its own rules. If the rule is that every letter gets a reply, send 30 000.	Policy issues are flagged by sudden shifts in the need to respond, or sudden shifts in demand for resources.
Ridicule is humanity's most potent weapon. There's no defence. It's irrational. It's infuriating. It also works as a key pressure point to force the enemy into concessions.	Political and bureaucratic discomfort, and adverse publicity are prime indicators of a policy issue in formation.
Keep the pressure on. Never let up. Keep trying new tactics to keep the opposition off balance. As the enemy masters one approach, hit them with something new.	Consistency of discomfort is an indicator of real or perceived influence.
A good tactic is one your people enjoy. They'll keep doing it without urging and come back to do more. They'll even suggest better ones.	
Pick a target and freeze it, personalise it, polarise it. Isolate the target from sympathy. Go after people, not institutions. People hurt faster than institutions.	Unfortunate, but often accurate advice.

5 Policy analysis

'Policy analysis is an art,' argued Aaron Wildavsky (1987:15). His purpose was to introduce an important paradox about the policy process. Often, he noted, the subject matter of policy analysis is 'public problems that must be solved at least tentatively to be understood'. Looking for a solution may be necessary before we understand the nature of the issue. To structure a problem is to give it shape and meaning through policy analysis. By the time we have tied down the issue we can already see solutions that might follow.

'Policy analysis' implies a rigorous method. There are indeed important and valuable analytic techniques available to public policy practitioners. But judgment must precede application of any analytic device. How important is this problem? How much time and effort should be expended in seeking a solution? What is the appropriate approach? Sometimes the art is deciding how much science will be required.

Policy makers develop shortcuts for these judgments. Emerging problems may be addressed by small changes to existing programs, a process known as *incrementalism*. Decision makers sometimes cast around for solutions from other jurisdictions, appropriating ideas that have worked elsewhere (Schneider and Ingram, 1988). They recognise the significant investment required to analyse a new problem and develop options. Policy makers know perfect rationality is not available in a world of limited attention and contingent politics, and seek to minimise search time. The forces of new technology, globalisation, and the benchmarking and 'good practice' revolutions have combined in a way that now make policy

SNAPSHOT

Good decision making about complex issues requires analysis. This is a fundamental stage in the policy cycle, since research and logic are the basis for developing options and making decisions.

This chapter explores the role of analysis, sets out a practical series of steps for policy analysis, and locates this within the various analytic frameworks used by government.

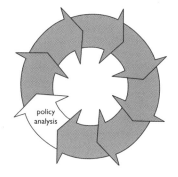

learning, diffusion and transfer an expected practice (see Rose, 1993; Meseguer, 2005). For example, a range of economic experiments occurred across Latin America during the 1980s and 1990s on the back of policy transfer and learning. This was a case of trial and error resulting in some dismal failure. Other instances evidence a more happy transfer of ideas. Initiatives to contain leprosy in Japan and the United States shifted dramatically midway through the last century away from isolation on the basis of policy learning and the importation of scientific ideas and practitioner exchange between the countries (Frantz and Sato, 2005).

Yet, those in the policy process must develop ways to approach new problems and to rethink old ones. There are issues that do not lend themselves to modifying current practice or to stealing other people's solutions. While perfect rationality may not be available, a sequential approach to policy analysis at least ensures definitions, implications, goals and possible outcomes for a policy have been worked through systematically. In solving public problems, art is important but method helps.

THE PURPOSE OF POLICY ANALYSIS

Most government departments have 'policy experts', people who study policy problems and offer solutions. They may comprise a special section of the organisation as a policy unit or each division can assume this role as it develops material for consideration by senior managers. Ministerial offices also take a strong interest in policy analysis, and will seek staff with detailed policy knowledge. Meanwhile clients, interest group advocates, third sector practitioners and media commentators are also contributing their own perspectives on what needs to be done and how.

But policy analysis is not decision making. Politicians seek considered advice about issues, a task usually assigned to the bureaucracy, although it may be undertaken by political advisers, external inquiry and even by management consultants (Boston, 1999:36; Saint-Martin, 1998). Typically the results will be conveyed in a briefing note to a minister or an information paper for cabinet.

Analysis provides data and advice for decision makers. It involves a professional commitment to presenting information in an objective and impartial manner. The purpose of analysis is to help others appreciate the costs and benefits of a range of approaches to a policy problem.

RATIONALITY

The ideal of a scientific approach to problem solving—logical, value-free, reliable, available for a wide array of problems—is attractive for many. Who would not prefer rational solutions to pressing public problems? How could anyone defend ad hoc, incremental decisions over those reached through careful analysis?

Yet experience suggests rationality is an unusual thing in the complex, quasi-political world of public policy. Rational decision making only occurs when there is agreement on objectives and a clear understanding of means. Such circumstances are rare. They may occur when established policy communities, dealing with familiar problems, develop consensus about an appropriate solution to a problem within shared resource constraints. Most public policy choices do not rest on such firm foundations, as governments seek to balance contending interests and manage expanding demands for resources.

> To be rational in any sphere, to display good judgment in it, is to apply those methods which have turned out to work best in it. What is rational in a scientist is therefore often Utopian in a historian or a politician (that is, it systematically fails to obtain the desired result), and vice versa.
> Berlin (1996:30)

Prescriptions for a 'rational' policy process remain influential but unrealised. In its classic form, as illustrated in Figure 5.1, this approach is known as the 'rational *comprehensive* model—rational because it follows a logical, ordered sequence, and comprehensive because it canvasses, assesses and compares all options' (Davis et al., 1993:160–1). While many variations appear in the policy literature, all share six basic and obligatory steps:

> The familiar notion of planning is that done by experts, with scientific knowledge. We have seen the results of that rational planning: tower blocks, food additives, valium—the list of horrors is endless.
> Sheila Rowbotham, British sociologist

1. A problem is identified and defined.
2. The values, goals and objectives of those making the decision are made explicit and ranked in priority order.
3. All options that could achieve the goal are identified.
4. The costs and benefits of each option are made explicit.
5. Costs and benefits for each option are then compared.
6. With information about costs and benefits, the decision maker can choose the option that best achieves their values, goals and objectives.

Figure 5.1 The rational comprehensive approach to decision making

This model appears regularly in textbooks. So do the criticisms. A rational comprehensive model assumes things about the world that often do not hold true—that problems are clear, separate and stable; that decision makers are certain of their values; that goals are hierarchical rather than multiple, conflicting and circumstantial. The model requires consideration of all options, which can be difficult or impossible, and the comparison of options that may not be readily quantifiable.

In practice, decision making is rarely rational (we do not always undertake every step in the model) and hardly ever comprehensive (political realities, budgets and time usually limit those options worth serious consideration and human frailty seldom yields the vision needed to accommodate a truly comprehensive list). Yet in setting out a useful sequence for making choices, the model at least forces policy makers to work systematically, and to provide some justification for favoured options. The following sections offer a simplified version of the model, one without the virtues of strict rationality but with the advantages of order and process in addressing policy problems.

A SEQUENCE FOR POLICY ANALYSIS

There are cycles within the policy cycle. Policy analysts typically work through problems in an orderly way. The analyst's cycle might include the following stages:

- Formulate the problem.
- Set out objectives and goals.
- Identify decision parameters.
- Search for alternatives.
- Propose a solution or options.

This sequence, however, does not end the process. Subsequent steps in the policy cycle, such as the selection of instruments, consultation or the political decision making process, may change aspects of the analysis, or even require a fresh evaluation of the problem. Policy analysis is not a 'once and for all' step; as agreement on the nature and scale of the problem varies, so the analysis must shift to take account of new realities.

> I find that approximately no one knows what is going on. That's why we have been leaving it to the politicians to make the world work.
>
> Buckminster Fuller, American futurist, inventor and author

Policy analysis is invariably iterative, because in practice 'things are seldom tidy' (Quade, 1982:49). Information is often incomplete. People disagree over objectives. Parameters shift. Policy analysts must be reconciled to developing options, testing them against departmental and ministerial opinion, and then working through them again and again.

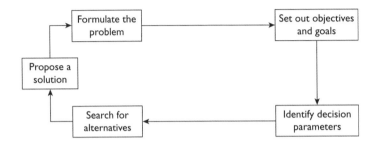

Figure 5.2 Policy analysis iteration

Formulate the problem

The first step to policy advice is to *formulate the problem*. Generally some external process—lobbying by an interest group, media campaigns or a persistent failure of programs to achieve objectives—draws the attention of decision makers to an issue. Ministers then seek advice from the bureaucracy about the nature, scale and characteristics of the concern.

There is no single method for formulating problems because the particular scale and content of the issue, and the way it is originally discussed, tend to frame the research which follows. Each problem may be unique.

Formulating a problem immediately raises questions of ownership. Departments have characteristic ways of seeing the world, and may define issues in ways that complement existing missions. Jeremy Taylor (1993) has explored how health, welfare and education departments in three Australian states respond to the question of early intervention programs for children under five years of age with intellectual disabilities. He demonstrates that each department formulates the 'problem' in a way that draws these children into its own programs and priorities. It requires a major

COMMON QUESTIONS TO CLARIFY ISSUES
- How did this situation arise?
- Who is affected by this issue and why?
- What do the main players in the field say about the issue?
- Are there data suggesting trends?
- Do local or international studies indicate the probable trajectory of this issue?
- Can the problem be broken into smaller parts and dealt with as a series of related issues?
- Are there existing programs or processes that can be applied to this problem?
- To whom within government does this problem belong?

See, for example, Brewer and deLeon (1983:43ff).

commitment to cross-departmental coordination before target children receive multidisciplinary treatment that begins with their needs rather than bureaucratic convenience.

Australian governments rely on a number of institutional constraints, including consultation prior to cabinet decisions and evaluation of policy proposals by central agencies, to restrain too narrow or self-interested problem specification. There remains, though, a professional obligation on policy analysts to offer options that can be defended on their own terms, and do not simply reflect personal or departmental values.

Set out objectives and goals

Defining objectives is fundamental to making policy choices. The objectives selected will 'determine what priorities are assigned and what policies are selected, provide guidelines for the implementation of the chosen programs, and determine the criteria for program evaluation' (Brewer and deLeon, 1983:48).

Just as problem definition can be elusive, so tying decision makers to particular objectives may prove difficult. Problems tend to pose precise questions ('How much will we spend to address this concern?') while politicians prefer to keep answers general ('Let's look at it in an overall budget context'). Government policy documents set out principles but often do not provide sufficient information to inform policy development in a specialised field.

Further, all policy decisions are taken in a wider setting. Since an ideal health care system would consume much of the national product, health system solutions are compromises. The goal—quality of care—remains unchanged, but in practice this objective is balanced against other, non-health, considerations.

As Wildavsky (1987:216) observes, 'the objectives people have, the goals they seek to achieve, are a function not merely of their desirability but also of their feasibility. What we try to do depends to some degree on what we can do.'

To deal with ambiguous or conflicting objectives, policy analysts typically produce a range of options for decision makers. Each option presents a different configuration of problem

---

Objectives are not just out there, like ripe fruit waiting to be plucked; they are manmade, artificial, imposed on a recalcitrant world. Inevitably they do violence to reality by emphasising some activities (hence organisational elements) over others. Thus the very step of defining objectives may be considered a hostile act. If they are too vague, no evaluation can be done. If they are too specific, they never encompass all the indefinable qualities that their adherents insist they have. If they are too broad, any activity may be said to contribute to them. If they are too narrow, they may favour one segment of the organisation over another. Strategically located participants often refuse to accept definitions of objectives that would put them at a disadvantage or in a strait-jacket should they wish to change their designation of what they do in the future. Arguments about which really, but really and truly, are the objectives of the organisation may stultify all future action.
Wildavsky (1987:216)

definition, policy objective and proposed solution. Ministers can then choose among an array of values and opportunities. As with problem definition, shaping options imposes an ethical requirement on analysts to treat the alternatives fairly.

Identify decision parameters

Policy advisers can frame options once they know:

- the likely objectives of the minister and government
- the possibilities for obtaining additional resources
- the time frames required for consideration and action
- the relative priority of the problem.

Often departments prepare briefing notes to test the minister's concern and resolve on an issue. If the minister indicates interest, further options or a single policy proposal are then prepared.

If the minister does not take up the invitation, the department must either find ways of rearranging its own priorities or leave the problem unaddressed. A new problem must push on to the agenda of government, already crowded with more demands than ministers can satisfy. The iterative process of notes and briefings between the department and the minister's office provides an indication for policy analysts about the relative importance of some new issue.

As constraints on a policy program become clear, analysts can judge how much time and attention a problem deserves. If the issue is unlikely to attract strong interest, policy makers may lean to an incremental solution—a minor modification of an existing program, or an extension of familiar procedures to a new domain. This minimises search and analysis time.

On the other hand, policy makers may confront new problems for which incremental solutions are not available. Analysis is required to create new laws, programs or institutions. Much greater investment must occur in research and evaluation before a policy approach emerges (Hayes, 1992).

Sometimes, even with that investment, viable policy options are not available. This may reflect a lack of reliable information about the problem at hand, leading to:

GOOD POLICY ADVICE

Michael Keating (1996:62), suggests four key elements to good policy advice:

- Is the advice timely, forward looking, correctly recognising emerging issues and problems?
- Does it identify implications of options, alternatives and cost effective solutions?
- Does it form part of a clearly defined and coherent strategy, including a strategy for achieving acceptance of the policy?
- Is it practical to implement?

- inability to break the problem into separate, manageable units
- lack of confidence in the causal models informing policy options
- incapacity to cost various courses of action.

When analysis fails, and the parameters affecting a decision remain unclear, this is usually a warning. It suggests policy makers are dealing with a wicked or intractable problem likely to defy policy intervention. At a minimum, it indicates more research and thinking is required.

It would be wrong just to ignore such problems, but policy advisers must be honest in their appraisal. A minister needs to know if a problem has no solution. US President Johnson accepted advice from his cabinet and staff that the war in Vietnam could be won. In retrospect, he lacked accurate information about the problem. The White House did not have a reliable causal model about the likely course of events or a realistic assessment of the cost of victory. Had the president's advisers been more honest about their limited knowledge of the region and its history, and provided a wider range of options, Johnson may not have elected to destroy his presidency pursuing a tragic, deadly and doomed policy. He might instead, as one Republican senator proposed, 'declare victory and leave'.

Honest appraisal may include a retreat to issue identification. Sometimes failure to develop viable options reflects muddy thinking about the nature of the problem itself. Revisiting issue identification is probably a necessary reality test even when viable options are developed. Many policy issues present in the form of a solution that is born of high ideals but unrealisable in the complex reality of government's limits and overall resource constraints. Real solutions may lie in reconceptualising the underlying policy problem and moving afresh through the policy cycle.

Search for alternatives

The *search* phase of analysis requires research. The objective is to acquire as much relevant information as required, and to identify possible responses. Given that problems often have multiple faces (economic, social, environmental, legal, technical, political), a team approach to analysis can be important.

Sources for ideas may include:

- current policies, locally and in other jurisdictions
- international findings on best practice in the field
- recent reviews and reports on the issue
- academic journals
- discussions with experts within and outside government
- consultation with clients.

> Listen, I'm a politician which means I'm a cheat and a liar and when I'm not kissing babies I'm stealing their lollipops. But it also means I keep my options open.
> *Jeffrey Pelt (played by Richard Jordan),* Hunt for Red October, *(1990)*

The search phase identifies possible options. It also narrows down the possibilities, compressing the potential universe of responses into those choices judged most likely to meet the objectives of decision makers. This judgment is inevitably subjective, and so requires supporting argument and evidence. The Australian National Audit Office has attempted to model various phases in gathering information to inform objectives.

In many (but not all) policy areas, it is possible to model the consequences of a particular course of action. Models assist comparison of options. Modelling is often strongest when dealing with financial or technical information and at its least effective when trying to calculate the social or political consequences of an option. Governments can model the cost of a new road, the likely usage and the environmental consequences of choosing one route over others. Despite sophisticated local consultation programs and social impact studies, calculating the community response (and subsequent political fallout) remains less reliable.

Providing models—or at least logical arguments—for each option imposes an important discipline on policy analysts. The requirement to model consequences ensures explicit statements about causation, with assumptions spelled out and reliability specified.

Propose solutions

Finally, robust policy analysis should point to potential courses of action. Some problems have a single solution, but most can be

66   The Australian Policy Handbook

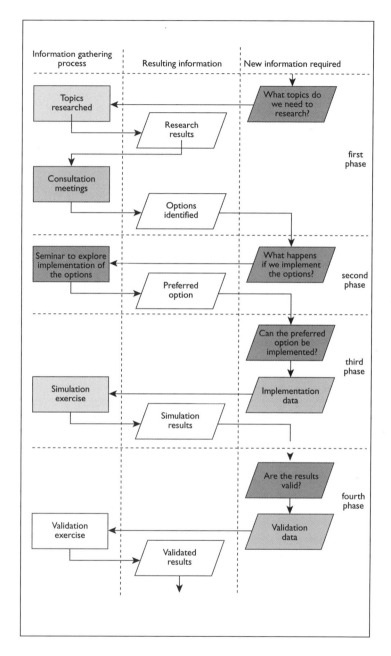

Figure 5.3   Developing policy advice

(Australian National Audit Office, 2001, *Audit Report No. 21*, Canberra, Commonwealth of Australia. The figure is on page 76 of the report, which can be sourced online at www.anao.gov.au.)

addressed in various ways depending on resources and enthusiasm. The product of a policy analysis is usually a briefing paper or report following the steps in analysis—that is, it formulates the problem, establishes objectives, identifies parameters, states alternatives and concludes with one or more recommendations.

Such recommendations should be accompanied by a comparison and, if appropriate, an 'on balance' finding for one choice over others. Ministers will not feel bound by bureaucratic findings, but at least they know how a professional policy analysis has dissected the issue and weighed the alternatives.

If the choices on offer are unpalatable, politicians may seek further information or change some aspect of the equation; often we need to see options to become certain of our objectives. So policy analysts are reconciled to iteration, to reworking the material in the search for workable choices.

EVIDENCE-BASED POLICY

The election in the United Kingdom of the Blair government in 1997 provided impetus for a renaissance in the idea that policy making should be better informed by research and evidence over the ideology and conviction approaches of the Thatcher and Reagan eras (Sanderson, 2006). Thus was born the global movement of evidence-based policy (Marston and Watts, 2003; Nutley et al., 2003).

The movement is strongly associated with the concept of evidence-based practice in the human services sector and in medicine. It advocates that policy processes can be improved by forging stronger links between researchers and public policy decision makers and between research and practice. A number of general trends driving efforts to improve such links include:

- sweeping public sector reform and capacity constraints
- competition for funding—search for a 'rational' means of allocating scarce resources
- recognition of the growing complexity and interdependence of public policy problems
- increasing use of specialists and experts in a more contested and competitive policy domain

Nutley et al. (2003) adapted the work of evaluation expert Carol Weiss to establish the following models of research utilisation to show different occurrences when governments might resort to evidence-based research in the policy making process:

- *Instrumental use*—research feeds directly into decision making for policy and practice
- *Conceptual use*—research used to change practitioner understanding of a situation, provide new ways of thinking and offer insights into the strengths and weaknesses of particular courses of action. New conceptual understandings can then sometimes be used in instrumental ways
- *Mobilisation of support*—research becomes an instrument of persuasion, a political tool or to legitimate particular courses of action or inaction
- *Wider influence*—research has influence beyond the institutions or events being studied. Evidence may be synthesized, come into currency through networks of practitioners and researchers and alter policy paradigms or belief communities. Research adds to the accumulation of knowledge which ultimately contributes to large-scale shifts in thinking and sometimes action.

> Experts are just trained dogs.
> *Albert Einstein*

- globalisation and heightened impact of international organisations sharing and shaping practice and assessing policy and organisational effectiveness
- moves towards 'knowledge economies' that have promoted emphasis on obtaining, sharing and trading knowledge.

Specific instances also propel action. Sometimes governments struggle to find enough policy resources, or to find satisfactory sources: there is a deficiency in policy supply. In these instances, research communication and dissemination are often emphasised and the role of 'policy entrepreneurs' or 'policy brokers' becomes critical. Sometimes the demand side of the research-policy interface is the key problem. For these instances a culture of 'policy learning' within government becomes the centre of attention. When there are problems in both supply and demand sides of the equation, wider socio-political and socio-cultural contexts are stressed and the emphasis in policy research shifts to cooperation, collective action and capacity building.

Using research and evidence to inform policy making appears self-evidently desirable, begging the question of why an evidence-based policy movement emerged. Why is there such a disjuncture between research and policy outcomes? The answer lies in the research and policy worlds having different priorities, different languages, different timescales, different reward systems and different ends (Burton, 2006). Interface between these two worlds is often fraught. Research emphasises knowledge advancement and understanding whereas policy is motivated to practical action. Politics rarely has the luxury of time and calm, scientific rationality. Political subjects are not able to be controlled or tested in the manner demanded by research.

It is often assumed that evidence-based policy making is attractive when there is not enough information to guide policy. However, the political nature of policy decision making also suggests that evidence-based policy making has uses when there is *too much* research, screening out irrelevant or discursive information. Knowledge-management, in effect, becomes the key.

There are strengths and weaknesses associated with evidence-based policy:

Strengths

- *Asking the right questions*. The requirement to conduct research and find evidence places a discipline on policy makers to take time to sit down and ask what exactly the problem is that they are trying to address. This discipline encourages more targeted policy making.
- *Efficiency and effectiveness*. Evidence-based policy can result in more efficient and effective policy making, leading to improved value for money and avoidance of wastage. Transparency in policy making can also be enhanced.
- *Means of inclusion*. Evidence-based policy making connects researchers, policy makers, decision makers, the public and other interest groups, yielding better informed and more inclusive policies.
- *Appraisal and risk minimisation*. Evidence-based policy can assist in appraising the potential reactions of stakeholders and can therefore contribute to risk minimisation in the policy making process.
- *Best practice*. Searching for evidence encourages policy makers to look for best practice and to learn from others' mistakes and successes. Innovation often emerges as a consequence.
- *Defensability*. Evidence-based policy making provides a sound basis for providing objective answers to policy questions.

Weaknesses

- *Time pressures*. Governments are under constant pressure to address problems, both in terms of identifying issues and resolving them in an adequate manner. Yet the time allocated to problem solving is usually short, denying policy makers the luxury of waiting for detailed research results before decisions must be made. Moreover, liberal democratic governments are usually subject to electoral cycles that can make research seem a luxury.
- *Temporal disjunctures*. The problems confronting governments are usually sweeping, interconnected social issues that have far-reaching impacts and implications. The evidence

required in such public policies should preferably be based on robust, long-term research. In reality only short-term studies are possible or no research is available. Time series research is often impossible due to changes in datasets or measures used, meaning that policy makers must start again. The lack of largescale, detailed and long-term research means results are often piecemeal and open to manipulation. Indeed, time series analysis may understate the severity of existing problems requiring an immediate or short-term action. Furthermore, the static nature of research often has to fit into a shifting context or environment that demands flexibility and applied decision making on the part of policy makers. Sometimes it is better or more appropriate for policy makers to rely on their ability to apply research lessons rather than rely on research findings per se.

- *Contesting evidence.* Unanimity in research and evidence is not common. Differences in research methodologies and differences in scientific interpretation of data can lead to conflicting information being presented to decision makers. It is all evidence but which is to be chosen as the basis upon which the policy should be made?
- *Subject matter limitations.* Many policy initiatives involve assumptions that are fundamentally untestable. People and programs cannot always be isolated into test groups, causality cannot always be established, appropriate sample sizes are often impossible to obtain given the nature of the programs, and key drivers affecting the future and uptake of certain policies cannot be measured or predicted with accuracy. Instead, policy makers often have to rely on best guesses. The subject matter of policy making, in other words, is often not open to empirical methods. Expectations that demand precision in evidence based on empiricist approaches to research result in unreasonable and sometimes damaging effects on policy making.
- *Public sector requirements.* Attention to due process, ethics and public accountability is a mainstay of public sector decision making, meaning that governments often cannot use or access certain pieces of evidence. Ethical and political dilemmas apply to experimental approaches to public policy:

different treatment of different groups in society and the potential misapplication of public funds constrains what is possible or desirable. The cost of research is significant. Governments must increasingly demonstrate value for money and there is an almost inherent expectation that new research must be cost-beneficial, which might be impossible to show in developing a research program.
- *Politicisation and downplaying democracy*. Recourse to evidence and managerial approaches to policy making can conflict with democratic participation and public opinion. Parsons (2002) notes that 'whose evidence? and what counts as evidence in the first place?' are important questions to ask. Evidence can be a rhetorical flourish masking pragmatism: what counts is what works; another tool of power manipulating perception. Thus evidence can constrain what is possible.

There is obviously a debate over the use of evidence in policy making. The policy process is not a simple, stratified matter of accumulation, assessment, assimilation and presentation of research. A dynamic, organic approach is more applicable. Fischer (2003:201, 202) suggests that evidence should not be understood solely as the gathering and presentation of scientifically rational information. Rather 'policy analysis can be understood as "crafted argument" ... [there is a] logic of policy deliberation, emphasizing the force of "the better argument" ... The goal is to improve policy discourse by illuminating contentious questions, identifying the strengths and limitations of supporting evidence, and elucidating the political implications of contending positions.'

Overall, the strengths and weaknesses of the evidence-based policy approach suggest the need for a balanced regard for what counts as evidence. From a strictly scientific research perspective, governments are variously choosing, puzzling and constructing policy in a relatively haphazard manner. Complex problems are, however, of their nature not amenable to cause–effect analysis. In developing solutions to complex problems policy makers often have to rely on post-hoc observation because it is more powerful than science.

ANALYTIC FRAMEWORKS AND EXAMPLES

Economic framework
- cost-benefit
- cost-effectiveness
- opportunity costs
- market competitiveness
- regulatory impact

Social framework
- community impact
- interest group impact
- community values
- social justice principles
- cultural heritage impact

Environmental framework
- environmental impact analysis
- ecologically sustainable development principles
- environmental quality
- habitat preservation
- biodiversity
- sound management of natural resources

Legal framework
- constitutionality
- head of power
- fundamental legislative principles
- certainty, equality and fairness of the law
- access to the law
- enforceability

Political framework
- consistency with governing party principles and policies
- consultation with political advisers
- agreement among policy elites
- electoral impacts
- expected media reception

THE ANALYST'S TOOLKIT

Many tools are available for policy analysis. Here we describe the major frameworks commonly used by analysts. No policy professional will possess all the expertise identified in these frameworks. Instead, policy advisers should call on the expertise of others, and draw a breadth of teamwork advice into their work. This collegiate approach exposes assumptions to scrutiny and tests them. It is a significant step towards building a robust policy, a policy that can engage the real world in the way decision makers intend.

The most fundamental of all analysis takes place in the substantive context of the policy itself. Educational, economic, health, agricultural and legal issues each require focus from relevant policy professionals, who should bring substantive experience to bear on the matter, and who can advise on secondary issues such as transaction costs associated with a policy choice. For example, if the policy will alienate a significant group, its opposition may result in financial or legal impediments that bring the option undone, or that need to be accommodated by incorporating effective dispute management strategies within the policy.

Economic framework

The analytic hegemony of our times is clearly economic. Much public debate is about economic and financial management, so governments need continuing advice on economic and budgeting policy choices. Accordingly, many government initiatives are framed through the perspective of analytical tools based on economic models. These are outlined in Table 5.1. These models in turn influence the major policy instruments used by government. Table 5.2 indicates how economic policy objectives are translated into public sector initiatives, often designed to reduce the scope and outlays of government.

Another potentially powerful economic analysis tool is based on examining the market for goods or services, and the incentives for participants in the market. This allows policy makers to examine the secondary effects of policy proposals, and adds a significant veneer to the more focused approach of cost-benefit analysis. This approach asks about the demand for and supply of goods or services, who provides and purchases them, and what the incentives (and disincentives) are for the participants in the market. It is not always easy to identify the goods and services, and it can be very complex to identify purchasers and providers.

The example of private prisons illustrates some of the complexity, and some of the power, of this approach. Traditionally, state governments manage prisons. They hold offenders convicted under both state and Commonwealth laws, and there is a national system for transfer of prisoners between jurisdictions. Prisons are very costly to build and run. Holding offenders in secure custody requires a lot of infrastructure and staff: a prison needs cells, walls, yards, kitchens, sick bays and recreation areas, and properly skilled and equipped staff to secure these areas. Rehabilitation of offenders, to ensure they re-enter society able to participate in a lawful and responsible way, may also be costly. Professional attention and quality programs to help offenders manage their behaviour and reduce prospects of re-offending are also resource intensive.

Table 5.1   Economic analysis tools

Cost-benefit analysis	Cost-effectiveness analysis	Opportunity cost
Cost-benefit analysis measures whether a policy has economic benefits for the society. It allows comparison of options to determine which will produce the greatest economic benefit. It does so by using dollars as a measurement of policy proposals. Policy makers can then explore the cost to benefit ratio of alternatives.	Cost-effectiveness is a variation on cost-benefit analysis. It recognises that not all options can be compared. The relative merits of a dam versus an untouched natural river cannot be decided by assigning dollar amounts to each. Yet decision makers need to know whether the options are viable in their own terms.	Opportunity cost is a necessary reminder for decision makers that in buying one thing they must forgo another. The decision to fund A is also a decision not to fund B (though perhaps not recognised as such).
Cost-benefit analysis requires significant technical skills, and important subjective judgments about the discount rate to be applied. The discount rate equates present values with future costs and benefits: set too high, and future benefits become unimportant compared with immediate cost; set too low, and government may waste resources chasing the future, losing the	Cost-effectiveness analysis examines the merits of a particular proposal. It measures the costs of a policy proposal against the expected benefits in traditional financial terms, the likely return on investment by government. Through cost-effectiveness analysis, decision makers can learn whether a given option will achieve its goals efficiently (Weimer and Vining, 1992:221).	Politicians are familiar with the calculus of budgeting—a submarine purchased is a new dam, hospital or school that cannot be built. Economists have developed ways to model opportunity cost, understood as the value placed on the best alternative that must be forgone.

More difficult to comprehend is the cost of *not* taking action. Yet if government decides against construction of a dam, it should be possible to estimate the |

prospect of other, immediate gains: see 'opportunity cost' in this table.

There is substantial literature on cost-benefit analysis, much of it hostile to the technique. Critics observe the difficulties of rendering some intangible benefits, such as the aesthetics of an unspoiled wilderness, in dollar terms. They question the emphasis on efficiency as the key criterion for evaluation compared with equity, equality or justice (Anderson, 1994:256).

Though clearly of limited applicability, the utility of cost-benefit analysis should not be underestimated. Many public problems are open to cost-benefit studies, and foolish decisions can be avoided if simple cost and benefit data are made available. Cost-benefit analysis is not a substitute for political decision making, but it can provide important evidence to inform better those who must choose between alternatives.

The results of cost-effectiveness studies can then be compared—if not directly, then against objectives set by government. Cabinet may decide, for example, to spend $20 million on new drought relief programs. A cost-effectiveness analysis will help identify the policy option that gains the most for the available cash.

Alternatively, cabinet may decide on rural adjustment, such as assisting small-scale farmers and their families to leave their farms and learn new skills for alternative occupations. The farms are thus available for integration into larger-scale, and more efficient, enterprises. Applying a cost-effectiveness test to the options may indicate which alternative will achieve the required outcome for the minimum cost.

As with cost-benefit analysis, there are limits to applicability. Not all benefits can be measured, nor all costs anticipated. Producing a benefit at the lowest cost may conflict with other goals such as providing employment opportunities. Yet cost-effectiveness analysis can provide important information to inform decision making.

subsequent losses to the economy. Government knows how much it saves, but also how much is lost in the long term. The net benefit (or cost) becomes the real measure of the policy option.

As with cost-benefit analysis, there is subjectivity hidden in the apparently technical certainty of opportunity cost measurement. The approach requires policy analysts to model a best alternative that never happened.

Still, the opportunity cost concept provides some rigour when making choices, because it provides information about the full cost—not just the cash required up front—of a course of action.

A cost-benefit analysis might identify significant fiscal savings to a government if prisons are built, operated and managed by private operators. There are several such prisons in Australia. The savings may be achieved through work practice changes, reducing overall staff costs, and use of contractors for specialised services. What does a market and incentive analysis add to decision making about private prisons?

Table 5.2 Australian public sector initiatives based on economic objectives

National Competition Policy
NCP is a national template aiming to remove unnecessary barriers to commercial competitiveness, such as restrictive licensing schemes. Within the public sector, NCP opens up government monopoly for competition. The schedule agreed between the Commonwealth and states imposes a phased program to improve performance by public sector utilities and local government authorities.

Among the related components of NCP are mutual recognition laws, which provide validity for qualifications across Australia, so that a lawyer trained in one jurisdiction can practise in other states or territories. The same laws also facilitate interstate trade in goods and services. As with NCP generally, the objective is to ensure efficiency through competition across national markets.

Competitive neutrality and commercialisation
Close relatives of NCP, competitive neutrality and commercialisation aim to ensure the management of government does not distort the market. Thus government entities are to be treated in ways equivalent to private sector participants. They will be structured along commercial lines, subject to equivalent tax regimes, and required to meet the performance, accountability and dividend expectations applicable to companies. The objective is to improve their competitiveness and reduce bureaucratic 'distortions' of decision making.

Regulatory impact
Legislation about economic activity carries costs, frequently borne by the business sector. Regulatory impact studies examine such costs and typically apply cost-benefit methods to assess the need for adjustment or removal of the regulation.

Reduced outlays and debt redemption
Governments at all levels have expressed their intention to reduce overall outlays and, in particular, to diminish debt. Less debt frees money currently committed to debt repayment. Some economists argue (though the evidence is equivocal) that lower public sector borrowing will reduce pressure on interest rates. This policy has encouraged the sale of many government assets, budget cuts to remaining operations and a reduction in the services and employment offered by government.

Competitive Service Delivery
To ensure efficiencies in public funded programs, governments are promoting Competitive Service Delivery (CSD). Government agencies compete for contracts to deliver a service, or the service is outsourced entirely and awarded on a regular basis to private providers through a tender process. CSD has been applied to many areas of social policy provision, including domiciliary services, labour market programs and even forms processing.

Shifting away from government monopoly creates a market where previously there was none. The market is for provision of custodial services. Decisions can be made in new ways about how a court-ordered sentence can be fulfilled, because there are alternatives. Each alternative is a prison, but the cost structures of imprisonment are decided differently for state and private facilities. It is possible for specialisation to emerge—for example, in the treatment of sex offenders.

The government has a *demand* for custodial services, and will *purchase* them, maybe from another government (as with Commonwealth prisoners held in state facilities), from a private provider or by building and managing a state facility. The demand is met by *supply* of prison beds in various facilities. The *provider* may be a government agency or a private operator. The *incentive* for providers is to manage the prison efficiently. There are high cost outcomes to be avoided: fights, self harm by prisoners, riots. There are events like escapes that impose externally derived costs. This will inform decision makers (purchasers) in structuring the contract for services with the providers, whether they are private or state facilities. These incentives may militate against the higher cost elements of imprisonment, such as rehabilitation. However, it may be cheaper to run educational programs, for example, because these can be facilitated by a single professional, such as a teacher, obviating the need for constant supervision by custodial officers. Privatisation may lead to more programs, but only for lower-risk populations such as long-term prisoners.

The power of this analytic framework also derives from the ability to attend to other perspectives. The corporate desire to expand and to gain economies of scale may create a *demand for prisoners*. Further, the demand is likely to be skewed to long-term prisoners, who are known to present fewer behavioural problems in prison once they have settled into the routine of institutional life (and whose management can be achieved through lower-cost education programs). Thus the *provider* has an interest in more and longer custodial sentences being given by courts. How does this interest express itself in the policy making process? How do decision makers interact with these providers and in which areas of policy?

The challenge for those using this framework is to avoid elevating *market* to an outcome. It is but a tool, albeit one that can be pushed until entire national and state governments are transformed into market analogues (e.g. Alford and O'Neill, 1994; Boston, 1995), with 'purchaser' and 'provider' being the ultimate definition of public sector participation. Yet this remains a tool, an instrument to achieve preferred ends. A good tool used well will make a task easier; used badly, it may destroy the original policy intent.

Ultimately policy analysis is more than budget and various indexes of economics; there are great dangers in analysing a problem solely in economic terms. Social, environmental, legal and political perspectives are also of crucial importance. Left to its own devices, economics can be reductionist, and drive all issues towards a binary choice between market and intervention (Freebain, 1998).

Social framework

Analysing policy issues and options from a social perspective recognises those dimensions that are difficult or impossible to accommodate in the economic framework.

The analyst is challenged by the consequences an option may have for specific sectors, such as women, indigenous Australians, rural communities, culturally and linguistically diverse peoples, people with mobility problems or the poor. Where these groups are not necessarily the target of the policy, the options are examined in terms of how each will affect the relevant social sector, and whether unintended impacts can be avoided.

'Social infrastructure', the institutions and physical resources through which social programs are delivered, is also important. A program to rationalise, say, local post offices, can have an important impact because of the many ways a community uses this resource.

Analysts often find 'social justice principles' useful to anchor their analysis of an issue or options. These principles are:

- *Rights*. Does the policy protect or advance individual rights, and educate about social obligations?
- *Equity*. Have interested community groups and individuals been identified and empowered in the policy process? How does each option affect them?
- *Participation*. Full participation in society is a goal of social policy. Thus options are examined in terms of their impact on people's ability to participate, and the resources they need. This is especially true of those who traditionally lack resources through distance, poverty, lack of social institutions validating their participation, or poor language or numeracy skills.

- *Access.* Individuals need access to social services. Well-structured access allows the service provider to respond more effectively to the needs and expectations of the target groups.

Environmental framework

Policy options may affect the environment, especially if considering approval for a major project. Analysis must therefore cover not just the economic feasibility of a proposal, but its potential impact on the environment.

It may be good economics to build a third or even fourth runway to manage Sydney air traffic volumes, but what does such a proposal mean for the environment? The environmental impact study (EIS) is the major tool for answering this question.

In its various forms, an EIS seeks to specify the consequences for the environment, and for communities, of a course of action. This may bring together scientific measurement of a habitat, and population data about fauna and flora, with an evaluation of the environmental consequences of a particular project. How many koala deaths from a proposed new road are acceptable? Is it a number which does not threaten the overall local population, or is even one roadkill an unacceptable price?

Environment evaluation includes not just land, air and water pollution, or pollution by noise and light. *Biodiversity* must also be considered, bringing specifics of plant and animal habitat into the analyst's frame.

The idea of *ecological sustainability* is also important. Human activity has significant and even irreversible ecological impacts. The idea underpinning ecological sustainability is that our activities should be structured in a way that allows regeneration and preservation of ecology. Other important considerations for environmental policy are *habitat preservation* and *environmental quality*. All these considerations will be incorporated into a well-structured environmental impact study.

Natural resource management has emerged as a further key concern over recent years, with emphasis not only on soil, water, forests and fisheries, but on the interaction that runs to environmentally sensitive areas, such as river catchments.

Too often in politics, there are fallacious either/or arguments put up as a justification or an excuse for an action or view which is skewed in such a way as to suggest that there is only one acceptable choice.
Peter Garrett, MP

Legal framework

Modern notions of government are founded on the resources available to fund programs, employ staff and build infrastructure. More traditional descriptions of the body politic start with the idea of power, exercised by the parliament in the form of law making.

Many policies require legislation to give them effect, and all policies take place in a legal context because governments are themselves subject to the rule of law.

Fundamental law, the constitutions of the Commonwealth, the states and the territories, describe the limits of governmental power. For example, the Commonwealth may possess the most powerful parliament in our federation, but it is unable to make laws that discriminate on the basis of religion, because the Commonwealth Constitution prohibits it from doing so. States may wish to protect their markets by imposing excises, but this option is not constitutionally open.

As well as a constitution, each jurisdiction in Australia has laws of general application, setting certain requirements on the policy process. For example, there are laws requiring the auditing of public funds. Policy officers must be aware of such laws when recommending policy options, and ensure any program design conforms to government accountability obligations. Similarly, each jurisdiction has a framework of criminal law, and myriad requirements covering employment, workplace health and safety and other matters. Decision makers must be confident options meet the principles in these laws, but need not specify all the relevant legislation when offering policy advice.

There are also legal principles that apply when developing a legislative proposal for a policy option. As one example, the Queensland parliament stated fundamental legislative principles in its *Legislative Standards Act 1992*, shown in Table 5.3.

Some of the questions asked in legal policy analysis include:

- What is the administrative and constitutional law framework?
- What institutional structures and relationships are necessary?
- Who is accountable to whom and for what? What are the mechanics of accountability?

- What are the relevant decision making frameworks and how are they to be stated?
- How does the proposal relate to fundamental legislative principles (see Table 5.3)?
- How are human rights and liberties affected, directly and indirectly?
- What is the legal and administrative efficacy and propriety of the proposal and the proposed instruments?

Very little work has been done on policy jurisprudence. We posit that there are general principles that may guide legal policy analysis beyond the more specific questions. These include:

- *Democracy*: ensuring our system of representative democracy subject to the rule of law is recognised and protected in policy development; that the nature of the franchise and the authority of electors is fostered; that governance principles are clearly stated and understood.
- *Justice*: looking to the institutions and rules that support social order and allow the exercise of rights; access to justice; understanding of the law; cost of justice; celerity and relevance of legal force and sanctions.
- *Reform*: ensuring the law reflects and develops society.
- *Service*: providing professional advice to decision makers.

Some of the other analytic frameworks need to be understood in their legal context, too. For example, the economics of competition policies are implemented in a complex legal framework, including the trade practice and fair trading laws. Social policy manifests itself in laws such as those prohibiting discriminatory behaviour and laws about social order.

> Even when the experts all agree, they may well be mistaken.
> Bertrand Russell, 'On the Value of Scepticism', from The Will to Doubt, 1928

Political analysis

Political analysis of options takes place in the political domain, and is not the task of the policy analyst employed in a government body. Politics is nonetheless fundamental to policy analysis. Good advice is sensitive to the policy goals of a government, without necessarily seeing these as optimal. The policy analyst's role is to ensure political input is made at appropriate times

Table 5.3   Fundamental legislative principles

Fundamental legislative principles require that legislation has sufficient regard to the rights and liberties of individuals and to the institution of parliament.

Parliament

Does the legislation:
- provide clarity and precision?
- limit delegations to make legislation?
- provide for parliamentary scrutiny of delegated legislation?
- reserve power to parliament to amend Acts?
- provide adequacy of the head of power to make subordinate legislation?
- provide for subordinate legislation's consistency with its principal legislation?
- contain only matters appropriate to subordinate legislation?
- provide for subdelegation of power under subordinate legislation only in certain circumstances?

Individual rights and liberties

Does the legislation:
- provide sufficient definition and provision for review of administrative power?
- provide consistency with the principles of natural justice?
- allow only appropriate delegation of administrative power?
- not reverse the onus of proof in criminal proceedings?
- provide judicial supervision by warrant of powers of entry, search and seizure?
- provide adequate protection from self-incrimination?
- apply retrospective laws?
- confer immunity from prosecution without adequate justification?
- provide for fair compensation for compulsory acquisition of property?
- have sufficient regard to Aboriginal tradition and Torres Strait Islander custom?

during the analysis stage of policy development, and that policy choices show awareness of the governing party's principles and platform, and sensitivity to the issues that are important to the political domain. 'How will this look as tomorrow's headline?' is often a sobering and relevant question for the astute policy adviser to ask.

AGREEMENT: AN ANALYTIC TOOL

American economist Charles Lindblom proposes a very different method for testing policy options—agreement. Lindblom's (1959, 1965) influential work on incrementalism began as a critique of the rational comprehensive model. Lindblom observed that ends and means in policy making are rarely clear. Often our objectives are defined by available resources, or shift as we learn more about the problem. Real and lasting solutions are rare; most problems receive only amelioration until they fade from view or are superseded. The urgent tends to crowd out the important.

Further, there is never enough time or energy to conduct a comprehensive search for alternatives. We do not address each new problem by starting from first principles. Policy makers prefer 'successive limited comparisons' with current practice, modifying existing programs to deal with new issues. Sometimes these modifications are tested through pilot programs. Policy proceeds by small experiments to see whether familiar responses can resolve an emerging problem.

What, then, is the test of a good policy? Not a strong cost-benefit ratio or specification of lost opportunities, argues Lindblom, but agreement. A successful policy is one which commands consensus among policy makers and interest groups. Table 5.4 compares an incrementalism approach with an ideally rational policy process.

In this view, policy makers build up a bank of knowledge about a policy area, and programs to match. This makes policy makers reluctant to move suddenly 'in an entirely different direction'; it is better to experiment with small changes than to seek major policy departures (Hayes, 1992:18). An incremental approach builds an inherent conservatism into the policy process.

Like the rational comprehensive model it sought to displace, incrementalism has many critics. Some critics argue that small steps may produce only circular movement. Others argue that agreement among elites is no guarantee that broader social interests are being served by a policy, and major problems facing society may need a radical push, not an incremental approach.

> Policy making is a process of successive approximation to some desired objective in which what is desired itself continues to change under reconsideration.
> *Lindblom (1959:86)*

> The decision maker almost always has information and insight not available to the analyst. Decision makers and political leaders are likely to be keenly aware of the constraints that the context imposes, which must be taken into account in formulating policy. Such constraints are not always evident to the professional analyst ...
> *Quade (1982:59–60)*

Table 5.4 Two models of policy analysis

Rational policy making	Incrementalist approach
Clarification of values or objectives distinct from and usually prerequisite to empirical analysis of alternative policies.	Selection of value goals and empirical analysis of the needed action are not distinct but are closely intertwined.
Policy formulation is therefore approached through means-end analysis: first the ends are isolated, then the means to achieve them are sought.	Since ends and means are not distinct, means-end analysis is often inappropriate or limited.
The test of a 'good' policy is that it can be shown to be the most appropriate means to desired ends.	The test of a 'good' policy is typically that various analysts find themselves agreeing on a policy (without their agreeing that it is the most appropriate means to an agreed objective).
Analysis is comprehensive. Every important relevant factor is taken into account.	Analysis is limited drastically: • important possible outcomes are neglected • important alternative potential policies are neglected • important affected values are neglected.
Theory is often relied upon heavily.	A succession of comparisons greatly reduces or eliminates reliance on theory.

(From Lindblom, 1959:81)

Despite these and other complaints, incrementalism probably most accurately describes how policy making proceeds. It stresses the expertise of bureaucrats and the economy of working out from familiar programs. To use only incrementalism would be as serious a mistake as relying too heavily on cost-benefit or cost-effectiveness analyses to make decisions; but sometimes, as Lindblom suggests, policy analysts must use judgment about how much time and thought to invest in a problem. The quick and rough calculations of incrementalism may be the most effective way to proceed.

WHY ANALYSIS?

Policy issues are usually complex and costly to address. The process of analysis ensures decision makers are well informed and can choose from an array of potential solutions, each explored thoroughly.

Through analysis we give shape to a problem—establishing its characteristics, drawing boundaries, bringing crucial

PRACTICAL HINTS FOR PRESENTING POLICY ADVICE

- Consider the nature of the times (e.g. electoral cycles, issue agendas).
- Ensure you understand ministerial and/or senior management requirements.
- Network and consult about ideas and/or proposals.
- Clarify whether the minister's office should be involved. If unsure how to proceed, advise senior management or the minister's office.
- When determining the key components of policy advice (e.g. objectives, scope, costing, implications), ensure administrative logics take account of political sensitivities; do not present purely partisan advice.
- Consider timing and/or alert senior management to timing issues.
- Briefs to ministers may become early drafts for cabinet submissions. Consider the requirements of cabinet when briefing ministers.
- Written and oral advice must be succinct, coherent, clear and support well-reasoned recommendations.
- Assess the policy's life. Is it a closing decision, a policy with a limited life or an open-ended proposal?
- Anticipate future needs/requirements.

Wanna et al. (1994:2.14)

variables into clear relief. Analysis allows a policy professional to 'frame' an issue, stating it in terms that make the problem open to possible policy approaches.

When solutions are not obvious, analysts learn to reframe the question, stating the problems in different ways to gain a broader sense of the question. Often the initial presentation of an issue constrains the range of options too tightly. Sometimes, too, a problem is first presented in terms of a solution. 'We need to amend the Act to impose a night-time flight curfew,' laments one person. 'Money is needed to build a new airport,' cries another. Each is proposing a solution, rather than stating the problem in policy terms.

The analyst starts with a problem and a policy objective, then expands and contracts the dimensions of the issue by asking questions, gathering and analysing data, and seeking opinions and views. The aim is to frame an issue in terms that make it intelligible to others, and open to the analytic tools available to policy professionals.

Sometimes political exigencies direct that the starting point is a solution, dictated by a desire to act in a particular area, and the availability of money or other resources. A government may, for example, dictate that it has $2 million available to foster cultural development through community grants. The analyst's task is thus inverted, being stated first as boundaries around the solution. One must work back to desired outcomes (what is 'cultural development'?) and underlying principles such as social justice, and forward again to state the outcome in full context.

Discussions of technique in policy analysis tend to imply a rational and sequential process. Experience, however, tells policy analysts to expect iteration. As problems are defined and redefined, solution parameters shift and objectives waver. This is not a counsel of despair, just a warning that the way of policy analysis rarely runs smooth.

Policy analysis is a balance between art and science. Some problems deserve sustained attention from teams, with full modelling and careful consideration of all variables. Others can be resolved quickly, with minimal search for alternatives. There is no magic that distinguishes one type of policy from the other, only the benefit of thought and experience.

Eminent practitioners discussing policy analysis usually conclude with a plea for judgment—that indefinable mix of experience and intelligence said to guide good policy analysts. One might also call for attention to ethical scruples, in particular the importance of objectivity both when selecting and presenting options. The potential conflict between the two (judgment requiring subjectivity, ethics preferring impartiality) is a paradox of professional life (see Waller, 1996; Keating, 1999). Good policy analysis presents options without spin, but it does not present all options, only those judged most likely to meet stated objectives.

Policy instruments

SNAPSHOT

Policy instruments are the means governments use to achieve their ends.

Here we describe four types of policy instrument:

- *advocacy*—arguing a case
- *money*—using spending and taxing powers
- *government action*—delivering services
- *law*—using legislative power.

Good policy advice relies on choosing the right mix of instruments for the problem at hand.

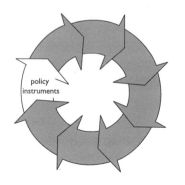

The excitement and bustle of politics and the technical judgment of policy advice must yield eventually to the more measured process of turning ideas into reality if a policy is to take effect in the world. A policy idea means nothing if it cannot be converted into practical application. This chapter is concerned with that conversion, and with the range of 'policy instruments' available to government to achieve its ends.

Governments influence what happens in society through their repertoire of policy instruments. If results are the *ends* of the policy process, instruments are the *means*—the programs, staffing, budgets, organisations, campaigns and laws giving effect to policy decisions.

The policy cycle asks policy professionals to consider policy instruments once they are clear about objectives and goals. Analytically, it is important to keep objectives separate from instruments. There may be more than one way to achieve the same goal, and some means carry political costs that are simply too high.

In the United Kingdom, for example, the conservative government of Margaret Thatcher was committed to reform of local government financing. Despite warnings from cabinet colleagues, the prime minister chose a poll tax as her instrument to achieve this objective. The subsequent urban riots and the clear unworkability of the scheme were significant factors in her downfall as prime minister. Mrs Thatcher's successor readily found less provocative instruments to pursue the same goal.

The temptation to call on an instrument from the repertoire before analysing fully the nature of the issue is also risky for the policy analyst. The means become the end; the instrument is a solution in search of a problem. Experience suggests that choosing the approach first and analysing the problem later is more common than might be expected—especially with legislation as a first resort for public service staff.

All instruments have strengths and weaknesses. As with selection of options, professional judgment is required when advising on choices. Decision makers need to know whether policy options are viable, and the comparative merits of alternative approaches.

CLASSIFYING POLICY INSTRUMENTS

Arguments over typologies may seem irrelevant to the main game of making public policy—a sport for professors. Yet, as Hood (1983) argues, government options are limited by available instruments. Great policy ideas are of little use without appropriate means. Knowledge about the range of choice is therefore essential.

No typology captures fully the complexity of policy instrument choice, but categories are important. They help make sense of various government actions. They display the array of instrument choice and draw attention to alternative ways of achieving goals.

There are myriad policy instruments, from the very broad to the highly specific. Howlett and Ramesh (2003:90) identify some 64 different instruments in the field of economic policy alone. Economic writings warn that instruments must be matched precisely to objectives—even though governments inevitably have more goals than available instruments.

There are important trends in policy instrument choice. Canadians Atkinson and Nigol (1989:111) note that 'governments, under pressure to restrain expenditures, have sought to employ less obtrusive means of intervention'. Further, 'politicians prefer to employ the least coercive instruments possible'. Thus the more coercive regulation, taxation and public ownership approaches are no longer politically favoured.

Despite the fact that Australian statute books are growing at a seemingly alarming rate, there is also movement away from law toward other forms of policy instrument. In the Australian

WHAT IS A POLICY INSTRUMENT?

Policy instruments are the methods used to achieve policy objectives.

Poor instrument choice

A public education program about alternative crops will have little effect on illegal marijuana production. Increased criminal penalties have also been shown in an overwhelming number of criminological studies to have little effect on crime rates.

Multiple instruments

Even simple policy proposals may use multiple instruments. Addressing speeding by motorists might require legislative amendments to allow the use of new speed detection equipment plus increased penalties, coupled with public announcements and education programs about the change.

context, the strengthening of the parliamentary committee systems, and parliamentary scrutiny of legislation committees in particular, has fostered this bias towards less intrusive instruments.

AUSTRALIAN POLICY INSTRUMENTS

In a federal system, policy instruments differ across jurisdictions. The Commonwealth has powers and responsibilities not open to the states, and exclusive access to important revenue streams.

Commonwealth powers have grown over the decades, aided by successive centralising governments, High Court support for Commonwealth legislation and, very occasionally, successful referenda. The Commonwealth has come to dominate the federation, particularly in financial matters. States might spend large amounts on education, transport and health, but they rely on the Commonwealth for most of their income, creating a 'vertical fiscal imbalance'.

This financial dependency allows the Commonwealth, through 'tied grants', to dictate policy in areas which are nominally the responsibility of states.

Local government is the silent partner in the division of powers. It draws authority from state Acts and is not even mentioned in the Constitution. The 1999 Commonwealth tax reform package included a fundamental shift in the basis of funding for local government. Much greater autonomy was given to states in deciding the distribution of financial assistance grants. Local government financial dependence shifted back to the states.

The federal division of powers is a major constraint on selection of policy instruments in an Australian setting. The Constitution, and subsequent intergovernmental arrangements, limit the choices available to state and local governments. In recent times, a number of innovations in 'cooperative federalism' have taken place in the Australian federal model to accommodate and achieve policy goals in new ways. The federal government utilised this approach to encourage uniform national competition policy implementation as well as the introduction of national markets in key essential infrastructure industries such as electricity. While the states and local governments signed up

---

Christopher Hood (1983:4–6) identifies four broad classes of policy instruments:

- 'nodality'—use of information to influence public behaviour
- 'treasure'—use of government money or resources to shape actions
- 'authority'—legal or official powers
- 'organisations'—policies delivered by government agencies.

... governments can achieve their policy goals in a number of ways. Students of policy instruments have argued that the means chosen affect not only the success or failure of policies, but also the political fortunes of decision makers.
Atkinson and Nigol (1989:107)

to the deal and had some discretion in implementation as well as political reasons for collaborating, nonetheless the basic tilt in favour of federal power remains (Hollander, 2006).

Drawing on Hood (1983), we identify five common types of policy instrument used in Australia:

- policy through *advocacy*—educating or persuading, using information available to government
- policy through *network*—cultivating and leveraging relationships within and across government and with external partnership bodies to develop and implement desired goals and behaviours
- policy through *money*—using spending and taxing powers to shape activity beyond government
- policy through direct *government action*—delivering services through public agencies
- policy through *law*—legislation, regulation and official authority.

POLICY THROUGH ADVOCACY

Advocacy instruments argue a case rather than force a result. Often they draw government into working closely with interest groups. Anti-smoking campaigns, for example, bring together state and federal departments of health, the Heart Foundation and the Australian Medical Association.

Such consultation is a growing feature of policy formation. In some policy areas, government agrees not to impose laws in return for sector agreements about shared objectives (for example, 'self-regulation' by various professions).

The power of advocacy as a policy instrument should not be underestimated. In the contemporary political realm, the currency of emotion is just as significant as the power of rationality or informed debate. Perceptions hold sway as much as ideas. Relational bonds, including trust, do much to cover the fears and insecurities created by uncertainty and growing sociological trends in the direction of the 'risk society' (Beck, 1992; Giddens, 1990). Under this environment, policy can be achieved using the currency of 'moral capital'. The idea is that moral capital (an element of political capital) is a resource that can be employed by leaders to legitimate some players or issues and to delegitimise others, 'for mobilising support and for disarming opposition, for creating and exploiting political opportunities that otherwise would not exist' (Kane, 2001:11).

Leadership, here, involves symbolism that moves and motivates people to pursue or support a certain path or cause. Moral capital might impel the moral susceptibility of followers to take certain action or adopt a particular conviction and is a valuable commodity for policy and political leaders. Deployment of moral capital can result in a policy position being accepted or preferred over alternatives. It can turn a respectable option to indecency just as it can turn unacceptability to trendy preference.

Table 6.1 Policy through advocacy

Instruments	Examples
Commonwealth	
• funding for public education promotional activity	• publicity campaign to encourage electors to vote
• establishment of consultative bodies	• hosting meetings of farm groups to discuss drought policy
• ministerial speeches and events to attract publicity for causes and ideas	• ministerial presentation to annual conferences of industry groups
• policy announcement	• issuing a discussion paper on new vehicle regulations for discussion
State	
• funding for public education promotional activity	• anti-smoking advertising campaigns
• establishment of consultative boards	• meeting with Ethnic Communities Council
• ministerial speeches and events to attract publicity for causes and ideas	• premier's announcement of proposed inquiry into health system reform through Leaders' Conference
• policy announcement	• launching a green paper on land clearing for consultation
Local government	
• funding for public education promotional activity	• community workshops to examine community safety issues
• promotion of council initiatives through suburban newspapers	• 'town hall meeting' initiatives to discuss local planning and development issues
• establishment of consultative bodies	• financial support for regional economic development committees

POLICY THROUGH NETWORK

The traditional policy process presumes a hierarchical government bureaucracy interacting with society to repetitively and uniformly carry out government objectives. This command-and-control model established a 'them and us' approach where public officials were kept at a strictly discrete and anonymous distance from those they served. The recent shift to network governance has challenged this system. Public sector officials can and should deal with external constituencies. Policy is enacted through the input and energy of a range of parties carrying out different duties and functions in order to achieve the desired goal.

Networks range from tightly integrated policy communities (an envelope or subsystem of discrete players and dynamics where stakeholders coalesce with departmental structures and processes and focus on, or promote, an agenda) through to loose conglomerates of interested parties joined around an ad hoc issue (Rhodes, 1997). Networks function vertically as well as horizontally within government and intergovernmental settings. In addition they include and match external parties such as third sector organisations, private sector participants and citizens with government/s to achieve policy ends.

Policy occurs through the medium of networked configurations built on relationships and information and resource exchange. Parties usually have some form of incentive to communicate and participate and the mutual interaction and joint exchange that occurs impels policy making. Using networks, governments often become policy facilitators rather than necessarily carrying the dominant role in service delivery or policy enactment (Goldsmith and Eggers, 2004).

POLICY THROUGH MONEY

Governments have multiple objectives when making fiscal decisions. At the broadest level, they hope to influence the economy, though deregulation of financial markets and a reduction in tariffs have diminished greatly the capacity of the Commonwealth to control macro-economic outcomes.

A second objective for government is to ensure sufficient revenue. Tax policy must strike a balance between encouraging

---

A governance network is:

1. a relatively stable horizontal articulation of interdependent, but operationally autonomous actors;
2. who interact through negotiations;
3. which take place within a regulative, normative, cognitive and imaginative framework;
4. that is self-regulating within limits set by external agencies; and
5. which contributes to the production of public purpose.

Sørensen and Torfing (2006:9)

It's clearly a budget. It's got a lot of numbers in it.
George W. Bush, 5 May 2000

Table 6.2 Policy community and policy networks: the Rhodes typology

Type of network	Characteristics of network
• Policy community/territorial community	Stability, highly restricted membership, vertical interdependence, limited horizontal articulation
• Professional network	Stability, highly restricted membership, vertical interdependence, limited horizontal articulation, serves interest of profession
• Intergovernmental network	Limited membership, limited vertical interdependence, extensive horizontal articulation
• Produce network	Fluctuating membership, limited vertical interdependence, serves interest of producer
• Issue network	Unstable, large number of members, limited vertical interdependence

(Rhodes, 1997:38; reproduced with permission of Open University Press)

enterprise and funding government programs. People want services but are often reluctant to pay. Tax increases are unpopular, and governments often struggle to balance their books.

A third objective is to influence individual behaviour through financial incentives or disincentives. Assumptions about market behaviour are seldom rigorously tested, however, and often such measures are driven as much by revenue possibilities as by their influence on behaviour.

Governments also use resources to achieve outcomes. Tax dollars fund industry development, schools, universities and other instruments of government policy. Groups and institutions outside government spend much time lobbying for money, arguing about the contribution they could make if appropriately funded.

POLICY THROUGH GOVERNMENT ACTION

While much money held by government is used for transfer payments—to other levels of government, to private organisations, to individuals—a significant proportion is invested in public sector programs and agencies. The Commonwealth's 2006/07 budget reveals estimated expenditure of $53 857 million on goods and services, and $130 387 million on subsidies, benefits and grants.

Such public sector activities are considered in a budget round, and settled by cabinet before presentation to parliament.

Table 6.3   Policy through money

Instruments	Examples
Commonwealth	
• fiscal powers to shape macro-economic outcomes	• asset sales, with proceeds redeeming public sector debts
• taxing powers on individuals, organisations and businesses	• raising tobacco tax to discourage smoking because of health impacts
• incentive payments for private sector activity	• research and development grants for new industries
• grants programs for state activity	• Commonwealth payments to private schools
State	
• limited taxing powers on land, financial transactions, gambling, levies and fines	• increase in pay-roll tax thresholds to attract business
• incentives to attract major industrial, commercial and tourism developments	• reduction in electricity tariffs or provision of cheap land in return for investment
• infrastructure spending for economic development	• construction of new rail and port facilities
Local government	
• rates, levies and limited other income sources	• rate rebate to encourage fitting of sprinkler systems in boarding houses
• user-charging for council facilities	• charges on building plan approvals, and for inspection of property
• limited capacity to offer financial incentives for local government attraction of business sponsorship to support local activities	• finding a company to sponsor a new art exhibition

Governments deliver services through the public sector, accounting for expenditure through annual reports and parliamentary scrutiny. Though government influences much in society, the main points of contact for citizens are often with such services, from transport to hospitals.

At all levels of government, there is movement away from direct government action. Governments choose to 'contract out' functions, relying on private providers who deliver services to a standard specified in a contract. As a result, the size of the public sector is diminishing in most jurisdictions, even though the reach and scope of government remain unchanged. Gary Sturgess (1996) describes this trend as 'virtual government', in which the public service funds, but does not deliver, services traditionally associated with government.

Table 6.4 Policy through government action

Instruments	Examples
Commonwealth	
• cabinet decisions	• providing direction on waterfront reform
• creation of new institutions	• universal health coverage through Medicare
• public service programs	• customs and quarantine inspection service
• funding for service provision by statutory bodies or non-government agencies	• allocations to family counselling agencies
• administrative decisions	• guidelines on dealing with sexual harassment in public sector workplaces
State	
• cabinet decisions	• setting up a rural adjustment program
• creation of new institutions	• establishing an Environmental Protection Agency
• public service programs	• schools, hospitals, rail services, road construction
• funding for service provision by statutory bodies or non-government agencies	• grant to community body supporting women prisoners
• administrative decisions	• directions banning smoking in government buildings
Local government	
• service delivery either by council or through contractors	• waste disposal, sewerage, curbing and guttering
• cultural services	• libraries, child care facilities, meeting rooms

> ... governments in the future—and citizens making demands on those governments—may need to become more aware of what is in government's toolbox in order to develop a better understanding of the possibilities and limitations of what government can do.
>
> ... success in government, in the future as in the past, will depend on its ability to apply a relatively fixed set of basic tools imaginatively to each new situation as it arises.
>
> *Hood (1983:168)*

POLICY THROUGH LAW

The law is the traditional instrument of government policy, and the final guarantee that policy intent can be translated into action.

Laws can facilitate, allowing a course of action; coerce, requiring or prohibiting certain behaviour; or create and govern institutions. Some laws are symbolic, stating aspirations and social values. In passing laws, parliament empowers the government to act and provides a framework for enforcement through the police and courts. Laws are also binding on government, and many impose specific and unique obligations on the political, policy and administrative domains. Freedom of information legislation, for example, opens government documents to public scrutiny.

Laws establish a framework for government action, but much of the detail is contained in regulations—delegated legislation authorised by an act and implemented by officials. Delegated legislation includes regulations, by-laws and ordinances. Local governments, for example, make by-laws, using the authority delegated to them by state government legislation. More detail is found in discretionary administrative decisions made by ministers and officials.

To interpret this universe of laws requires courts and quasi-judicial bodies such as the Human Rights and Equal Opportunity Commission and literally hundreds of administrative appeals tribunals. Such legal bodies make independent judgments, even though they are funded by government.

CHOOSING A POLICY INSTRUMENT

The criteria for selecting the best policy instrument in given circumstances involve a combination of technical efficiency and political nous. Some simple questions help guide the choice:

> If the only tool you have is a hammer, soon every problem begins to look like a nail.
> *Proverb*

- *appropriateness*—is this a reasonable way of proceeding in this policy area?

Table 6.5 Policy through law

Instruments	Examples
Commonwealth	
• legislation	• *Immigration Act*
• subordinate legislation (regulation)	• regulations governing applications for refugee status
• parliamentary resolution	• creation of parliamentary committee of inquiry
• administrative acts	• visa application refused
State	
• legislation	• *Workplace Health and Safety Act*
	• *Fair Trading Act*
• subordinate legislation (regulation)	• regulations governing fishing in national parks
• parliamentary resolution	• formal apology to the Stolen Generation for past wrongs
• administrative acts	• firearm licence granted
Local government	
• legislation	• local laws (by-laws) under *Local Government Act*
• zoning and development approval powers	• zoning land for residential development
• town planning and building approvals	• rejecting a building approval as inconsistent with the character of an area

- *efficiency*—will this instrument be cost-effective?
- *effectiveness*—can this instrument get the job done?
- *equity*—are the likely consequences fair?
- *suitability*—will there be any conflict with existing processes or policies?
- *workability*—is the instrument simple and robust, and can it be implemented?

The choice of policy instruments matters. It is the link between an objective and its attainment. The right set of instruments will be appropriate, efficient, effective, equitable and workable.

Like much else in the policy cycle, judgment as well as science is required to select the best available instrument. As Hood (1983:163) notes, however skilfully policy instruments are used, they do not enable government 'to shape the world outside in any way that it likes. There are some inherent limitations.' The simple application of a government toolkit cannot solve wicked or intractable problems nor address poorly structured issues. Policy instruments need to be backed by sufficient authority and money, and chosen in a framework of rigorous thinking about ends as well as means.

Some policy objectives are simply beyond government. The surrender of economic controls over the economy, for example, may have long-term benefits for growth and competitiveness, but it means government has only limited ability to influence important (and politically sensitive) variables such as inflation or interest rates.

It is imperative, then, to choose the right policy instrument. But it is equally important to be plain-spoken when no such instrument exists. Good tools cannot rescue bad policy.

7 Consultation

The defining feature of Australian representative democracy is free, fair elections. Yet increasingly citizens want a say between elections on choices affecting their community. Governments are learning to include participation in the policy cycle.

Whereas secrecy was once the hallmark of the political and policy domains alike, community expectations have shifted. Groups outside government expect involvement in decision making. The legitimacy of much public policy now rests on an exchange between citizens and their government. Public servants and politicians must find ways to discuss with relevant communities of interest and draw them into the policy process, while avoiding unreasonable delays, simple vetoing by unrepresentative groups and abrogation of responsibility to vested interests.

SNAPSHOT
Consultation takes place throughout the policy cycle. However, as policy problems are analysed and options emerge, government may wish to test its choice with a wider community. The main tool for this testing is consultation.

THE ROLE OF CONSULTATION

The pressure on governments to consult about public policy is considerable. New forms of accountability, including developments in administrative law, encourage consultation as a phase within the public policy cycle. Seeking a viewpoint from those affected by a policy decision is sometimes a legal requirement, and often just smart policy making. Governments are realising that taking positive action to give people a voice and allow them to be heard can improve trust as well as enhance policy development and implementation. In the age of networks and policy communities, consultation is not so much a stage in the policy cycle but an important dimension to the whole process.

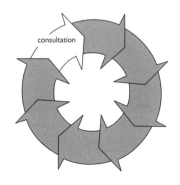

CONSULTATION

Consultation is used by governments for one or more of the following six objectives:

- supporting democratic values
- building consensus and political support
- improving regulatory quality through information collection
- reducing regulatory costs on enterprises, citizens and administrations
- quickening responsiveness
- carrying out strategic agendas.

OECD (1994:6–9)

> When a political leader who holds a public meeting is dubbed a 'revolutionary'—as Mark Latham was in 2004—we know something has gone seriously wrong with Australian politics.
>
> *Young (2004:6)*

A consultative process offers policy makers a way to structure debate, and to develop a solution more likely to 'stick' because it reflects the realities of the problem and the competing interests of those involved.

Consultation also provides an opportunity for policy makers to invite and obtain stakeholder input into the calculation of whether any particular policy is feasible. Policy makers can utilise consultation feedback to help develop a feasibility study prior to the actual implementation of the policy in order to verify policy viability. In project planning, a feasibility study is a way to avoid costly mistakes while grasping the full range of economic, technical, cultural and legal issues at stake. Feasibility information helps improve the confidence of decision makers that a policy is not going to be riddled with embarrassing problems even before it commences the implementation phase. Feasibility information also aids planning for the policy's future.

However, consultation carries costs, especially expenses and delays inherent in managing a large consultation exercise, and the risk of debate dominated by committed but unrepresentative voices.

While consultation is valued by government for addressing legitimacy problems over contentious decisions, consultation has its own legitimacy issues (Davis, 1996:16). Who can claim a voice in consultation? If government alone decides, it risks imposing its preferences and so undermining the benefits of consultation. If self-appointed spokespersons for 'the public interest' dominate the process, the results may not reflect broader community feeling.

There are also problems of how to weight differing voices. Access to the consultation process and capacity to state a case are seldom distributed evenly. It is always easier to deal with interest groups who can speak authoritatively for their membership. However, there is a risk such groups will eclipse other representative but less organised interests, or fail their members and not be representative at all. According to Stoker (2006), there has been a certain degree of professionalisation of activism such that participation may occur solely through experts: 'What they have created is a large pool of activist experts who jointly inhabit with technical, professional and business experts a world of high-intensity engagement' (2006:116). The original intention behind consultation and participation can get lost in the rush to secure tangible evidence of engagement, defeating the purpose of consultation. Politics is for amateurs, too.

An important development in consultation practices has been the recognition of diverse publics. Cameron and Grant-Smith (2005) argue for layers of consultation in order to capture two views of citizenship, the *transcendent* (where the citizen acts with unreflective self-interest, thereby promoting beneficial difference in the community) and the *transformative* (where the citizen is reminded of others' claims and is open to their own identity being transformed through reflection on other people's perspectives). They suggest a number of consultation phases. Separate engagement activities aimed at giving marginalised groups the opportunity for 'safe spaces' in which to explore and establish identity and ideas with like-minded people should be encouraged. At the same time, open forums should also be held that enable diverse groups to express and learn from alternative views and 'respond to the perspectives of others in a process of public deliberation' (2005:30).

Participation and consultation are not simple and once-off. Nor are there any templates that determine the approach. Time, energy, dedication and growth are demanded for meaningful and productive consultation, and paying attention to the unique characteristics in each consultation exercise is likely to pay dividends.

Deciding whether to use consultation requires analysis of the costs and benefits, based on the type of decision and the value of sharing the choice with interested individuals and groups. Formal cost-benefit studies may sometimes be appropriate. However, recourse to such methods should enhance the process rather than represent an excuse for not making an informed effort. In their analysis of the community consultation associated with the Murray-Darling Basin, Crase et al. (2005) propose a number of tools to improve the cost-benefit analysis of consultation in order to overcome criticisms of the Murray-Darling process that saw it labelled as 'a new benchmark for tokenism'.

A consultation strategy is driven largely by the nature of the problem at hand. Deciding when to consult (or whether to

> The important question is, How many hands have I shaked?
> *George W. Bush,* New York Times, *23 October 1999*

consult at all) is as much political judgment as a procedural issue. Decisions about public participation in decision making need to be made in a dialogue about the technical requirements of public service advisers and the political needs of elected officials. Consulting serves specific policy making purposes. Often it can improve the effectiveness of policy delivery and produce 'better' policy outcomes. Several policy improvements have been recognised through effective community consultation achieved in Tasmania in the case of community involvement in tourism infrastructure such as the Strahan Visitor Centre (see Fallon and Kriwoken, 2003). Meanwhile, political objectives are just as important as the policy imperatives. This was the case in the massive two-and-a-half year community consultation exercise associated with the *Tasmania Together* blueprint developed to secure a shared vision for a 'new Tasmania' for the period to 2020 (Althaus, forthcoming).

DELIBERATIVE DEMOCRACY

Consultation also reflects other values, particularly those of open and transparent government. The deliberative democracy movement is an example of governments focusing on 'the democratic right [of citizens] to be involved in the public policy process and the importance of all barriers to such involvement being reduced or withdrawn. The emphasis here is on enabling access to the policy process, encouraging the take-up of that access and ensuring that such participation makes a difference to policy outcomes' (Rydin and Pennington, 2000). Examples of deliberative democracy include focus groups, deliberative polling (see Fishkin et al., 2000) and citizens' juries (Smith and Wales, 2000).

This form of participation serves as a measure of the overall legitimacy of the policy process (Fischer, 2003). It is assumed to reduce conflict as well as build consensus. It is also a form of 'public education' that encourages citizens to sympathise with the plight of elected officials. Deliberative democracy techniques help citizens appreciate that politicians face the complex task of making decisions in the interests of the common good and not just based on their own, or a select group of, preferences. Sometimes a community is involved in a consultation exercise that spirals destructively as vested interests emerge and conflict with

---

Direct citizen participation captivates our attention and imagination. There is something very seductive about the idea that people ought to be directly involved in the decisions that affect their lives . . . The practice of direct citizen participation is another matter. We struggle to ensure that our public deliberations are inclusive of all citizens, not just a subset . . . The gap between our ideal and its practice appears to have energized us rather than deterred us. The deliberative democratic project, our social experiment, is still very much alive.

Roberts (2004:341)

increasing intensity and without an arbiter. The notion of deliberative democracy supports the importance of having people develop a community view either in spite of, or without having, a direct interest in the issue.

The deliberative democracy project, however, is fraught with its own tensions. The concept of representative government is sometimes pitted against consultation. Politicians can claim their role as representatives of particular electoral communities supersedes the necessity for consultation. Information gained from political antennae and informal political polling can hold preference over formal bureaucratic consultation processes. The system provides no clear answer to the dilemma. Practice will determine which route results in better policy outcomes.

Some examples serve to illustrate practical instances of deliberative democracy in the Australian context. In 2000, the minister for environment in New South Wales commissioned the Institute for Sustainable Futures to undertake an independent review of container deposit legislation as part of statutory requirements to review the *NSW Waste Minimisation and Management Act 1995* (Carson and Hartz-Karp, 2005). There was a hostile policy environment given that producers, the packaging and beverage industries, were opposed to the introduction of new container deposit legislation which would place responsibility for container collection in their hands. Local government and environmental groups supported introduction of such legislation.

A combined televote of 400 people and a citizens' jury, consisting of eleven participants involved in discussion over three days, was conducted in 2001 to provide a synthesised deliberative democracy exercise to ensure information could not be dismissed as either uninformed or too small a sample. A stakeholder group of disparate parties was used to vet the questions and jury charge to ensure independence. In both cases, the more people learned about the topic, the more they inclined towards introduction of container deposit legislation.

Citizens' forums or juries 'seek to bring a small panel of randomly selected lay citizens together to deliberate on a policy issue' (Hendriks, 2002:65). The forums 'are viewed in terms of

> The degree of group involvement desirable in making a decision depends on the attributes of the core problem; some problems demand more involvement, others less.
> *Thomas (1990:435)*

their advisory capacity to policy development, rather than as a means to replace existing decision-making processes or representative forms of government' (Hendriks, 2002:64).

The process typically involves experts, who may include academics or interest groups, making presentations to the forum, which in turn develops policy recommendations on the basis of the information provided. In this case, Hendriks describes how commercial interest groups found the process threatening and ultimately withdrew. The interest groups were accustomed to directly communicating with government and were hostile to the idea of information being interpreted by people 'who have no knowledge or interest in the issue'. It is these very characteristics, according to Hendriks (2002:69), that make citizens' forums 'effective for the democratic project'.

Another example is that provided by the experiment of Perth *Dialogue with the City* (Carson and Hartz-Karp, 2005). In 2003, 1100 people participated in a '21st Century Town Meeting' to discuss town planning for Perth for the period to 2030. Computer technology helped determine key themes and also enabled participants (one-third stakeholders, one-third mail invitees and one-third advertisement respondents) to engage in a planning game that required each to take the role of a planner and determine where and how the future growth of the city would occur. The feedback was overwhelmingly positive with 98 per cent of participants indicating they were willing to participate in similar community engagement processes in the future. Over one-third indicated a change or significant broadening of their views as a result of the dialogue.

Dialogue with the City had been commissioned by the minister for planning and infrastructure, together with the Western Australia Planning Commission and her departmental chief executive officers of road, rail, ports, land development, redevelopment authorities, and planning and infrastructure. Strategic partnerships were also struck with a commercial television station, the major newspaper, several computer companies and a key mining corporation to both broaden ownership and lessen the financial burden on the state.

The Town Meeting was the culmination of a process that had included a survey of 8000 residents, an interactive website, a one-hour television broadcast, a series of full-page newspaper stories, art and essay competitions in schools, as well as 'listening sessions' with youth, indigenous people and non-English speaking communities.

Overall, these two projects show innovative application of multiple deliberative democracy techniques that aided the respective governments to claim 'a mandate to act'. Key protagonists of the projects, Lyn Carson and Janette Hartz-Karp (2005:122), suggest there are three criteria that guide effective deliberative processes:

1. *Influence*—the process should have the ability to influence policy and decision making
2. *Inclusion*—the process should be representative of the population and inclusive of diverse viewpoints and values, providing equal opportunity for all to participate
3. *Deliberation*—the process should provide open dialogue, access to information, respect, space to understand and reframe issues, and movement toward consensus.

DELIBERATIVE POLLING

A deliberative poll is an intensive or enhanced opinion poll. The process consists of a random selection of participants via telephone numbers, followed by an initial telephone interview after which people are invited to meet to discuss or deliberate on the topic. The process is designed to address the limitations of traditional polling by providing adequate time and information for more in-depth consideration of issues. The key characteristics of the deliberative poll are as follows:

- A statistically significant sample of citizens (usually several hundred) is selected and provided with briefing material.
- Participants meet at a single location for one or two days, with expenses paid, to hear and question witnesses and debate in small groups.
- Participant views are polled before and after the event.

A major deliberative poll was conducted on the issue of an Australian republic in October 1998. Initially, 1220 randomly selected voters were interviewed by Newspoll about their views on the republic referendum question. At the conclusion of the interview, people were invited to Old Parliament House in Canberra, all expenses paid, to participate in a deliberative process involving small group discussions and televised plenary sessions. A total of 347 people accepted the invitation to participate. After the deliberations, the initial telephone poll questions were again put to the delegates. Opinions had changed dramatically. The initial poll showed that 20 per cent approved of the republic referendum question. After the weekend-long deliberations, approval had increased to 61 per cent.

PLUSES AND PROBLEMS OF CONSULTATION

Consultation offers a wide array of advantages as well as posing challenges. Determining the need for consultation is an initial step in calculating the most appropriate consultation tool to utilise. Sometimes it is useful to consider how a decision reached in isolation might look as tomorrow's headline, and reflect on whether some consultation might be warranted. Of course, consultation can be frustrating too, adding time to already difficult processes, and risky to technocratic sensibilities, shifting control away from ministers and bureaucrats to those invited into the policy process.

The reality is that under traditional policy process models a lot of policy development takes place within the public sector. It is public servants who write the documents on which decisions are based. Ministers relate extensively to the community, their political party, their constituents and the stakeholders in the portfolio, but rely on public servants to manage the process, especially in the early and later stages of policy development. This results in a narrow band of time during which public participation expands, as shown in Figure 7.1.

Traditional bureaucracies are inherently ponderous and bound by process. These features dampen consultation processes and the rules of engagement can complicate the effectiveness of consultation efforts. Bureaucracies must accommodate due process while also adhering to confidentiality and privacy rules and other public accountability requirements. Accountability mechanisms do not always lend themselves to the community

During the middle stage, there is a greater public participation in policy development. Assumptions are tested through consultation. The foundations are laid for community acceptance of the ultimate policy, and additional data gathered.

Early stages are more intensely internalised to the public sector, as the options are explored and discarded or developed.

Later, the public service assumes greater control as the formal documents of decision making are prepared and submitted to cabinet.

Figure 7.1   The consultation diamond

engagement undertaking. Public sector staff are often left frustrated and helpless as they try to be proactive, engaged and innovative in how they consult and achieve community empowerment while adhering to rules and regulations that defeat the engagement intent.

Meanwhile, there is the continuing drama of intense consultation activity without any real change. Managerial silos continue to dominate the policy making realm despite the imperative of joined-up government. Consulting may just be cherry-picking acceptable responses. In one instance, a representative group from a community in northern New South Wales was used to increase the coalface skills and knowledge available in the local policy making process for health policy. Consultation was used to create ownership for policy choices about what to do with a white elephant country hospital. When the option of hospital closure was posed by this group of community representatives, they found to their chagrin that they were 'beaten up' by their own community! They were seen to be as bad as any other 'noxious' politician; the consultation exercise saw greater polarisation occur instead of positive change.

Consultation is not a panacea for policy making success. Creative thinking and high level skills are needed to resolve the tensions in practice.

> I not only use all the brains I have, but all I can borrow.
>
> Woodrow Wilson, 28th President of the United States

DIFFERENT TYPES OF CONSULTATION

An Organisation for Economic Cooperation and Development (OECD) study by Shand and Arnberg (1996:21) suggested that public involvement in government action can be placed on a continuum, from minimal interaction through to complete cooperation. This is shown graphically in Figure 7.2.

Information involves informing people about government policy. An advertising campaign to encourage safer driving—and announce the introduction of lower urban speed limits—is a familiar example of a government information campaign. This is a one-way process, educating the public about some policy initiative and its objectives. It does not allow client input to a choice. Information campaigns are part of the advocacy policy instrument described in Chapter 6.

Consultation seeks input from individuals and groups to a policy decision. Here consultation involves an exchange, though the decision makers remain in charge of the agenda and outcome. The process may involve surveys, public hearings or, more typically, meetings with interest groups representing various players in the policy arena. The goal is to improve policy, and enhance its acceptability, by taking into account the comments and interests of those likely to be affected. Regulation covering workplace health and safety, for example, is developed in this mode, with regular discussions between government, industry and unions.

Partnership hands some control of a decision from public officials to the public. In this mode, clients can do more than just express opinion. They have some say over policy content, working in cooperation with decision makers. Often this is achieved through consultation structures, with clients and experts sitting on advisory boards, helping shape policy and its implementation. Many welfare services, for example, use advisory boards of clients and public servants to decide priorities within the government's overall framework. Partnerships can be part of the network policy instrument described in Chapter 6.

Figure 7.2 **A consultation continuum**

Delegation hands control of the policy agenda to an outside group. In Australia the commission of inquiry is a familiar instrument for making policy choices. So too are statutory authorities, which may perform the function of keeping government at arm's length from some contentious area. In most states, for example, parole for prisoners is determined by a community board, with no direct role for politicians. Fisheries management, a perennially intractable policy matter, is also often handled by a statutory authority. Monetary policy is managed by the independent Reserve Bank.

Finally, it is possible to pass *control* of a policy issue entirely to the public. Section 128 of the Australian Constitution establishes the referendum as a means for direct decision by the people. There have been 21 national referenda since federation, offering 44 proposals for constitutional change. Only eight proposals have been accepted.

Referenda can also be used to determine issues that are not constitutional, such as the choice of national anthem, the introduction of daylight saving and extended trading hours. Popular control of a policy issue is an important way to settle controversial topics in which the policy process is unlikely to reach a satisfactory, or legitimate, resolution.

Another currently popular method for transferring policy control of the more commercial government activities is privatisation. Control here is vested in the shareholders of a new entity rather than the public at large, shifting the policy dynamic from the public domain to the powerful world of large corporations. Examples include Telstra and electricity generation.

CONSULTATION INSTRUMENTS

With the continuum for consultation options identified, it becomes possible to identify the various instruments that help achieve consultation objectives. These are set out in Table 7.1.

Information

Information campaigns adopt the standard techniques of marketing. *Surveys* provide data on public opinion. This work is almost always done outside government, by market research companies competing for government contracts. Companies

---

The literature on consultation includes all the following techniques:

- public information campaigns
- focus groups
- surveys—key informants, clients and citizens
- circulation of proposals for written comment
- advisory committees
- interest group meetings
- town hall meetings
- public hearings
- public inquiries
- citizens' advisory committees
- impact assessment studies
- policy communities
- referenda.

Table 7.1 Consultation objectives and instruments

Information	Consultation	Partnership	Delegation	Control
• surveys • focus groups • public information campaigns	• key contacts • interest group meetings • town hall meetings • circulation of proposals • public hearings	• advisory committees • policy	• public inquiries • impact assessment studies • communities	• referenda • privatisation

(From Davis, 1996:18)

EXAMPLES OF NATIONAL PEAK BODIES

- Business Council of Australia, representing industry
- Australian Council of Trade Unions, representing workers
- Australian Council of Social Service, representing the welfare sector
- National Farmers Federation, representing rural producers.

EXAMPLES OF PUBLIC INQUIRIES WITH POLICY IMPLICATIONS

- Coombs inquiry into the Australian government administration (1974–75)
- Royal Commission into Aboriginal Deaths in Custody (1991)
- Royal Commission into the failure of HIH Insurance Limited (2002)
- Royal Commission on the Building and Construction Industry (2001–02)
- Cole inquiry into certain Australian companies in relation to the UN Oil-for-Food programme (2006).

also provide *focus group research* to test and refine a message. Focus groups bring together people chosen for their demographic characteristics, who discuss a particular issue, view a trial advertisement or respond to key words and phrases. Such groups indicate how the intended audience will respond to the government's message. Finally, with the research completed, governments use a mix of advertising avenues to present a *public information campaign*.

Information campaigns are a necessary, and sometimes controversial, part of governing. One example is the Howard Government's workplace relations reform campaign of 2005, costing somewhere in the vicinity of $55 million, making it the most expensive publicity campaign undertaken to date by an Australian government (Wilson, 2005). Often policy success relies on implementation by the public (as in obeying new laws). But information campaigns are not consultative because the flow is only one way. Such campaigns have a role in the policy process, but will not satisfy those looking for more meaningful interaction.

Consultation

The consultation mode seeks to solicit, and respond to, views about a policy proposal from relevant people and groups.

Those who advise and make policy build up contacts with players in their policy area. These *key contacts* become an important conduit for information, both informally and through representation on advisory boards. Since key contacts may be a limited group, however, policy makers also arrange other forums such as *interest group meetings* to exchange views on a policy area with those who represent a viewpoint on government action. Should a policy proposal have implications for a community, as in an urban renewal or freeway project or the construction of a new dam, policy makers may also organise *town hall meetings* so the local community can hear about, and express views on, a proposed course of action.

If the constituency is too diffuse or the players too many to allow face-to-face meetings, government may introduce a more formal consultation process. Many proposed regulations, for example, are made available through *circulation of proposals.* An intention to change a subordinate law is advertised in the press, with a date set for responses. Interested parties can put their case and these are considered in the final policy decision. The discussion paper or 'green paper' is a traditional means of consulting about a policy proposal. Alternatively, a process of *public hearings* is established, in which policy makers or specialist outsiders like judges listen to points of view and consider the various cases before making recommendations.

Whichever combination of techniques is adopted, the consultation method always involves opportunities for public input. Yet policy makers remain in control of the process and its results. Faced with opposition to a proposal, policy makers may find it wise to withdraw. They are under no obligation, however, to do so. Consultation offers input but not a veto for individuals or interest groups on policy choices.

Public consultation about a universally unpopular policy will often result in tokenism and a concomitant lack of legitimacy in the process. When the Commonwealth government tackled the problem of where to locate a 'low level' nuclear waste dump, strict boundaries were set for consultation. Twenty years after the initial formation of a Commonwealth–State Consultative Committee, a process that saw a number of changes of government, false starts, significant timeframe overruns and periodic ad hoc public consultation, three sites were selected for detailed environmental impact assessment in 2000. The consultation process was deliberately limited to the siting decision, which did not allow for the expression of wider concerns people had about the issue. The process was also based on a 'scientific' approach which acted to sideline any debate about social or political aspects of the issue and dismiss most community concerns as 'wrong' (Holland, 2002).

In 2005, the Commonwealth government introduced legislation to facilitate siting of the dump in the Northern Territory. This legislation overrode the powers of the Northern Territory government which claimed some 9000 citizens wrote letters and petitions against a waste dump. According to the *7.30 Report*'s Murray McLaughlin (2005):

> Public information sessions by Commonwealth scientists and bureaucrats up and down the Territory, have failed to quell community fears. At a meeting in Katherine in August, an official from the Federal Department of Science acknowledged that the select three sites in the Territory has been a consequence of flawed process, that the Commonwealth's preference for a site at Woomera in South Australia would have been better.

The technically preferred Woomera option was ruled out by a legal challenge by the South Australian government. Legal challenge is not available to the Northern Territory government.

Partnership

Partnership strategies draw the community into decision making. The standard mechanism for inclusion is the *advisory committee*. Community representatives on an advisory committee can provide policy makers with direct and unfiltered views. Various OECD studies emphasise the widespread use of such committees as the primary vehicle for consultation (OECD, 1994a, 1994b). Governments appreciate the two-way exchange provided by committees—greater community input into policy, but also an opportunity for policy makers to explain their approach and objectives.

Over time, advisory committees can become *policy* communities—regular meetings of the key interests in a policy field—with an opportunity to broker agreements (Sabatier and Jenkins-Smith, 1993). Governments see their role as providing a forum for discussions, ensuring the participants are representative of the broader community's interests, and proposing policy ideas that can be debated, modified and adopted with some measure of common support.

Contentious policy areas, such as the environment and industrial relations, particularly suit this form of consultation. Policy communities allow the players to understand each other's concerns and interests, and seek agreements balancing competing interests. In environmental policy, for example, industry needs and conservation goals are brought together, with depth of understanding developing on both sides, while policy makers benefit from both improved information and developing accord on central points. Another example is the Hawke government's accord with the union movement through its peak body, the Australian Council of Trade Unions. Policy communities can be slow and difficult forums for policy discussion, but they may find resolutions where otherwise only conflict and disagreement prevail.

Representativeness must be carefully considered when consulting through partnership bodies. Can a public housing client or an employee's representative claim to speak for others? Why, when discussing people with disabilities, should one organisation but not another have a voice in the consultation? Governments often address this concern by asking peak bodies to represent their sector.

To assist with consultation, governments sometimes create peak bodies. The Consumers Health Forum, for example, was founded and funded by government to represent consumer interests in various health policy discussions.

Delegation

Delegation aims to shift policy responsibility to an institution or process outside political control. This may be as close as the policy cycle ever comes to an ideal 'rational' process, in which evidence is collected and weighed, and judgment provided with supporting arguments.

Public inquiries are a standard feature of Australian policy formulation. They provide an impartial forum to explore an issue and settle on authoritative recommendations (Weller, 1994). Inquiries seek submissions to obtain evidence and views.

> The idea of direct democracy proposes a more continuous, active role for citizens. Theorists who call for the implementation of such an idea are proposing much more significant levels of participation than prevail in a representative democracy, through such institutional mechanisms as direct local assemblies or the extensive use of referenda. In contemporary political life, such ideas have achieved considerable prominence because of the size, impersonality and power of modern governments, whose elected politicians do not always appear accessible and, in any case, seem to have become dominated by non-elected parts of the governing system, notably bureaucracies.
> *Painter (1992:22)*

Public hearings provide opportunities for consultation. Reports typically list the range of arguments and evidence put before the inquiry, indicating the dimensions of the policy debate. Of course, inquiries can also be a way for governments to defer contentious issues. British Prime Minister Harold Wilson's famous formulation was that royal commissions 'take minutes and waste years'.

The use of *assessment studies* is a more recent style of delegation. Here, governments impose a process on decision making. Proposals for a new tourism development, airport or mine must meet certain threshold standards before government will issue the necessary approval or lease. Independent consultants study the proposal and consult with the local community. Their detailed reports form one important basis for government's decision.

Environmental impact studies (EIS) are the most familiar such form of assessment, and social impact studies are becoming important to policy making (see, for example, Holden and O'Faircheallaigh, 1995; see also Chapter 5 about policy analysis frameworks). Such studies are particularly useful when communities are sharply divided on the merits of a proposal, since the study provides detailed and authoritative data on all aspects of the choice, including the views of interested parties. Assessment studies provide government with grounds for a decision on technical rather than political criteria.

Control

It is rare in Australia to hand control of an issue directly to the people despite the constitutional provision for referenda.

In principle, referenda could be used to resolve issues that are too fundamental or too contentious for the usual business of politics. Without a controlled approach to consultation, such issues result in non-decisions, reflecting the unwillingness of politicians to tackle very divisive subjects. Laws about moral issues such as abortion, prostitution, euthanasia and same-sex relationships, for example, often have little relation to actual practice. It is easier to leave the old statutes in place—but ignore them—than to open touchy debates to the popular will.

In Australia, citizens cannot force government to put issues to a vote. The referendum mechanism entrenched in the Common-

---

Most governments have not articulated very clearly their objectives for consultation. This lack of clarity has both good and bad implications. On the one hand, the general acceptance of consultation as inherently desirable, even without clear goals, demonstrates its powerful appeal within modern societies. It is supported by strong and fundamental values that, in some countries, mean that the value of consultation is virtually unquestioned. This encouraging environment makes reform and expansion of consultation easier. On the other hand, the failure to establish clear objectives means that consultation programs are more likely to be inappropriately designed, inefficient, difficult to evaluate, and disappointing or even disillusioning in results to public and public administrators alike. These kinds of outcomes serve only to discredit consultation efforts.

OECD (1994:5–6)

wealth and most state constitutions can only be activated by parliament. This contrasts with practice in the United States and New Zealand, where forms of citizen initiated referenda allow individuals and groups to propose propositions for ballot. Yet, as Franklin (1992:59) argues, 'reducing all policy questions for voters to a simple yes/no form is hardly an appropriate method of government or political discussion. Few issues lend themselves to simplification in this way.' The resounding 'no' to the 1999 republic referendum, for example, presented no clear political direction.

Privatising government activity removes government control, and vests it in the hands of a select group—shareholders. This cuts out potential conflicts of interest between government as trading entity and government as regulator and policy maker. Privately owned and operated airports are not amenable to government's direction, and policy can only be directed by government through regulation or cooperative arrangements with the new owners.

SOCIAL CAPITAL AND COMMUNITY ENGAGEMENT

More recently, governments have begun experimenting with new techniques for obtaining views and information and constructing meaningful dialogue with communities. Robert Putnam's work has stimulated political commentators, theorists and practitioners to debate the role and status of civic community under the conceptual expression of 'social capital' (Putnam, 1995, 2000).

Notions of social capital have also been influential for governments. Social institutions and practices are often central to government operations, the glue that binds together society in a coherent and positive manner (Productivity Commission, 2003:1). There is civic value in the connections and networks that spring from human interaction. Sporting associations, churches, professional societies, unions, school groups, voluntary and service clubs all express social capital. A well-connected society can leverage individuals and local communities towards higher aspirations and better outcomes through reciprocity, trust, cooperation and mutuality of support. Employment opportunities, welfare nets, healthcare, parenting, and educational circumstances—to name but a few areas of impact—can be enhanced, impacting on governmental efficiency and effectiveness. Putnam claims that social capital 'operates through psychological and biological processes to improve individuals' lives ... Social capital appears to be a complement, if not a substitute, for Prozac, sleeping pills, antacids, vitamin C, and other drugs we buy at the corner pharmacy ... Mounting evidence suggests that people whose lives are rich in social capital cope better with traumas and fight illness more effectively' (2000:289).

Putnam assembled a case for bemoaning decline in social capital towards growing solitarism and rank individualism. Putnam and others (see McLean et al., 2002) suggest the trend is driven by consumerism, media impact, explosion in market logic, economic inequalities and globalisation.

Disintegration of social capital can cripple communities and place much greater demands on governments to fill the void, however caused. But government programs are no real replacement for social capital (Winter, 2000). 'Social capital cannot be legislated, bought, taught, or standardised' (The Allen Consulting Group, 2006:37).

It is contestable whether government action 'crowds out' or complements and strengthens social capital (Productivity Commission, 2003). Governments can assist, support and encourage personal relationships, though they cannot stand in their place. Social capital agendas have generally encouraged government to be seen as a facilitator or enabler (see for example Botsman and Latham, 2001), though others suggest government could play a role in directly creating social capital (Cox, 1995) or that government should 'withdraw ... to give the community more "room to breathe"' (Norton, 1998).

Community engagement programs explicitly attempt to address social capital disintegration. This form of consultation serves several purposes. It can act as a means of kick-starting local communities in forming or rejuvenating their own social capital. For example, the *Be Strong, Be Heard* program saw the Queensland Police Service assist in empowering 'individuals and groups within remote indigenous communities to report sexual assault and child abuse'. The program has seen a dramatic increase in the reporting of sexual assault and ill-treatment as well as expanded partnerships to provide support networks in child and family welfare. It did so by utilising the support of Auskick to assist in delivering socially and culturally sensitive workshops in local communities to provide information and promote awareness of issues in order to enhance the lives and safety of the most vulnerable in the community (Queensland Government, 2006).

Latest trends suggest the use of cultural stories, narratives and creative arts technologies as ways of encouraging community engagement and development of social capital. In 2003, the *Creative Democracy—Homelessness* project was launched. It used 'art and creative processes to engage the citizens of Brisbane to find solutions to the issues of homelessness in our city ... A professional photographer, writer and community cultural development worker were employed to create and collate photos and stories of homeless people and some of the service providers.' The images and text was screened in several outdoor locations around Brisbane and also distributed through Brisbane City Council libraries and regional business centres. Homelessness continues to be part of the council program but as a result of this initiative direct donations to organisations of blankets, household items and funds occurred. Civic dialogue was achieved allowing the aspirations of homeless people as well as the broader community to be uncovered in a positive manner. New ideas could then be explored rather than continuing to treat homelessness only as a problem (www.getinvolved.qld.gov.au/share_your_knowledge/keyinitiatives/showcase_ce/brisbane/homelessness.html).

Community engagement also represents a form of consultation that aims to supplement political participation by providing ongoing mechanisms for communities to participate in government decision making. In this sense, it serves to aid the cause of deliberative democracy. For example, the Brisbane City Council has an online community reference panel (*Your Say Online*) which currently features some 12 500 members who contribute their ideas and views and participate in consultations that occur in the Brisbane region (see www.brisbane.qld.gov.au/BCC:BASE::pc=PC_76).

Yet again, community engagement programs can be a means of governments securing improved accountability mechanisms. Experimentation with 'community cabinet' models demonstrate an attempt to provide a forum for local communities to see and hear what their elected representatives are discussing and deciding, to contribute in some form to the process, and to raise issues of concern in order to hold decision makers to account and provide direct input. Indeed, community cabinet has become a central plank of state government activity across Australia: see Queensland (www.thepremier.qld.gov.au/community_consultation/), Victoria (www.premier.vic.gov.au/cabinet/), South Australia (www.ministers.sa.gov.au/pagephp?id=101), the Northern Territory (www.communitycabinet.nt.gov.au/dcm/communitycabinet/index.html), and New South Wales (www.cabinet.nsw.gov.au/meetings).

E-CONSULTATION

In his influential book, *The Wealth of Networks*, Yochai Benkler (2006) states: 'The change brought about by the networked information environment is deep. It is structural. It goes to the very foundations of how liberal markets and liberal democracies have coevolved for almost two centuries'. His argument outlines how the current production and exchange of informa-

> I can't think of anything except kissing babies that you can't do online.
> Michael Cornfield, political scientist, George Washington University

Table 7.2 Advantages of citizen participation in government decision making

	Advantages to citizen participants	Advantages to government
Decision Process	Education (learn from and inform government representatives)	Education (learn from and inform citizens)
	Persuade and enlighten government	Persuade citizens; build trust and allay anxiety or hostility
	Gain skills for activist citizenship	Gain legitimacy of decisions
Outcomes	Break gridlock; achieve outcomes	Break gridlock; achieve outcomes
	Gain some control over policy process	Avoid litigation costs
	Better policy and implementation decisions	Better policy and implementation decisions

(Irvin and Stansbury, 2004:56; reproduced with permission of Blackwell Publishing)

Table 7.3 Disadvantages of citizen participation in government decision making

	Disadvantages to citizen participants	Disadvantages to government
Decision Process	Time consuming (even dull)	Time consuming
	Pointless if decision is ignored	Costly
		May backfire, creating more hostility toward government
Outcomes	Worse policy decision if heavily influenced by opposing interest groups	Loss of decision-making control
		Possibility of bad decision that is politically impossible to ignore
		Less budget for implementation of actual projects

(Irvin and Stansbury, 2004:58; reproduced with permission of Blackwell Publishing)

tion, knowledge and culture are fundamentally different from the modes of market production and exchange that characterised the industrial information economy. Phenomena such as blogging, wikis, and the free software movement are symptomatic of the flourishing nonmarket environment that defies traditional economic rules. Material capital no longer stands as the pre-eminent building block of the economy. Instead, cooperative knowledge exchange, development and creativity are dominant forces in the production of economic value. 'Why can fifty thousand volunteers successfully coauthor *Wikipedia*, the most serious online alternative to the *Encyclopedia Britannica*, and then turn around and give it away for free? Why do 4.5 million volunteers contribute their leftover computer cycles to create the most powerful supercomputer on Earth, SETI@ Home?' (Benkler, 2006:5).

These trends towards a networked economy have been influencing policy making circles and challenging traditional ways of conducting political and policy activity. Virtual policy networks (VPNs) is a term used to describe interactive policy collaboration that is coordinated via the internet and mediated utilising online technology (McNutt, 2006). While web-based politics and policy making has a long way to go, governments

If we don't understand [how people make decisions and formulate policy] then we may be wasting time with the technology... Each new generation of nerds thinks it has the answer, only to run into the same brick wall of human behaviour. We must understand people and organisations before we can determine how to meld them with technology.

Frank Bannister, senior lecturer at Trinity College Dublin and e-democracy expert, January 2002

> e-Government and e-governance can be defined as two very distinct terms. e-Governance is a broader topic that deals with the whole spectrum of the relationship and networks within government regarding the usage and application of information and communication technologies (ICTs). e-Government is actually a narrower approach dealing with the development of online services to the citizen, more the e on any particular government service—such as e-tax, e-transportation or e-health. e-Governance is a wider concept that defines and assesses the impacts that technologies are having on the practice and administration of governments. It also includes the relationship between public servants and the wider society, such as dealings with the elected bodies or outside groups, like not-for-profit organisations, NGOs, academic institutions or private sector corporate entities. e-Governance encompasses a series of necessary steps for government agencies to develop and administer in order to ensure successful implementation of e-government services to the public at large.
>
> Sheridan and Riley (2006)

have been testing the usefulness and impact of networked technology, especially in the context of the consultation phase of the policy cycle.

The last few years have seen a flurry of Australian and international research into e-governance and e-democracy. Research has included some trial community consultation via the internet, or 'e-consultation'. An innovative trial was conducted in the late 1990s by the Moira Shire Council in Victoria, where an internet bulletin board was used by constituents to post questions for question time.

Other states are looking to Queensland's experience in e-consultation initiatives and frameworks. Queensland has established an E-democracy Unit within the Department of the Premier and Cabinet to deliver the e-democracy initiative of conducting community consultation online (www.getinvolved.qld.gov.au). The e-democracy policy framework states a commitment to:

- post a number of issues on the website on which the government desires wide consultation and feedback
- provide online access to government consultation documents relevant to those issues, such as discussion and policy papers and draft bills.

The issues identified as key considerations are: equitable access, responsiveness, and security and authentication. e-Petitions and webcasting of parliamentary proceedings were successfully trialled in 2002 and continue to provide important tools for the community via the Queensland Parliament website. Meanwhile, the Office for Youth has recently launched an interactive youth website, *Generate* (located at www.generate.qld.gov.au/about/office_for_youth_generate.html), for 15 to 25 year olds. *Generate* aims to 'support young people to shape and develop the community of Queensland'. As well as discussion forums and email news, the site hosts an event submission and organisation function to assist young people to create personalised events for National Youth Week.

There is still some way to go in use of online mechanisms for consultation and participation (see Weiksner, 2005). Access to technology and technology literacy are important considerations. The credibility of data and the anonymity of participation are dilemmas for elected representatives and other public sector officials. Meanwhile there is a need to translate mouseclicks into action and to ensure continued participation; take-up and meaningful interaction and 'e-conversations' are difficult and expensive to sustain, especially over time. Nonetheless, as these problems are overcome and e-consultation demonstrates benefits, its use will no doubt increase.

DESIGNING A CONSULTATION PROCESS

Consultation is a two-way exchange. When active participation or direct control is part of policy making, governments have to balance their own process needs with those of the consulting parties. Effective consultation is unlikely to be characterised by a lopsided balance of power where the government dictates a predetermined agenda onto an unsuspecting public. Nevertheless, to avoid the pitfalls of consultation, processes must be tightly structured, with clearly specified terms of reference, time lines and outcomes. This lets parties to the consultation know the process to be followed and keeps the discussion focused (Byrne and Davis, 1998). The following outline of consultation design issues is taken from the perspective of an insider public sector official; the emphasis is on the official putting themselves in the shoes of the parties with whom they will be consulting. Policy makers are likely to achieve better results when they 'look ahead and reason back' (Crase et al., 2005:235).

> Deliberation—a problem-solving form of discourse that involves problem analysis, establishing evaluative criteria, and identifying and weighing alternative solutions. Deliberation focuses on policy choices.
>
> Dialogue—form of speech is not as concerned with solving a problem as with bridging linguistic, social, and epistemological chasms between different subgroups of the potentially deliberative body. Dialogue seeks accommodation, reconciliation, mutual understanding, or at the very least, informed tolerance.
> *Levine, Fung and Gastil (2005: 282–3)*

Purpose

Policy makers may decide on consultation to:

- improve the quality of policy decisions through access to relevant information and perspectives, including exchange of problem and solution definitions, alternatives and criteria
- ensure understanding, acceptance and legitimacy of proposed policies

- promote consensus about policy choices
- anticipate challenges to the policy process by providing transparency, accountability and opportunities for participation.

From the purpose, and the problem to be addressed, flows the appropriate type of consultation.

Method

- The resources to be spent on consultation must reflect the nature and significance of the problem to be addressed, and the time available.
- Most consultation processes use a range of instruments, aiming to limit the inherent biases of any one approach by seeking opinion through a range of different avenues.
- Agencies should be clear about their objectives. These can range from disseminating information through to consultation, partnership, delegation or control.

Identifying stakeholders

- While consultation material may be distributed to those identified by policy makers as relevant interests, there must be avenues for others to self-identify as parties to the consultation process.
- Barriers such as language, physical and education disadvantage, resources and time may keep some stakeholders from contributing. The mix of consultation methods must address inclusiveness in the process.
- It is important to advertise the consultation process, even if most who see the advertisement will choose not to participate.

Beginning consultation

- The objectives and parameters of consultation should be clear. Documentation should establish in advance the purpose, process and outputs of the consultation phase.
- Policy makers must identify the full impact of a proposal so all affected interests understand the issue at stake.
- The process of consultation should be transparent throughout.

- Consultation should begin early enough to permit consideration of comments and suggested alternatives.

Consulting with individuals and groups
- Policy makers should meet with the main interest groups to discuss their views. The purpose and agenda of such meetings should be clear in advance, as well as the kind of information that will be useful.
- Reaching an 'unorganised' public is more difficult, and may rely on circulating written proposals, calling public meetings, using talkback radio and other techniques designed to solicit opinions.
- Agencies must avoid 'consultation overload', particularly with voluntary community groups, by coordinating processes, stakeholders and schedules among departments.
- Enough time is needed for representative bodies to consult their members. For most consultations, three months should be the norm and two months the absolute minimum.
- Consultation places a burden on those consulted. To minimise these costs, any written information should be concise and clearly show the issues at stake.

When consultation is complete
- Comments should be acknowledged as soon as possible.
- It is important to 'close the loop'. Interest groups and the public should know how their input has been used. This is essential for building trust and credibility.
- Details of the outcome should be provided to commentators. Feedback should include a summary of the views and information collected, and the resulting proposals or action.
- Processes for listening to citizens after policies are implemented can help identify problems on a continuing basis, and ensure continuous improvement.

Consultation traps
- Not all citizen action groups or industry spokespersons are legitimate representatives of their community. The basis on which people claim to speak for others must be clear.

- Highly organised and expert interest groups are most likely to participate in the process, digest the information offered and provide substantive comments.
- There is a risk professional lobby groups will dominate consultation processes, particularly if the issues are technical, complex or otherwise difficult to communicate for less organised or financed groups.
- Credibility for the consultation process depends on sound reputation. Consultation strategies that pay lip-service to drawing communities into the policy process should not be expected to return positive outcomes. This was the case with the New South Wales Police Accountability Community Teams (PACTs) established in 2002 to 'create an effective mechanism for broad-based community consultation'. The initiative has so far failed to provide evidence of improvement in community consultation or police accountability. The majority of PACT meeting reports show discussion of community issues but 'police responses seemed limited to explaining what they were already doing in the relevant area or denying that the issues were relevant to them' (Walters, 2005).
- Policy makers should not presume they already know the issues or the answers. Just like any human relationship-building exercise, second-guessing and making assumptions are unhelpful. All parties to the consultation process should be given the chance to think through and communicate their views and ideas.
- A fundamental trap is the failure to consult relevant parties, including other agencies of government, opinion makers or affected bodies.

CONSULTATION AS PARTICIPATION

Consultation is essential but often not easy. It can be difficult to identify all the stakeholders in a policy area. Often there are multiple interests at stake—those who will benefit from a new toll road, but also people living in the path of the development; businesses along the old road that will lose custom; environmental concerns about a forest or area of cultural significance along the way; lobbies for and against greater access to the new transport corridor. Each will criticise the process if they do not achieve their desired result.

Without consultation, legitimate and workable solutions to many problems prove elusive. Rather than despair at the complications, policy makers must develop better tools for consultation, providing opportunities for greater participation in the policy cycle.

8 Coordination

SNAPSHOT

Governments strive to work in a coordinated way, so the parts pull together. They institutionalise coordination through routines and structures. Routines are procedures required of policy advisers. Structures include those central agencies that manage the routines and provide whole of government advice to key ministers.

This chapter describes the routines and structures used in Australian governments, and the relationship between bureaucratic coordination and political control.

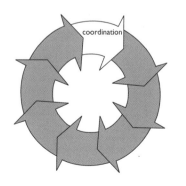

Policies are based on shared goals. Government programs should work together, not at cross-purposes, and priorities must be assigned between competing proposals. Coordination in government is a virtue.

Coordination takes many forms. It can refer to a sense of *coherence* in overall government direction; it can speak of a sense of *consistency* in the specific objectives and policies of government; it can reflect ideas of *efficient interaction* between multiple parties working together to achieve a common goal; or it can refer to the need to *consult* with multiple parties to allow input that will ensure a particular policy is a workable proposal.

The traditional model of policy making is premised on an operation of government activity through hierarchies, with politicians exercising sovereign authority passed down through the chain of command from minister to heads of departments to frontline public officials and onto the populace. This view of policy is a centralised, top-down application of rules and directives. Citizens periodically exercise their voting power thereby handing sovereignty to elected representatives.

While this is a neat description of sovereignty, representation and society, it hardly provides an accurate picture of the layered complexity that characterises the role and actions of the state, let alone the workings of the policy arena, including the role of other actors. Alternative views and maps of the system have emerged in recent years.

NETWORK GOVERNANCE

The notion of network governance has emerged as a dominant portrayal of how contemporary policy making occurs in practice.

Network governance premises government action on loose, decentralised associations of interconnected parties (from the private sector, third sector and from the community itself) negotiating and bargaining their way to, or through prisms of, shared values and policy ideas. The model offers the possibility of a bottom-up conceptualisation of how policy comes into being. On some views, the government takes on more or less the role of another player in the system. Certainly, the theory proposes that government exercises a less imperial style of sovereign authority than that envisioned in the traditional model. There is also a shift in focus away from institutions towards relationships, and emphasis on the dynamism of policy making. 'Whereas the institutional language implies stability, networks imply fluidity' (Hajer and Wagenaar, 2003:5).

Under the network governance model, the coordination task becomes critical. In addition to the coordination challenges of bringing consistency, coherence, efficiency and consultation, networks demand high levels of communication to ensure synchronisation of tasks and response and alignment of core objectives and goals. If hierarchical models presuppose high levels of unity (because there is only one organisation), networked governance relies more on shared information and trust, raising issues of privacy, accountability and collaboration.

COHERENCE

Even under a more traditional view of the state apparatus, modern governments are networks of loosely linked organisations rather than a single hierarchy amenable to command and control (Painter, 1987:9). Departments and statutory authorities have their own goals and perspectives. Coordination amid this complexity requires rules about giving advice to decision makers. The policy process must include ways for advisers to:

- acknowledge potential conflict over policy goals
- consider the arguments in a structured way
- arrive at a recommendation.

> ... More is at stake than implementation success, as policy coherence also relates to the consistency with which policy intentions are signalled ... a lack of policy coherence sends confusing messages to potential policy targets ... As such, policy coherence and policy politics are intertwined.
> *May et al. (2006:381)*

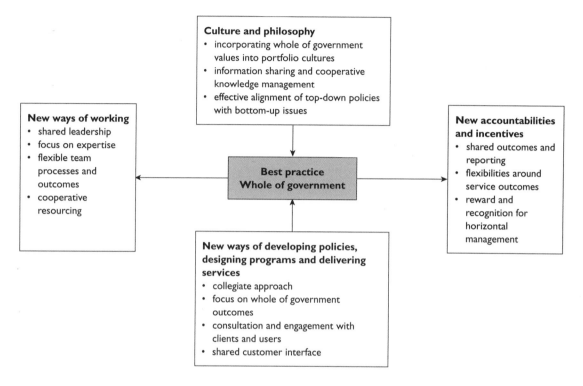

Figure 8.1 Best practice: whole of government
(From MAC, 2004:13; copyright Commonwealth of Australia, reproduced by permission)

Ideally a government will have a well-developed and widely distributed policy framework, setting out economic, social and environmental objectives. It will behave corporately, a unity with multiple parts in pursuit of the same goals.

In practice, such overall policy frameworks are rarely documented cohesively, although attempts by state governments have been made in recent times to turn to strategic management and planning frameworks (Gallop, 2006; Althaus, forthcoming). Strategic planning exercises such as *Tasmania Together 2001*, *Growing Victoria Together 2001*, *Western Australia's Better Planning: Better Services 2003*, *South Australia's Creating*

Opportunity 2004 and *New South Wales State Plan 2006* all attempted to provide an overarching guide to the priorities and strategic agenda of the respective governments. These frameworks are meant to signal policy commitments, outline targets and measures of performance, and provide direction as to how the government and the community will interact to achieve a shared vision going forward.

Usually, however, policy goals are scattered through many sources—budget papers, major statements such as white papers, electoral pronouncements, social justice strategies and recent legislation. Occasionally a prime minister or premier makes a landmark speech outlining a comprehensive program. More often, overall policy objectives must be inferred from various sources and tested through consultation and coordination.

Central agencies work to key ministers, in particular the prime minister and treasurer, who are key players in establishing this overall framework. Like line departments, central agencies often work from clues rather than explicit statements of intent. But proximity to decision makers and consistent involvement in policy development across government ensure central agencies are well informed about government pronouncements and intentions. Hence central agencies act both as a resource for departments about policy frameworks, and advise cabinet on the fit between a proposal and the heritage of policy choices.

> Central agencies have the particular responsibility of bringing a whole of government perspective to policy advising and advising on the overall coherence of policy. Their contribution is most often found in those areas where the interactive effects of individual policies cross portfolio boundaries. This is, of course, typical of the issues which need cabinet attention. In addition, central agencies may become involved if the issues have significant implications for the government's overall strategy.
> *Keating (1996:64)*

As networks have assumed greater significance in the practice of policy making, efforts to create coherence have also gained a critical position. Clear objectives and stated goals are essential for shaping multiple actors towards the requirement of united behaviour. Governments cannot utilise networks if they are not clear about what they seek to achieve. Coherence in the overarching framework provides the necessary ground rules within which the creativity and adaptability of networks can be employed to their full advantage. Coherence can be brought by different methods other than a single unifying framework. Government processes, direction statements or whole of government policy initiatives present alternatives. Yet the point remains; policy making demands a degree of coherence if results are to be achieved.

CONSISTENCY

Government consistency is about:

- internal congruity of policies and decisions
- equal treatment of citizens or regions within the jurisdiction
- appropriate behaviour by officials
- adherence to due process and official procedures
- projecting a public image showing that government knows what it is doing and what it wants (Wanna et al., 1994:1/14).

Achieving consistency by coordinating *within* government is not easy. Meanwhile governments in a federal system such as Australia must also grapple with the coordination task *across* governments of different levels. Coordination of relationships, functions and goals between federal, state and local governments must be managed if outcomes in many policy fields are to be achieved. Under the networked governance approach to policy making, governments are also discovering the need for consistency *between* government and external providers and policy actors. Established arrangements in supra-national and transnational networks continue to develop, making multi-dimensional governance a common reality.

The complexity and scale of government, and the need for specialisation, make it impossible for any one person—or even a committee such as cabinet—to keep all the relevant variables in play. The considerable cost of perfectly meshing policies and programs can outweigh the benefits. Coordination may be necessary, but it is an ideal realised only with many compromises. Governments have multiple and sometimes conflicting goals. Decision makers and policy advisers must learn to live with some incoherence. Coordination at least aims to minimise harmful inconsistencies.

CONSULTATION AND EFFICIENCY

Governments include a coordination phase in their policy cycle because they seek tolerable compatibility across activities. Coordination is institutionalised through a combination of procedures and structures, in particular government departments charged with a coordinating role.

Power which flows from the practices of governing depends on the mundane but orderly world of routines, those repetitions which institutionalise behaviour. Routines give purpose to actions, making them part of a wider process. By habitualising us to play a role, routines provide predictability within an organisation, and the possibility of coordinating a wider enterprise. They link individuals to process and values, and so make coordination possible. Through routines which turn rules into habits, the centre can act at a distance.
Davis (1995:135)

❛I am extraordinarily patient, provided I get my own way in the end.
Margaret Thatcher

A first step in coordination requires agencies to consult within government, since this allows other departments to offer suggestions about the appropriateness of a new policy proposal and draws the proposal into the framework of existing programs administered by those other agencies. In the networked environment, departmental consultation might incorporate the views and input of collaborators and partners in the network, or these parties would be separately consulted.

Review by central agencies follows. This imposes a 'whole of government' perspective, in which a particular policy idea from a line department is compared with the overall policy direction of government.

Central agencies ask a number of simple questions—usually imposed by the format of cabinet submissions—about the policy, financial and administrative implications of a proposal. Is the submission consistent with existing objectives? Can it be afforded? Are there legal or organisational issues? Are there consequences for particular interest groups? Who was consulted and what was their response?

The answers—those supplied by line departments and those reached by central agencies—form the basis of policy briefs to senior ministers. Such briefs are one of the instruments of coordination. They let cabinet decide about consistency.

Central agencies use standardised routines to gather the information needed to test the consistency of a submission with other government objectives. Routines require agencies to state, for example, whether funding is available, or the social, economic or environmental implications of the proposal. Central agencies coordinate intergovernmental discussions through mechanisms such as the Council of Australian Governments (COAG), the Council for the Australian Federation or one of the many ministerial coordinating committees that bring representatives of the Commonwealth, states, territories and sometimes local government into policy forums.

The routines of coordination are little more than checklists of questions asked by central agencies about policy proposals. These query the importance of an issue, the quality of the original policy analysis, the choice of instruments and the depth of consultation. If the submission lacks information or does not answer serious concerns about the proposal, central agencies request more detail from the originating department. The objective is not to obstruct policy ideas but to ensure submissions address all relevant aspects of the proposal, and thus empower cabinet to make well-informed decisions.

Coordination is pursued through procedure, starting with the strict format of the cabinet submission, demanding detail against a range of headings. The draft submission is circulated to relevant agencies for consultation comments, then lodged with the central agencies which check information, evaluate content and suggest modifications. Only then will the submission proceed to cabinet for its decision.

Increasingly, cabinet submissions are but one form of making government policy. Especially under networked governance, the coordination task demands that all the network players are operating in harmony. While multiple players contributing to policy bring the benefits of flexibility and diversity, they also create risks of embarrassing incongruity or gaffes. Coordination is essential for guiding multiple partners towards an efficient and unified operation. Cooperation demands coordination.

Governments seek to avoid shoddy arrangements or scandal that might tarnish their reputation. Citizens demand and expect government action—whoever undertakes it on government's behalf—to be exemplary. Policy makers have to grapple with ensuring behaviour, processes and outcomes match government standards regardless of whether the provider is from the private sector, the third sector or from some other network partner.

A number of coordination tools are available to achieve this aim. Contract specifications, incentive packages and corporate governance structures are some of the ways in which agents can be directed towards the actions and behaviours desired by the government. A delicate balance must be struck between giving freedom and flexibility to network operators while at the same time exercising control over the process to ensure objectives are met without a hiccup and in an efficient and productive manner.

CENTRAL AGENCIES

Government is divided into departments, each with its own mission, culture and resources. Departmentalisation allows specialisation and focus, but it risks dividing government into contradictory programs, with pointless competition between units and inconsistent outcomes for citizens.

Central agencies work to resist this fragmentation by providing consistent rules and processes. They view government as a single undertaking that needs balance among devolved responsibilities and adherence to a shared set of norms.

Central agencies offer a whole of government perspective when dissecting financial, administrative and policy aspects of a cabinet submission in briefing papers to ministers.

From a policy perspective, central agencies check that proposals:

- are logical and well considered
- are consistent with other government announcements and programs
- are consistent with governing party policy
- are consistent with intergovernmental and international obligations
- meet cabinet guidelines
- have no presentational problems
- are suitably timed.

From a financial perspective, central agencies must ensure:

- money requested is really needed
- the initiative is cost-effective
- the right priorities are met
- the overall budget is not exceeded
- there are no hidden traps likely to require sudden funding increases.

Finally, from an administrative perspective, central agencies will report on any implications of a policy proposal for:

- public sector employment
- employment or industrial relations generally
- equity and fairness considerations.

The division of responsibility for examining these issues varies across jurisdictions. The list of 'central agencies' is flexible, varying between jurisdictions, and changing over time and by issue. Because all governments must address policy, financial, legal and administrative issues, agencies tend to be organised around these responsibilities. Generally, policy issues are pursued by the central policy agency, financial questions by treasury and personnel arrangements by the management agency. The prime minister will receive briefs from all three, along with political advice from the prime minister's office. An important job of the leader is to maintain the general strategy of the government. These briefs from central agencies are therefore an important coordination mechanism, a way to pull together the diverse threads of policy. A 'whole of government' perspective from the centre allows ministers, especially leaders, to impose consistency on the vast array of decisions before any cabinet.

Central policy agency

In Canberra, central policy coordination is the responsibility of the Department of Prime Minister and Cabinet (PM&C). In the states and territories, this task falls to the cabinet office, or to the department of premier and cabinet or chief minister. Some large local government authorities have developed a similar central policy capacity around the office of the mayor.

PM&C (Department of Prime Minister and Cabinet, 2006a) accepts a 'particular responsibility for policy coordination'. The department must ensure 'the prime minister has the best possible advice drawing from, and consulting with, appropriate sources across the whole of the government system'.

More broadly, PM&C's role is to:

- ensure policy proposals put to the prime minister, other ministers in the portfolio and to cabinet are developed in a coherent, informed and coordinated fashion
- coordinate the administrative response to government policies and decisions, recognising that ministers are responsible individually for the administration of their departments and collectively for matters decided by cabinet

- provide services to the prime minister and to the government to enable the business of government to be managed in an efficient, effective and coordinated manner
- monitor the implementation of the government's objectives where charged with doing so in particular areas such as science and technology policy and access and equity.

These objectives, shared by Commonwealth and state central policy agencies, require a structure that mirrors activities across government. The central policy agency needs experts in every major area facing government, to test views offered by line departments. These policy officers, often drawn from the agencies they monitor, are the core staff of policy coordination.

In Victoria, for example, branches within the Cabinet Office are explicitly designed to observe policy activities in particular agencies.

This structure allows the Cabinet Office to provide advice to the premier on every matter before government. It also provides a capacity to coordinate intergovernmental negotiations. The relevant branch will work closely with line agencies to ensure a consistent state position on various working parties, and to ensure the premier is briefed fully before attending government leaders' meetings.

Central policy agencies in other jurisdictions operate in similar ways. Indeed, the need to coordinate crosses jurisdictional boundaries. Senior officials from Canberra, the states and territories meet regularly, or converse on national telephone links to provide a measure of consistency in policy advice across borders.

Briefs prepared by the central policy agency are forwarded to the prime minister, premier or chief minister. There will be a brief on every item before cabinet, regular 'topical' briefs on matters of the day, and occasionally longer briefs that explore emerging or long-running issues. According to Peter Shergold (2004:10), the PM&C provides over 5000 written briefs every year to the prime minister and his assisting minister and parliamentary secretary.

Leaders thus chair cabinet armed with an array of information and analysis supplied by central agencies. They can question ministers on details of a proposal, or how it fits into the wider scheme of government.

Treasury

As the central policy agency advises on policy activity, so central financial agencies keep a close eye on the fiscal implications of existing and proposed policies. This function typically sits in the 'budget' division of the state treasury or Commonwealth Treasury and Department of Finance and Administration.

When a line department prepares a cabinet submission, it must consult with the central financial agency. Finance will certify that the costings on the proposal are 'agreed'—that is, the figures included in the submission accurately reflect the likely costs of the proposed program. Such agreement does not necessarily mean the treasurer will support the proposal in cabinet, nor that the department will brief its minister supportively, only that the sums are accurate.

Central financial agencies manage the annual budget cycle that sets priorities among all programs for the year ahead. Departments make bids for new policy funds, through their minister, as part of the budget round. The central financial agency is likely to oppose spending outside the budget process, since this upsets fiscal forecasts and undermines budget discipline.

Cabinet submissions put forward outside the budget cycle therefore focus on implementation of policy proposals included in the budget papers. Nonetheless, governments must respond to issues not anticipated in the budget, and maintain reserves (known in some jurisdictions as 'the Treasurer's Reserve') to deal with these contingencies. Alternatively, agencies with an urgent policy proposal are instructed to find the necessary funds within their existing allocation.

The treasury or finance department is likely to provide a brief for its minister on most matters in the cabinet agenda, just as central policy agencies brief the chair of cabinet. The advice will be concerned principally, but not exclusively, with financial considerations. The brief is forwarded to the treasurer, with a summary of any concerns from other departments incorporated into the leader's briefing papers.

Like cabinet offices, budget divisions generally mirror the structures of government. Budget officers become expert in the portfolios they monitor, working closely with line agencies on new proposals. The Commonwealth Department of Finance and Administration, for example, views the 'analysis and evaluation of new spending proposals' as one of its central tasks. A prudent department will discuss a policy proposal with Treasury or Finance and Administration before presenting a cabinet submission.

Attorney-General's Department

When submissions carry legal implications, or require new legislation, departments must consult with the government's legal agencies. Depending on the matter at hand, consultation may be required with the Attorney-General's Department, the Crown Solicitor or Solicitor-General and the Parliamentary Counsel, or the legal staff in the central policy agency.

It is embarrassing (and often expensive) for governments to make mistakes in legal issues, so great care is taken to ensure appropriate scrutiny before cabinet is asked to make a decision. The Commonwealth, for example, sets down very strict requirements in the *Cabinet Handbook* about consultation for submissions with legal requirements. It suggests legislation be considered only as a 'last resort'. The Attorney-General's Department is required to certify that the proposed legislation is necessary; not even a draft submission can be circulated for consultation 'until cleared by the Attorney-General's Department'.

Central personnel agencies

When a submission has implications for the public sector workforce, advice is sometimes sought from the agency with responsibility for personnel. In most jurisdictions this function is attached to the Premier's Department, though some states and the Commonwealth retain free-standing personnel agencies, such as the Australian Public Service Commission.

Such advice may be included in the brief provided by the central policy agency, or forwarded directly to the responsible minister. In the Commonwealth, for example, the minister assisting the prime minister for public service matters may take to the cabinet table a brief on any public sector consequences from a submission.

Employment implications may also attract the interest of departments responsible for employment or industrial relations. However, employees are increasingly treated as an element of budget rather than managed separately, and detailed personnel implications are left for the relevant line department to settle.

Other consultation

A line agency with a policy proposal to put before cabinet must consult the central line agencies. It must persuade the centre that a proposal makes sense from a whole of government perspective, and has been cleared for financial and legal consequences, with proper consideration of public sector implications. This is often a process of bargaining, with significant modification of a submission before it finally reaches the cabinet agenda.

The coordination process does not stop with the central agencies. Indeed there is a daunting array of Commonwealth agencies to be consulted if affected by proposals. These can include:

- Productivity Commission for regulatory matters
- Treasury and Australian Taxation Office for taxation issues
- Department of Environment and Heritage for proposals with environmental consequences
- Department of Foreign Affairs and Trade or Australian Agency for International Development (AusAID) for issues concerning assistance to other countries.

The list can be expanded almost endlessly at Commonwealth level and for each state and territory. This form of consultation is intended to assist coordination. It brings the proposals of one agency into alignment with practices elsewhere in government. Since agency boundaries overlap, prior discussions about policy proposals settle disputes and lock in support before cabinet deliberation. The machinery of government changes to accommodate issues as they rise and fall in political or public prominence. Keeping up to date with shifts in responsibilities is an ongoing task, but it is essential.

Like most parties, we tend to present our policies within departmental boundaries—health, education, transport and so forth. In an era of boundary crossing, however, this is no longer sufficient. People do not live their lives according to bureaucratic categories. Increasingly, political issues are crossing over into a range of policy disciplines. Labour and capital, education and economics, work and family—these are just a few examples of this process.
Mark Latham, May 2002

Coordination comments

Cabinet practice varies across jurisdictions, but in all Australian governments cabinet submissions must include detail of consultation with other government agencies. This introduces contestability into the policy process.

These 'coordination comments' advise ministers on views about a policy proposal from within and beyond government. They alert cabinet to any inconsistencies between the proposals in the submission and practices elsewhere in government.

As the Commonwealth *Cabinet Handbook* (Department of Prime Minister and Cabinet, 2004:21) states:

> Consultation is an integral part of the development of a policy proposal, from the outset of that development through to clearance of a final draft submission. Ministers and officers in departments with an interest should have ample opportunity to contribute to the development of the proposal and to resolve any differences before lodgement of the submission.

The *Cabinet Handbook* stresses that agencies must take on board coordination comments, either dealing with the objection or modifying recommendations accordingly. Should they fail to do so, 'Cabinet Office may reject a submission (unless there are persuasive mitigating reasons) where strong criticism by other departments has not been addressed in the submission or where significant issues have not been canvassed' (Department of Prime Minister and Cabinet, 2004:22–3).

Commonwealth cabinet procedures require dissenting coordination comments to be 'included in the submission as an attachment' (Department of Prime Minister and Cabinet, 2004:21). Ministers can thus read the views of interested parties when considering a submission.

Coordination comments allow cabinet to compare a particular policy proposal with the overall framework of government direction.

Coordination in departments

Every complex organisation must grapple with ways to bring its disparate parts together. This is as true for individual

> Co-ordination, while desirable, is not reform.
> *Noel Pearson, June 2006*

departments as it is for governments, though on a smaller scale. The policy domain within agencies is usually charged by the chief executive with orderly management of policy processes and documents, with fulfilling the centre's demands for routine and extensive intra-governmental consultation, and with testing the integrity and quality of divisional proposals to draw overall direction at this level.

Thus one finds policy divisions and liaison units within departments, usually close to the secretary or director-general, responsible for internal coordination, liaison with the centre, and smooth management of inter-agency and ministerial council negotiations. Finance divisions or economists in policy units may scrutinise costings; the advice of personnel sections may be required on human resource implications, mirroring their counterparts in the centre of government.

Like central agencies, departmental policy groups need to develop keen sensitivity to policy shifts, an ability to predict responses from within and without, and astuteness about the demands of the political and policy domains. Also, departmental policy specialists experience tensions as they strive to coordinate within, to find common ground and to arm their ministers properly for cabinet's deliberations.

POLICY ALIGNMENT

The demand for consistency and coherence in government policy making has seen various jurisdictions experiment with whole-of-government initiatives and 'joined-up' government. These programs are aimed at tackling problems of vertical and horizontal alignment, challenges identified by the National Institute for Governance (2004).

Horizontal alignment refers to the need for inter-organisational cooperation and collaboration in order to battle problems of 'silos' that stifle coordination and prevent 'outsiders' from positively contributing innovation, quality and new ideas. Vertical alignment, on the other hand, seeks to connect goals, resources and structures so that policy intent matches program design and delivery.

Child protection is a policy area that attracts policy alignment attention. In terms of horizontal alignment, it has been identified that there is benefit in police, health officers, social and youth workers, as well as education specialists, uniting to help develop tailored packages for 'at-risk' children to help them preferably avoid, or alternatively navigate their way through, government systems. Unless specific attention is given to each case, many children run the risk of falling into the cracks of government program fragmentation. Through information sharing and joint approaches, government programs can assist in identifying early on which children require enhanced preventative care. Success in early detection helps prevent abused children or children in foster care falling out of the welfare system straight into the judicial system. This type of coordination can have a profound impact on vulnerable individuals who otherwise might face deterioration in their life prospects and who could easily spiral into adverse circumstances.

On the vertical dimension, child protection policy demands alignment between policy objectives and resources and service structures. Government faces a choice: should it enact a framework for child protection aimed at early detection and prevention or should it emphasise post-crisis care and government intervention? In making its choice, a government has to match resources with its selected framework to ensure that its objectives are met in an efficient and effective manner.

Policy alignment is a traditional objective underpinning coordination and consultation. However, there has been a re-focusing of these ideas across the globe. Faced with the reality of fragmentation in public sector structures and service delivery, contemporary government perceptions suggest a need to recalibrate public services. Policy alignment becomes a tool for this recalibration.

'Joined-up government' became globally fashionable after the Blair government introduced the concept as a central plank of its plans for public sector reform when it came to power in 1997 (Ling, 2002; Perri 6 et al., 2005). Meanwhile the Australian Commonwealth government relies on the terms 'integrated government', 'connected government' and 'whole of government' which it defines as 'public service agencies working across portfolio boundaries to achieve a shared goal and an integrated government response to particular issues' (MAC, 2004). Centrelink, created in

1997 to deliver integrated services for sixteen Commonwealth agencies and all State Housing authorities, is an Australian example (see Podger, 2002).

A range of models (see Barrett, 2003; MAC, 2004) can be employed to provide joined-up or connected government arrangements:

- *lead agency model*—One department provides leadership, often with other agencies represented on a taskforce. These are specialist teams brought together to deal with complex or sensitive policy dilemmas requiring coordination. The governance arrangements will often be tightly determined by the lead agency. Taskforces may last for months or years depending on the issue. Recent taskforces have tackled biofuels, health, people smuggling, welfare to work and the 2007 Asia–Pacific Economic Cooperation meetings in Sydney (Department of Prime Minister and Cabinet, 2006b).
- *committee model* (including interdepartmental committees (IDCs) but also including committees with non-government players)—These involve a loose confederation of players charged to consider a particular policy area or problem. Governance arrangements are usually shared among the parties.
- *board model*—The policy and coordination tasks are handed over to a separate entity with independent governance arrangements designed to ensure clear and comprehensive responsibility for the particular relationship that exists with the government and for the activity that is being undertaken on behalf of the government.
- *case management* and program linkages model—Whole-of-government action focuses on the client or individual; rather than the client making individual multiple contacts with agencies, the services are coordinated around the individual in a way that avoids duplication and provides complementary support. Agencies often have agreements or protocols among themselves to coordinate packaged service for the client.
- *one-stop-shop model*—Shifts whole-of-government activity away from coordination among multiple agencies towards

coordination of multiple functions within one agency. This form is often used in regional centres as governments attempt to give 'seamless service' to citizens. State governments have experimented with this model in the creation of social service 'mega-departments' such as the Victorian Department of Human Services which combines the portfolios of health, housing, aged care, children and disability services under the one umbrella.

Coordination is essential for policy alignment. Crisis management has a particular need for fast, synchronised and effective government responses. Terrorist incidents like the Bali bombings and natural disasters such as Cyclone Larry in north Queensland heighten the need for government to prepare for the unexpected. Cooperation and consistency are critical. The demands are not just for technical procedures and institutional interaction but also enhanced bonds built on trust and clarity.

Citizens also expect better policy alignment. Technological change and innovation have facilitated service improvements but have also raised expectations. Citizens used to online, fingertip service from the private sector expect no less from governments. In many ways, this has prompted the logic behind the joined-up governance phenomenon.

Our discussion of network governance at the beginning of this chapter suggests that the public sector has to increasingly confront the task of managing multiple players in the policy making process. But the presence of networks does not automatically result in the practice of network governance (Damgaard, 2006). Coordination is a key skill that deserves greater attention and prominence on a case-by-case basis.

Coordination and politics

Some issues cannot be resolved through consultation or central agency coordination. When disagreement centres on politics rather than policy, central agencies can only present the facts and leave the argument to be settled by ministers.

Many policy arguments reflect the clashing agendas of departments. A proposal to increase woodchip exports might

> Politics is not the art of the possible. It consists in choosing between the disastrous and the unpalatable.
> *John Kenneth Galbraith*

Table 8.1 Factors determining choice of a governance model

Factors favoring network model	Factors favoring hierarchical model
Need for flexibility	Stability preferred
Need for differentiated response to clients or customers	Need for uniform-driven, rule-driven, response
Need for diverse skills	Only a single professional skill needed
Many potential private players available	Government predominant provider
Desired outcome or outputs clear	Outcome ambiguous
Private sector fills skill gap	Government has necessary experience
Leveraging private assets critical	Outside capacity not important
Partners have greater reach or credibility	Government experienced with citizens in this area
Multiple services touch same customer	Service is relatively stand-alone
Third parties can deliver service or achieve goal at lower cost than government	In-house delivery more economical
Rapidly changing technology	Service not affected by changing technology
Multiple levels of government provide service	Single level of government provides service
Multiple agencies use or need similar functions	Single agency uses or needs similar functions

(From Goldsmith and Eggers 2004:51; reprinted with permission of the Brookings Institution Press)

attract support from the agriculture and forestry portfolios but strong opposition from Environment and Heritage. Consultation will highlight differences in opinion rather than create consensus. The central agency brief can point to the strengths and weaknesses of the proposal, to national and international agreements, to scientific evidence and expert opinion. They may sometimes propose one or more compromise recommendations, but only cabinet can make the final, difficult choice.

In some cases, governments decide to live with inconsistency. For decades, state governments funded public health campaigns against smoking while also subsidising tobacco farmers. Governments have many clients, often with incompatible demands. Coordination is essential, but in the end, politics rule.

THE CENTRE VERSUS THE PERIPHERY

Coordination routines seek consistency in government. They require line agencies to consult other affected departments and key stakeholders or other network participants. Submissions must then be discussed with the central agencies, which look to the policy, financial and administrative implications from a whole of government perspective. Those central agencies brief their ministers on the compatibility of a new policy proposal with the existing policy framework. If the benefits of coordination are to be realised, the coordination task must address all facets of its concern: coherence, consistency, efficiency and consultation, and policy alignment on horizontal and vertical dimensions.

Coordination systems inevitably create tension between service agencies and those at the centre. For line departments and network partners, coordination routines can seem frustrating impediments, causing delay and adding to the reporting burden. Ministers, unused to questioning, may bristle. Such tension is unavoidable. The desire for whole of government consistency means little to a line manager, struggling to deliver a program with stretched resources, yet required to seek cabinet approval for some modification or staff appointment. In any coordination process, the costs are felt by those in the field, while the gains belong to the centre.

This imbalance places a special responsibility on those in central agencies to use their authority lightly, to avoid unnecessary demands on line departments and network partners, and to explain the wider purpose behind their request for information or further work on a submission. Central agency arrogance is inappropriate and unhelpful. Government looks very different from the viewpoint of a line department than from the centre, because people are pursuing very different purposes. Central agencies matter because they help government to operate as a single unit. But unless line departments and network partners are allowed to get on with the tangible business of government—delivering services—coordination is a pointless paper exercise.

> My experience in government is that when things are non-controversial and beautifully coordinated, there is not much going on...
> *John F. Kennedy*

Decision

SNAPSHOT

Finally, it is time for a decision. This is a pivotal point: when the analyst's work is judged by cabinet. Yet this step in the policy cycle is also regulated and made routine.

Who makes the decision? What material is before them? How are decisions recorded? This chapter explores the routine of cabinet deliberations.

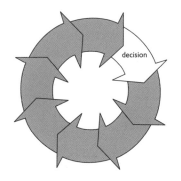

The apex of formal government decision making is citizen and parliamentary voting. In Australia a number of mechanisms are available that widen the scope of decision making beyond the tight constraints of the party system. Referenda are used for critical national issues that demand direct citizen participation, especially those needing constitutional change. Meanwhile, since 1955 the Australian parliament has utilised some 30 instances of 'free votes', known more commonly as conscience votes, on sensitive issues usually relating to social, moral and ethical issues such as abortion, capital punishment, euthanasia, drug reform, stem cell research, war crimes and homosexuality (McKeown and Lundie, 2002, 2007).

But government decision making is far deeper with much, like an iceberg, hidden below the visible parliamentary and electoral level. Here lies the day-to-day determinations of the myriad officials—police officers, teachers, health workers, welfare officers and diplomats—who shape the course of policy through their judgments and actions. More and more, networks elevate focus to dynamic relationship connections and interactions between multiple parties within the policy arena. Attention on these actors (and on players outside the formal channels of government) shows that they have a critical role in policy decision making and determining policy direction.

In between the punctuated formality of parliamentary voting and the day-to-day authority of street-level officials, we have cabinet.

Cabinet's decision is the pivot of the public policy cycle, the point on which all previous and subsequent work turns. Here, political judgment is delivered in light of all the technical advice, the options, the analysis, the comparison of possible instruments, the consultation and coordination efforts.

From the world of issues and problems, a small number have been selected, developed and stated for cabinet's decision about the future.

At any time, many thousands of proposals are before government. They occupy different places in the policy cycle, some nearing completion, others barely formulated. Most are working toward this moment: a place on the cabinet agenda.

For many jurisdictions, cabinet convenes each week to consider and decide on a dozen, or even fewer, submissions. A cabinet decision brings legitimacy and the prospect of implementation. If a submission passes over this all-important hurdle, it is on the way to becoming public policy.

The sheer volume of material awaiting consideration, and the need for at least minimum standards of information and analysis, mean that cabinets must operate by strict rules. Submissions follow a predetermined format. They are considered in a set order. Decisions are recorded and distributed according to a standard process.

Cabinet is the only opportunity for ministers, acting collectively, to consider the full range of ideas before government. In many ways, cabinet provides a regular, closed-door forum for frank debates about policy alternatives, assuming ministers are active and that the cabinet room has not been overtaken by a dominant premier or prime minister.

The political dimension to cabinet decision making should not be underestimated. Ministers and the prime minister all have their eye to determining the political risks and benefits associated with pursuit, or non-pursuit, of policy options. They take into account the political environment and political stringencies as much as they do any technical criteria. Meanwhile prime ministers and premiers use cabinet as they will and as they can: it can be a show of prime ministerial power or relegated to more formal matters. After all, 'cabinet was never intended to be democratic' (Weller, 2007:273).

When discussing submissions, ministers must balance political consequences, policy objectives, administrative convenience,

> Public servants who have the first word in policy-making may be as important in determining the outcome as the politicians who legitimately have the last word.
> *Corbett (1997)*

> ... cabinet remains one place where most of the time the most senior ministers meet to discuss the most pressing problems facing government and, indeed, the nation.
> *Weller (2007:232)*

media attractiveness and their own place in history. Given this pressure, ministers insist on proper process, so that all necessary data and advice are before them when choosing. The pressure on advisers is to ensure that cabinet activity is streamlined and that unnecessary disputation is mitigated. This often sees a lot of precursory work done within departments and with stakeholders to iron out problems and secure support. Sometimes, it may even seem that cabinet is redundant. Often, however, cabinet acts as a very necessary arbiter, bringing political perspectives into play.

Policy advisers must be thoroughly proficient in the rules governing cabinet. A good policy idea is not enough, even if consultation and coordination indicate widespread support. Proposals must answer all the questions posed in the format for submissions. They must be supported with financial, legal and social impact data, and any other relevant information. Ministers want to make informed decisions. The routines of cabinet government are designed to ensure consistency, coherence and clarity, and to reinforce the political nature of this pivotal moment. Neglecting these routines diminishes the effectiveness of cabinet.

CABINET ROUTINES

Cabinet routines are expressed as rules, and usually codified in the *Cabinet Handbook* (see, for example, Department of Prime Minister and Cabinet, 2004). These guidelines set out formats for all types of submission, and timelines for consideration.

Cabinet routines establish a timetable for business within government. Because cabinet meets regularly, agencies can organise their work agenda around the cabinet schedule. Cabinet also requires certain regular submissions—quarterly performance indicators, budget submissions, annual strategic plans and reports. Government is always prone to crisis and disruption, but the orderly business of cabinet provides some measure of stability and predictability.

The policy cycle has been in play long before cabinet considers a submission. Once an issue has been identified, a line department undertakes policy analysis and makes recommendations to the minister about an appropriate policy instrument.

A CHECKLIST FOR GOOD CABINET SUBMISSIONS

Ask yourself:

- Is the submission necessary?
- Should it be a submission seeking a decision or, alternatively, an information paper?
- Are the objectives of the submission clear?
- Does the submission achieve the objectives it sets for itself?
- Does the submission include all reasonable options and no unrealistic options?
- Has the necessary level of consultation inside and outside government taken place? Does it indicate whether the views of the major affected groups are known?
- Are winners and losers clearly identified?
- Are precedent considerations addressed?
- Has consistency with arrangements/directions in other jurisdictions been addressed?
- Are financial implications clear and proposals properly costed (in conjunction with treasury)?
- Are recommendations clear and uncomplicated? Do they flow from the body of the submission?
- Is the submission drafted clearly and is it well structured?

Wanna et al. (1994:2/27)

The ministerial office may offer views. The minister must approve further policy development. A discussion paper or draft submission may be circulated and feedback sought from related government agencies and key interest groups. Following consultation, the draft submission, by now well developed, is forwarded to the central agencies for consideration and comment. Only with the consultation and coordination phases complete is an agency finally ready to approach cabinet through its minister for a decision.

Of course, some cabinet submissions do not take so long to develop and submit. The wheels of government often do not turn as slowly as one might think. When crises and other circumstances require fast action, the cabinet process can accommodate speedy turnaround times. Nonetheless, an orderly process is usually followed, even for urgent matters following a truncated pathway.

The Commonwealth cabinet process provides a reasonably standard Australian model for cabinet deliberations:

- Once cleared by the central policy agency, a submission is lodged with the cabinet office at least five days before cabinet consideration.
- The submission must follow the standard format required in the *Cabinet Handbook*, with details of prior consultation and warning of any likely complications or objections.
- A submission is divided into three parts—a *cover sheet* summarising key points, a *body* spelling out the proposal, and any *attachments* with supporting data. Commonwealth cabinet rules restrict the combined cover sheet and body to just ten pages.
- A new electronic document management system called CABNET has been adopted for the lodging and circulation of cabinet submissions, agenda papers, minutes and business lists. 'While the CABNET system has changed the practicalities of lodging and distributing Cabinet documents, it has been designed to fit in with existing requirements and processes of the Cabinet system. It is essentially an improved tool for operating within established principles' (Department of Prime Minister and Cabinet, 2001).

Cabinet plays a number of different roles as a:

- focus of responsibility, as part of the political system (constitutional theory or legal approach);
- set of rules and bureaucratic practices and their implications for its workings (public administration or positional approach);
- maker of policy, and the search for better decision-making (public policy approach);
- political battleground, a centre for political power and reputation, particularly the weight of prime ministers and their ability to drive the cabinet agenda (political science approach); and
- network of influences and relationships (network analysis).

Weller (2007)

- Submissions at the cabinet meeting are considered according to an agenda prepared by the cabinet secretary and approved by the prime minister as chair of cabinet.
- The minister presenting a submission puts the case for cabinet acceptance, and debate may follow. At the close of discussion, the chair may sum up, perhaps suggesting words for the decision to reflect the meeting's mood. Votes in cabinet are rare; a submission with insufficient support in the room tends to lapse, or be deferred for further development.
- After the meeting, the cabinet secretary (along with two other note takers) draws up the minutes and, if necessary, confirms these with the prime minister. Decisions (known as cabinet minutes) are then circulated to agencies for action or information.

Of course routines vary slightly across jurisdictions and defence procurement has attracted separate attention at the Commonwealth level with its own rules for submissions and memoranda.

Cabinet is not discussed in the Commonwealth constitution, though key conventions are well understood and outlined in Table 9.1. The secrecy of cabinet meetings was challenged during the 1990s when a judge ruled in favour of disclosing 113 cabinet notebooks to test concerns the Northern Land Council had been unfairly dealt with through the passage of the *Land Rights Act 1976*. On appeal, though, the High Court held that the opening of this form of cabinet record was not in the public interest. Cabinet's privacy remained intact (see Weller, 2007:225–6).

There is no question cabinet retains a central role in the Australian system of government. The executive controls the numbers in parliament, so cabinet decisions are legitimate and authoritative. Cabinet sets the agenda for the executive and the public service. Cabinet is the forum in which choices are endorsed, information exchanged, initiatives coordinated, strategy endorsed and decisions made.

Within the policy cycle, cabinet's decision settles disagreement. A submission may have strong supporters and detractors within government but only cabinet can consider and finalise the issue. Cabinet consideration is one moment in the policy cycle when all perspectives focus on a single proposal, and the arguments translate to a decision.

The cabinet plays a key role in bringing together and in reconciling different viewpoints, but it requires an orderly process to do this.
Keating (1996:63)

Submissions are papers containing recommendations by the responsible minister(s) on action to be taken by the government.
Howard (1998:5)

Table 9.1 Cabinet conventions and procedures

Collective responsibility	Cabinet ministers must publicly support all decisions taken in cabinet, whatever view they advanced during the meeting. A cabinet minister who cannot accept collective responsibility should resign.
Ministerial responsibility	Ministers are responsible for the submissions they bring forward, even though others, mainly departmental officials, may have developed and drafted the material.
Portfolios	Ministers represent their portfolios in cabinet. Public servants or advisers cannot deputise for a minister in cabinet.
Policy approval	Major policy initiatives cannot be announced or implemented until approved by cabinet (unless cleared by the leader).
Confidentiality	To reach the best decisions, cabinet discussions must be frank. The meeting, together with all related documents, is subject to strict confidentiality.
Interests	In cabinet discussions, ministers must indicate any conflict of interest concerning a submission, and excuse themselves from deliberations if appropriate.
Committees	The decisions of cabinet committees are not binding until endorsed by cabinet.
Agenda	The agenda is usually approved in advance by the chair of cabinet, along with the contents of the cabinet folders.
Non-agenda items	An item not listed for discussion can be raised only with the prior agreement of the chair of cabinet.
Five-day rule	To ensure sufficient time for evaluation and briefing of ministers, submissions must be lodged at least five days before cabinet meets.
Circulation	Several days before each cabinet meeting the cabinet secretariat will circulate folders containing submissions, memoranda and other cabinet material. These are subject to secrecy provisions, and cannot be shown to others outside cabinet security protocols.
Submissions	Cabinet submissions must include all information specified in the *Cabinet Handbook*, be of no more than ten pages (excluding attachments), signed and, if concerned with policy, contain options and recommendations.
Secrecy	All cabinet submissions include a secrecy classification level and are marked 'cabinet-in-confidence'.
Secretary	The secretary of cabinet is bound by the same rules of secrecy as ministers, and must never breach the confidentiality of the cabinet process.
Note takers	The secretary may be supported by note takers, who are also bound by cabinet confidentiality. While notebooks may include comments that assist in framing decisions, no verbatim record is made of the meeting.
Officials	Officials other than note takers attend meetings only with the permission of the chair of cabinet, and only to answer questions about factual or technical matters. Officials should leave the room before any decision is taken.
Decisions	In theory the chair approves the wording of decisions before circulation. In practice officials write up cabinet minutes. Ministers can object to the wording at the next meeting or in writing to the prime minister.
Records	The records created by a government are only available to that government. New governments do not have access to the cabinet records of their predecessors.

See also Glossary

WHAT GOES TO CABINET?

Cabinet ministers sometimes complain of being overloaded, of having to read and think about too many different policy problems. Agencies, on the other hand, may be frustrated by an inability to get urgent business onto the cabinet agenda.

Establishing firm rules about what cabinet will consider is a difficult task. Ministers need sufficient information to feel in control, yet they also wish to maintain a strategic outlook, setting policy direction rather than trading in detail.

The Commonwealth *Cabinet Handbook* (Department of Prime Minister and Cabinet, 2004:13–14) sets out guidelines for agencies about what matters should be considered by cabinet.

In the Commonwealth, matters that must go to cabinet include:

- new policy proposals and proposed significant variations to existing policies
- proposals likely to have a significant effect on employment in either the public or private sector
- expenditure proposals, including proposals for major capital works and computer acquisitions (normally considered only in the budget context)
- proposals requiring legislation, other than minor proposals which the prime minister has agreed need not be raised in cabinet
- proposals likely to have a significant impact upon relations between the Commonwealth and foreign, state, territory or local governments
- proposed responses to recommendations made in parliamentary committee reports, except for responses which the prime minister agrees raise no significant policy questions
- government negotiation of, or agreement to, international treaties in accordance with Department of Foreign Affairs and Trade guidelines and the Commonwealth's treaties procedures
- requests from parliamentary committees for references, where the references proposed have significant policy or administrative implications.

Similar statements govern cabinet procedures in most states and territories. All emphasise reducing the volume of business. Where agencies can settle a matter between themselves, or when a concern is not of sufficient importance to make a demand on cabinet's time, it must be resolved at a ministerial level. As the Commonwealth *Cabinet Handbook* (Department of Prime Minister and Cabinet, 2004:13) notes, 'ministers should consider seriously the option of settling a matter by correspondence, particularly where it is likely that all interested ministers are in agreement'. If need be, the proposed solution can be then forwarded to the prime minister for approval.

As a matter of principle, cabinet declines to consider matters not listed on the agenda. The cabinet agenda shifts according to the interests of the chair and the issues before government.

In the Commonwealth, each type of submission has a specified format. Policy submissions are the most extensive, with fifteen or more different headings which must be addressed. *Policy submissions* are signed by ministers and seek to commit the government to a course of action.

Memoranda are prepared and signed by departmental officials, usually in response to a cabinet request for further information or more options in some policy discussion.

Committee reports reflect the increasing importance of cabinet committees. Cabinet may have a series of standing and ad hoc committees to deal with the volume of business, and to provide focused discussion on sensitive or detailed issues (Howard, 1998:5). Almost all are nominally chaired by the prime minister, though in practice a senior minister may take the running. Many submissions pass through a committee before they get to cabinet, providing a forum for debate and negotiation among relevant ministers. If subsequent cabinet consideration is required, the committee recommendation is printed on blue paper; otherwise it is simply noted by cabinet. Ministers are reluctant to reopen in cabinet an issue already settled at committee level (Codd, 1990:6), and cannot do so if they are a member of that committee.

Legislation submissions take several forms, depending on the stage of the proposal:

PREPARING SUBMISSIONS

Submissions and memoranda should:

- be presented in a familiar format
- be easy to 'navigate' around
- put forward an agreed basis of facts on which discussion may proceed
- succinctly identify the central issues
- indicate realistic policy options and their implications for achieving identified objectives.

There are various techniques to achieve this:

- use everyday language
- avoid long, complicated sentences and paragraphs
- avoid technical terms, jargon
- be concise; stick to key points
- build arguments step by step
- rework each sentence until every word counts
- edit ruthlessly
- test the finished product by having it read by a colleague unfamiliar with the subject.

Department of Prime Minister and Cabinet (2004)

Officials (other than cabinet officers) do not attend cabinet or committee meetings unless their attendance has been specifically requested by a minister and approved by the prime minister...

Officials are present only to aid their minister and, through him or her, to provide advice to the meeting if requested. They are expected to explain factual or technical matters on request, but not to participate in discussions. Officials normally leave the meeting before final outcomes are discussed.
Department of Prime Minister and Cabinet (2004:11–12)

- An *Authority to Prepare* submission invites cabinet to approve the broad outlines, and drafting instructions, for a new bill.
- Cabinet, or a cabinet legislation committee, may later consider an *Authority to Introduce* submission, which sets out the completed bill, outlines the consultation process and its results, and indicates how the proposed legislation differs from the outline originally approved.

In some jurisdictions there are also separate submissions for *Significant Appointments*, though in the Commonwealth this is handled through a letter to the prime minister (Department of Prime Minister and Cabinet, 2004:24–6). In either case there is still a standard checklist covering the name and qualifications of the candidate, the nature of the office, regional and gender balance considerations, and any matters likely to cause controversy.

Information Papers inform cabinet of discussions in ministerial councils and the Council of Australian Governments (COAG). As intergovernmental relations become more complex, ministers need to know what options are being considered by their colleagues. Such items are described as 'under the line' because they are usually listed for noting rather than for discussion.

Matters without Submission are an opportunity to discuss urgent business. The prime minister or premier may also address questions of political strategy or parliamentary business.

Executive Council Minutes are recommendations for appointments or expenditure required to be approved by the governor-general in council. In recent years these have been greatly reduced in number, and are not discussed by cabinet. Still, cabinet must ensure a schedule of ministers who will attend the formal meetings of the executive council. Cabinet may also allocate engagements for important events the prime minister is unable to attend, though this is typically handled through ministerial offices rather than in the cabinet room.

BRIEFING MINISTERS

Each type of submission carries a security classification. Only those advisers and public servants with appropriate security clearance can view a submission, and all governments have strict rules about the handling, distribution and filing of cabinet material.

Cabinet meetings last half a day or more, and can cover anything from national security to schedules of public appearances and media campaigns. Even ministers with no items on the agenda must be ready to discuss any proposals with cross-portfolio implications. Hence a key function of departments is to brief ministers on the contents of the cabinet folder. Ministers are not merely responsible for their portfolio: they are members of the executive council, and share collective responsibility for management of the entire policy agenda.

Each agency has its own format for briefings. Most keep a brief to a single page. The department will tell its minister what the submission is about, how it may affect the portfolio, indicate a position and possibly suggest amendments. The brief provides a script for the minister to participate in the debate, and a way for the agency to have its concerns heard in the cabinet room. Some briefs are the responsibility of the minister's office rather than the department.

For submissions prepared by the department, the brief will be more extensive. Ministers must be able to promote and defend their submissions. They need at their fingertips all the necessary facts and figures. Nervous ministers rehearse arguments with senior officials before going to cabinet. Later, senior line department managers cluster in the minister's office to learn whether cabinet accepted the departmental recommendations.

An important role for the prime minister in cabinet is to provide 'whole of government' scrutiny on submissions. As chair, the prime minister must stand above the interests of individual departments to consider the interests of the government. To assist in this, the prime minister is provided with extensive briefing notes on every agenda item. These include detailed analysis of the policy and financial consequences of a submission, and a recommendation for or against acceptance. These briefs are prepared by specialised policy officers from PM&C.

Many sources of advice make the prime minister the best informed participant in cabinet discussions, able to interrogate ministers about the detail and implications of their proposals.

ADVICE

There can be no doubt that a competitive environment has emerged for the provision of policy advice to government. In addition to individual government departments and agencies, ministers obtain advice from within their own offices, government-initiated reviews and inquiries and, in increasingly sophisticated ways, external sources such as interest groups, industry bodies and lobbyists. The revolution in communications represented by email has also led to a vast increase in direct contact by constituents.

This is a positive and healthy development. Elected representatives should canvass views and take advice from as wide a range of legitimate community sources as possible.
John Howard, June 2001

A cabinet meeting might follow the standard format published by the Queensland government in its *Cabinet Handbook*:

- apologies
- confirmation of collective minutes from the previous meeting
- policy submissions and memoranda
- cabinet committee reports
- legislative submissions
- significant appointments proposals
- information papers
- matters without submission
- minutes for executive council
- ministers to attend executive council
- invitations unable to be attended by the premier.

Office of the Cabinet (1995:23)

The treasurer and the minister for finance also take extensive briefing notes to cabinet, though with an economic and budget emphasis. Other ministers with cross-government responsibilities, such as the attorney-general and the minister for industrial relations, may also work from specialised analysis of submissions. Any concerns held by their agencies, though, are also incorporated into briefs prepared by the Department of Prime Minister and Cabinet.

While departments provide ministers with technical advice, ministerial offices supply a political perspective on cabinet business. In particular, the prime minister's office advises on the electoral and media implications of submissions. These political judgments are prepared in a briefing note that, along with the department's advice, is presented to the prime minister in the cabinet folder above the submission in question.

The submissions and briefing notes draw together political, policy and administrative advice and bring them to the cabinet process. Ministers enter cabinet discussion alive to the implications of proposals. They have the information required to balance political interests with sound policy and to avoid unmanageable proposals. Cabinet becomes a central focus of government, a time and place when a political perspective engages with line departmental submissions to produce public policy choices.

RECORDING CABINET DECISIONS

The practice for recording cabinet decisions varies across jurisdictions. Some state governments ban all public servants from the cabinet room, relying on the premier or a seconded member of parliament to note decisions. Most jurisdictions, including the Commonwealth, prefer to support cabinet with a professional secretariat. These public servants prepare, collate and distribute cabinet papers; take notes during meetings; retrieve cabinet material for confidential storage; write up cabinet minutes; and distribute these to departments and ministers.

By tradition, elaborate procedures are used to code cabinet decisions. Some jurisdictions use different shades of paper to indicate the significance of a decision. A record of decision on gold-edged paper is forwarded to the minister with implementation responsibility. Chief executives assigned tasks by cabinet

RECOMMENDATIONS

Cabinet submissions must contain recommendations. These follow a standard format: 'I recommend that cabinet agree/approve/note...'

A poorly crafted recommendation does not assist clear decision making: 'I recommend that cabinet adopt proposals (a) through (e), as set out on page 5 of the submission.'

A good recommendation sets out clearly what action cabinet is being asked to take: 'I recommend that cabinet approve an increase of 5000 places in the family reunion immigration program for the coming financial year.'

receive the relevant decision on silver-edged paper. For the rest, decisions arrive on blue paper—an interest in the decision but no implementation responsibility—or white for information only.

The Commonwealth does not follow such procedures with cabinet minutes, though the cabinet secretariat uses colour coding within cabinet folders to distinguish cabinet committee decisions from matters requiring cabinet consideration.

The record of cabinet's decisions is direct and to the point. A minute is framed in terms of submission recommendations: 'Cabinet decided to increase spending on rural drought assistance by $24 million in the coming financial year, subject to no break in current weather patterns.' It is imperative, therefore, that officers preparing submissions frame recommendations so they make sense when distributed as decisions.

The central policy agency will pay close attention to a submission's recommendations and conclusions because these state the action cabinet is being asked to take. They must be accurate, a logical product of the submission, and capable of being stated in the form of a decision.

As with submissions, access to cabinet decisions is also governed by security considerations. Very sensitive decisions, such as those with important defence or trade implications, may be circulated only to senior ministers, or not at all. In any case, all cabinet decisions must be secured using prescribed filing procedures. They are returned to the cabinet secretariat on a change of government, when the records of the outgoing administration are collated and locked away.

EXECUTIVE COUNCIL

While cabinet is the apex of decision making, Commonwealth and state constitutions vest formal authority in an executive council. It is this body that proclaims legislation, appoints people to statutory positions, changes administrative arrangements, and endorses international treaties.

The Federal Executive Council comprises the governor-general and the ministers. It is also known as 'the governor-general in council'. All ministers are sworn in as executive councillors, and so known by the title 'Honourable'. State executive councils are

EXTRACT FROM THE AUSTRALIAN CONSTITUTION

61. The executive power of the Commonwealth is vested in the Queen and is exercisable by the governor-general as the Queen's representative, and extends to the execution and maintenance of this Constitution, and of the laws of the Commonwealth.

62. There shall be a Federal Executive Council to advise the governor-general in the government of the Commonwealth, and the members of the council shall be chosen and summoned by the governor-general and sworn as executive councillors, and shall hold office during his pleasure.

63. The provisions of this Constitution referring to the governor-general in council shall be construed as referring to the governor-general acting with the advice of the Federal Executive Council.

the governor and ministers, and are called 'the governor in council'. The state bodies often meet weekly, while the Federal Executive Council, chaired by the governor-general, generally meets fortnightly at Government House in Canberra. Ministers are rostered to attend. Convention dictates that at least two executive councillors are required to provide a quorum (Howard, 1998:8).

As with cabinet submissions, there is a specified format for material being presented to executive council. This is set out in a federal *Executive Council Handbook*. The governor-general may seek assurances about recommendations in an executive council minute and may decline to approve the minute until further information is provided. Such interludes are rare; executive council is essentially a constitutional formality rather than a deliberative meeting.

Protocol requires that decisions requiring the approval of the governor-general in council are not announced until it has met.

CABINET

> ... it is necessary to avoid too technocratic a view of cabinet. The political agenda, to keep cabinet together and the supporters satisfied, may run counter to the technical benefits of particular decisions. No amount of good information will outplay a sense of political urgency or political fear. It is often possible to improve the technical level of cabinet debate, but for ministers that may not be the point. They need to contribute.
>
> Weller (2007:248)

Making cabinet decisions is a complex business. Most submissions take some weeks to work through the precabinet phase, to find a place on the agenda and then to be considered and settled. Public servants, ministers and advisers complain at times about the elaborate procedures, secrecy and ritual of cabinet deliberations. However, such routines are an important control mechanism. They introduce rigour. They spare cabinet from incomplete or inappropriate submissions. Routines ensure sufficient minimum information before a topic is discussed. They structure decision making, creating a sequence that invites analysis of proposals from a range of perspectives. Finally, cabinet rules establish clear responsibilities for implementation, making decisions the specific responsibility of particular ministers and agencies.

Through cabinet routines, governments pursue consistency. By bringing all proposals to the same meeting of ministers, and requiring information about objectives, finances, legal, regulatory, environmental, social and administrative consequences, proposals can be compared and tested. Ministers can use cabinet processes to demonstrate how a submission fits with government's overall strategy, and how its recommendations will be promoted to the community, interest groups and the media. A cabinet that works well is essential if a government is to survive politically.

SAMPLE COVER PAGE FOR A CABINET SUBMISSION

The following sample cover page illustrates the information required before a submission can go to cabinet. The format is drawn from the Commonwealth *Cabinet Handbook* (Department of Prime Minister and Cabinet, 2004). Note this would be followed by the body of the submission, spelling out each of the topics covered in greater detail, and by attachments containing necessary technical and financial data.

Although notes are taken during discussion for the purpose of writing up minutes (which record only the agreed outcomes), cabinet notetakers do not keep a verbatim record of discussions. For security reasons, any notes taken are recorded only in special cabinet notebooks that are subject to strict confidentiality requirements.
Department of Prime Minister and Cabinet (2004)

Submission Number	300056 [ASSIGNED BY CABINET SECRETARIAT]
Copy Number	1
Title	REVIEW OF TERTIARY EDUCATION CHARGES
Minister	Senator Scott Free Minister for Education, Science and Training
Purpose	• To establish a review of current charges for Australian university students • To announce no further fee increases until this review is complete
Program Context	• The Higher Education Contribution Scheme (HECS) is administered by the Funding and Student Support Branch within the DEST Higher Education Group • This review will test the viability of sustaining current Student Contribution Amounts (SCAs) under the HECS scheme
Relation to Existing Policy	• HECS was introduced with the *Higher Education Funding Act 1988* but was replaced with the existing legislation being the *Higher Education Support Act 2003*. The Scheme includes both student contribution amounts (SCAs) as well as a student loan scheme called HECS-HELP. This submission pertains only to the SCAs and does not address the HECS-HELP loans arrangements. • SCAs were expanded significantly in the 1996/1997 budget, with capped deregulation legislated in the higher education reform package of 2003 and taking effect in 2005. Overall the SCA represents about 45 per cent of the cost of a higher education course, although actual course costs vary between 27 per cent for nursing and 84 per cent for law. • While current budget strategy assumes revenue from SCAs, there are mounting problems with payment and evidence of disincentives to study. A review of the Scheme may improve long-term viability

Sensitivity/Criticism	• The current operation of SCAs is attracting criticism from students, parents and higher education institutions given proposals to allow a surcharge on SCAs • A freeze on further fee increases pending a review is likely to attract support from the National Union of Students (NUS) and Australian Vice-Chancellors' Committee (AVCC) • No public consultation has occurred, pending cabinet consideration of this sensitive issue
Legislation Involved?	• Any modification of the scheme will require amendment of the *Higher Education Support Act 2003*
Urgency: critical/significant dates	• As current Year 12 students consider post-education options, the annual cycle of criticism over SCAs has resumed • Recent media reports have highlighted alleged inequities in the present operations of the HECS scheme • A review must be established this month if a report is to be available for consideration in the next budget round
Consultation: ministers/ departments	• Finance • ATSIC • Prime Minister and Cabinet • Australian Taxation Office
Is there Agreement?	• No. Finance says the matter should be considered in budget context • Yes. ATSIC indicate concerns about current Scheme for disadvantaged students and support a review • No. Prime Minister and Cabinet acknowledge state concerns as expressed at COAG, but do not consider the issue critical • Yes. Australian Taxation Office acknowledges present collection difficulties and supports a review.
Evaluation Strategy Agreed	• Yes. Though Finance does not favour a review outside the budget context, it has agreed on a methodology and appropriate measures should such a review proceed
Timing/handling of announcement	• No announcement is anticipated until the prime minister has approved membership of a review committee • Once membership is settled, a review would be announced by the minister during a forthcoming national conference on higher education
Departments consulted	• A draft media release is included at Attachment A
Cost: • this fiscal year • year 2 • year 3 • year 4	• A review must be completed before Expenditure Review Committee deliberations resume in February if the findings are to be considered in the context of the next budget • Consequently, a one-off expenditure of $1.23 million is proposed, to be supplied from within the current resources of DEST. All money would be expended in the current financial year.

10 Implementation

Once a decision has been made, the policy cycle moves to implementation. People are informed of the choice, policy instruments are created and put in place, staff instructed, services delivered, money spent, and bills prepared for parliament. The machine of government smoothly implements cabinet's wish—in theory.

The story of implementation does not always run so well, however. The gap between intention and outcome may be large. Implementation failures in the public sector are the stuff of political debate, and quickly identified by political opponents and the media alike as examples of government incompetence.

To avoid this embarrassment, implementation issues must be considered long before a submission gets to cabinet. Policy makers must pay attention to the demands of implementation at every stage of the policy cycle. In fact, continuous implementation is a mark of robust policy making if the dynamism of the policy process is recognised and the benefits of learning are to be incorporated. The rigours of the real world are the ultimate test of a policy. Poor design means a policy will fail once implemented. Consequently, a submission that has not identified the appropriate policy instruments or the necessary resources for successful implementation should not be put before cabinet. Implementation begins with policy analysis, and must carry through to recommendations for practical, achievable programs.

SNAPSHOT
Good policies are meaningless unless implemented. Policy analysts must consider implementation needs early in the development of a proposal.

This chapter explores implementation methods, and some familiar pitfalls. Advisers should develop implementation plans during policy development to enable timely implementation once cabinet approves the policy.

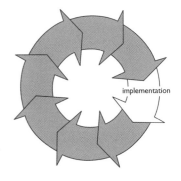

POLICY DESIGN INCLUDES IMPLEMENTATION

Despite occasional policy failures and the practical problems of design, public policies are intended to achieve their objectives. The task of the policy adviser includes identifying implementation and design problems, and developing strategies to meet these.

The challenges are many. Of particular importance is the division of authority between multiple, sometimes competing, agencies, differing objectives within government and the complexities of a federal system. In the Australian context, implementation must accommodate, and delicately balance, diverse regional claims with centralised systems (see Smyth et al., 2005). The wide disparities between urban and rural populations and their accompanying needs makes implementation a complex task. Linear, hierarchical systems of decision making do not always accommodate the fluidity of network delivery.

Noting these formidable constraints, some argue that public policies are largely doomed to fail. Academic studies have indeed found a high rate of implementation misfires, either because the policy design was fundamentally flawed or because government agencies lacked sufficient expertise and resources. It is one thing for politicians to promise, another for government agencies to deliver.

In science, no experiment is wasted—there is always something to learn. Pressman and Wildavsky's influential study *Implementation* (1973) focused on failure, but it inspired further studies and a series of important findings. Public policies will indeed fail if not designed carefully, with an eye to the many constraints on government action. Yet, through skilful analysis, evaluation and evolution, policy programs can improve over time and eventually meet their objectives. Policies are hypotheses that improve through testing and refinement.

POLICY LEARNING AND POLICY FEEDBACK LOOPS

In Chapter 5 the role of policy learning was considered as part of the policy analysis phase of the policy cycle. Policy learning is

---

Ten conditions for perfect implementation:

1. no crippling external constraints
2. adequate time and resources
3. a suitable combination of resources at each stage
4. a valid theory of cause and effect
5. direct links between cause and effect
6. a single implementation agency, or at least a dominant one
7. understanding and agreement on the objectives to be achieved
8. a detailed specification of tasks to be completed
9. perfect communication and coordination
10. perfect obedience.

Gunn (1978)

just as important to implementation and coincides with the emphasis on implementation as a continuous exercise.

Contemporary organisational theory emphasises the importance of *knowledge management* and the *learning organisation*. These ideas view policy making as a continuous process directly shaped by priorities for knowledge sharing and learning. The public sector has taken up these tools in its recalibration and in its need to meet greater demands for information and evidence to improve government success in the policy process (see Mulgan, 2003). As networked governance and the New Public Management have taken root in public sector practice, more attention has been paid to these management techniques.

Knowledge management is the process of an organisation embracing knowledge as a strategic asset that drives performance (in a private sector environment, competitive advantage) through the identification, capture and management of intellectual and human capital. For example, the Australian Family Law Council implemented a knowledge management strategy that reconsidered how knowledge was stored and transferred in its organisation (Osborne, 2004).

The learning organisation movement complements knowledge management by embracing the idea that organisations must value and encourage thinking and learning across horizontal relationships while incorporating knowledge vertically into appreciation for, and development of, organisational strategy. The learning organisation movement directly encourages interaction between operational and policy or foresight actors to encourage strategic organisational debate (Garratt, 2000) and to improve each other's performance (Doherty and Horne, 2002).

The connection between policy development and implementation is an age-old issue but its relevance has increased due to the fragmentary nature of contemporary governance and the conscious separation of purchasers from providers and policy from delivery.

Learning achieved through policy feedback links the practical experience of service delivery operators with the ideas of policy makers (Althaus, 1997). Having an institutional

> I think one of the things we lack in the public service at a Commonwealth and a state level is a consolidated focus on the efficient and timely and sympathetic delivery of services. We tend to look at service delivery as an afterthought rather than as a policy priority... I do see service delivery and the quality of it as an end in itself and not just something that is the end product of having taken a decision. And I've seen too many examples over the last eight and a half years of a good policy being compromised somewhat by inferior service delivery.
> *John Howard, 22 October 2004 (quoted in Wanna, 2006:347)*

> Members of the career service [have] ... the responsibility—in Aberbach, Putnam, and Rockman's lovely phrase, to 'take the dreams of politicians and bring them gently to earth'.
> *Ingraham (2005:19)*

connection or a transfer of expertise between policy and operational arms of implementation is essential if policy objectives are to be achieved effectively and efficiently. Without this connection, service deliverers can miss a policy goal, while policy makers can fail to translate into practice. Opportunities to improve service delivery are lost; the risk of implementation failures is heightened. In the age of network governance there are multiple, separate organisations interacting with each other to achieve certain goals. Feedback loops become critical for policy development and implementation to inform each other and to improve the policy making process.

The Job Network is an example in Australia of the application of purchaser-provider models and its associated underpinning of principal-agent theory (Burgess, 2003). It provides a concrete case of the need for policy feedback.

The Job Network was launched in 1998 and consists of a networked web of services provided to job seekers. At the centre of the hub is Centrelink, which coordinates and maintains the web and allocates job seekers with employment service providers. The federal government, through the Department of Employment and Workplace Relations, tenders out employment services on a rolling basis to a mix of private and not-for-profit providers. Contracts are awarded for fixed periods to provide a certain amount of services. The department uses a rating system to review providers' renewable tender applications. Providers receive a commencement fee and an outcome fee and 'these vary according to the type of service provided for and in turn are linked to the needs of the job seeker as determined by the Job Seeker Classification Instrument that is applied by Centrelink' (Burgess, 2003:228). Job seekers are either voluntary or conscripted through social security benefits being tied to job-seeking activities.

The Job Network initiative is an attempt to address unemployment through a supply-side focus and by framing unemployment as a commodified market. It demands clear specification of objectives, sustainability in a large number of competitive service providers who possess adequate experience and local knowledge and infrastructure, incorporation of a smart incentive package that matches provider interests with job seekers' needs, and a rigorous regulatory regime to monitor the system and ensure consistency as well as attention to the placement of long-term unemployed over 'quick-fix, quick-money' placements.

Over time, as experience informs policy design, the Job Network is 'evolving towards a system with both more regulations in some areas (such as minimum service provision) and less regulations in other areas (such as removing quotas and facilitating greater choice) . . . there has been and will continue to be adaptation to learning by doing in the terms of the development of the operational details of the model' (Burgess, 2003). Redesign, however, cannot hide problems in policy fundamentals. According to John Quiggin (2006:23), the repeated redesign of the Job Network 'has never overcome the fundamental problems of an incentive-based system'.

Yet this is perhaps the key feature of intractable and wicked problems. Sometimes even flawless policy design may not be able to combat structural issues. Demand for continuous implementation improvement endures. 'There are undoubted tensions within the contrived market, price versus quality, funding limits versus generating outcomes, flexibility versus process specification . . . Learning by doing, ongoing adjustment and process redesign have been and will continue to be features of the JN [Job Network] as they were for previous regimes for employment service delivery to the unemployed in Australia' (Burgess, 2003).

CABINET IMPLEMENTATION UNITS

Implementation has become more and more prominent in recent years as politicians have complained that the public sector is failing to deliver on the achievement of government objectives. In several jurisdictions, including the Commonwealth, cabinet implementation units have been established to 'work with agencies to ensure timely and effective implementation of government decisions' (McPhee, 2006).

These implementation units reside in the premier's or prime minister's department and provide a dual role. They alert cabinet through an early warning system about potential risks associated with implementation plans for particular cabinet

> . . . the implementation literature is a little depressing, because it is predominantly about 'implementation failure'.
> Colebatch (1998:56)

submissions. They also monitor progress of initiatives approved by cabinet and conduct in-depth studies of 'existing areas of administration, especially cross-cutting issues or where systemic implementation problems appeared [sic] to be delaying achievements' (Wanna, 2006:360). A 'traffic lights' system (green for satisfactory progress, amber for concerns and red for major problems or hold-ups) is used to rate, checklist and prioritise implementation concerns (Tiernan, 2006; Wanna, 2006).

Whether implementation units endure or not, their use signals the growing government concern for policy incapacity and the political damage inflicted by high-profile delivery failures. The fashion for implementation units is one manifestation of policy design being an anticipatory exercise that demands attention to real-world issues throughout the cycle.

POLITICAL DIMENSIONS TO POLICY IMPLEMENTATION

The concept of mandate is used by governments to support delivery of certain policies on the grounds of representative authority gained through the electoral process. The Constitution Commission of Victoria (2002:16) gives the following definition of a mandate:

- Government has the right and duty to organise and operate the machinery of government effectively, accountably, and subject to the supervision of parliament.
- A government has the right and the duty to govern, although not to do whatever it likes.
- A government has the right and duty to implement its specifically outlined initiatives and the broad directions of its election policy, subject to parliamentary supervision of detail.
- Electors are entitled to expect that a government will honour and implement its promises.

Policy makers must pay attention to a government's mandate as it often sets out the core policy program that the government of the day wishes to pursue. Chapter 4 considered a number of political drivers including the party political platforms that form a core part of a government's mandate. Implementation by policy makers of a government's objectives is not always clear and simple. Public sector officials might be 'servants' to their political masters but their service should not be uncritical compliance devoid of commitment to the public interest. The policy making process, and the implementation phase in particular, is not a mindless delivery arm of the political machine.

In 2004, the Secretary of the Department of Prime Minister and Cabinet, Peter Shergold, queried the status of public servants as 'lackies, careerists, political stooges'. He was drawing attention to growing criticism that has been aimed at the quality of public service in Australia (Barker, 2007). Quoting Melbourne *Age* journalist, Kenneth Davidson, Shergold (2004:4–5) summarised the critique as follows: 'Now, when the government says, "Jump", the response of the bureaucracy is "How high?" . . . The suggestion today . . . is that there now exists a conspiracy of silence between government and public service. It is alleged that public servants provide to government only the information and advice that it wishes to hear . . .'

This charge can be addressed on many grounds, but it highlights a central cautionary tale: implementation is full of subtlety and nuance and it demands a sensitive appreciation for, and application of, the obligation of public sector responsiveness. Diligent commitment to the implementation of government objectives neither precludes challenging defence of the public interest nor frank and fearless advice.

There is much scope for policy making in the implementation process. Translating policy decisions into legislation, for example, is a rich process that often involves a judgment on the part of policy makers charged with legal drafting. Parliamentary Counsel—who draft legislation—ask challenging questions of instructing officers in order to determine the precise intent of government. It is impractical to obtain cabinet feedback or approval on drafting minutiae. Instead, the instructor and drafter will decide how best to put the government's objective into practice. This often occurs on tight time frames and the selection of a particular word might have a profound impact on the future course of a policy.

SUCCESSFUL IMPLEMENTATION: INTRODUCING THE EURO

The introduction of the euro at midnight on 1 January 2002 represented the 'single biggest operation in the history of money'. 1.128 trillion in euro notes and coins flooded into Austria, Belgium, Finland, France, Germany, Greece, Ireland, Italy, Luxembourg, the Netherlands, Portugal and Spain, replacing their respective sovereign currencies. The transition was mostly smooth, although there was some public resentment over rounding-up of prices. Over 317 million people now use the world's second most traded currency unit after the US dollar.

CONDITIONS FOR SUCCESSFUL IMPLEMENTATION

A range of factors influence policy implementation. Along with broad contextual matters such as economic, social and political conditions, Howlett and Ramesh (1995:154–5) note that implementation is affected by:

- the nature of the problem
- the diversity of problems being tackled by government
- the size of the target group
- the extent of behavioural change required.

Those with implementation responsibility must work within cabinet objectives, available resources and competing priorities. Fortunately, a vast literature suggests a few key lessons for successful implementation (Ingram, 1990:462; Davis and Weller, 1993:17):

- All policies are built on implicit theories about the world and how it operates. If these theories are mistaken about cause and effect, the policy will fail. If, on the other hand, the model is simple, robust and tested through experience, then a policy can prevail.
- Policies should include as few steps as possible between formulation and implementation. The more complex the policy sequence, the more likely it is that misunderstanding or competition will arise, with deleterious effects.
- Policies frequently fail if responsibility is shared among too many players. This is particularly a problem in federal systems. As more agencies become involved, the complexity of coordination overwhelms the original policy intent. A successful policy will therefore be implemented by just one, or at most a small number, of agencies.
- There must be a clear chain of accountability. One person or agency must have responsibility for the success of the program, and a capacity to intervene when implementation runs into difficulties.
- Those who deliver a program should be involved in policy design. 'Street level bureaucrats'—the people who provide

the service to customers—must be informed, enthusiastic and cooperative if a program is to work.
- Continuous evaluation is crucial if a policy is to evolve and become more effective. As Sabatier (1988:131) notes, 'numerous studies have shown that ambitious programs which appeared after a few years to be abject failures received more favourable evaluations when seen in a longer time frame; conversely, initial successes may evaporate over time'.
- Policy makers should pay as much attention to implementation as to policy formulation: 'implementation cannot be divorced from policy. There is no point in having good ideas if they cannot be carried out' (Pressman and Wildavsky, 1973:143).

According to Meredith Edwards' cogent analysis of the development of social policy in Australia, the overseeing of implementation by politicians can be a necessary, but often neglected, component of ensuring policy success. Part of the problem lies in the fact that 'Politicians often lose interest after the main decisions are made. This can mean that, unintentionally, what they hope to achieve does not eventuate' (2001:182). Policy makers need to maintain the interest and support of relevant ministers if they are needed to champion a policy or give added weight to the seriousness of implementation. At the same time, programs can be used as political veneer to coat negligible policy change. For Quiggin, the Job Network exemplifies how a government can defuse unemployment as a political issue without making any 'real progress in addressing the fundamental problems. Compared to similar points in previous cycles there has been no real reduction in unemployment. When various forms of hidden unemployment are taken into account, it seems likely that unemployment has actually risen' (2006:23). Political dimensions in implementation can be both a boon and a hindrance to the policy making process.

IMPLEMENTATION INSTRUMENTS

The selection of policy instruments will largely dictate the mode of implementation. Early in the policy cycle, attention should address how the government wishes to address a problem and therefore, by implication, the implementation instruments to be used. The cabinet submission may, for example, recommend the use of legislation or changes in government spending. Such instruments are often specifically mentioned in the cabinet minute ('cabinet decided to approve the introduction to parliament of the Recognition of Overseas Tertiary Qualifications Bill'). However, cabinet will rarely consider the implementation instruments in great detail, leaving discretion to individual ministers and agencies. Further, there will often be more than one implementation instrument required for successful implementation, even for relatively simple policies. If cabinet alters the original submission recommendation, or provides a lesser level of resources, an agency may need to rethink the choice of policy instruments.

There are numerous instruments open to government when planning implementation. Table 10.1 provides examples based on coercive and non-coercive categories of implementation instrument.

The choice of instrument is inevitably a judgment about factors such as cabinet intention, available resources, the policy target group, the risks of failure and any likely constraints on particular courses of action, such as an overall government preference for markets over regulation (see Linder and Peters, 1989). Ideally, cabinet will make this calculation when it accepts or modifies a policy submission. In practice, departments often find themselves forced to remake the decision as they seek to turn general instructions into specific programs.

Often new policies require new organisational arrangements—either programs within a department or whole agencies. Table 10.2 outlines major program delivery choices. Each serves a specific purpose. Since the development of endless new institutions can cause coordination and accountability problems for government, it is important that policy design work only reach for such solutions when more modest avenues, such as incorporation of the new service within existing programs, are not feasible.

IMPLEMENTATION TRAPS

Just as the conditions for successful policy implementation can be identified, so there are recognised traps which can bring policies and programs to grief. Charles Lindblom (1980:65ff) identifies some of the most common. All relate to the agencies

---

Policies fail because:

- agencies lack the necessary expertise or commitment
- implementation mechanisms are too rigid and unwieldy
- people do not respond to the program in ways government expects them to
- the cost of realising the policy objective becomes too great
- the program assumes federal cooperation which does not occur
- the program assumes powers which are beyond government's control
- there are too few incentives to encourage compliance
- those implementing the program do not understand what is required.

Policies or programs fail because either the program could not be implemented as designed (program failure), or the program was run as designed but did not produce the desired result (theory failure).

Patton and Sawick (1993:365)

Table 10.1 Implementation instruments

Non-coercive forms of action	Examples
Communication	Press releases, advertisements, brochures, community meetings, staff training, instruction manuals—these all communicate the policy to affected individuals and groups.
Contracts	Legal agreements to regulate the private provision of government services.
Expenditures	The purchase by government of goods, services, equipment, land and other resources, and engaging staff to achieve policy objectives.
Inspection	The examination of premises, products or records to test whether these conform to officially required standards.
Loans, subsidies and benefits	Making public resources available to citizens or businesses for specific purposes.
Market operations	Government involvement in a market to buy, sell or provide goods.
Service delivery	Provision by government of services to the public, sometimes accompanied by enforceable rights.
Taxation incentives	Taxation benefits can be used as an incentive to sanction or encourage particular types of behaviour from citizens or corporations.
Coercive forms of action	**Examples**
Licensing	Government authorisation to engage in a business or profession.
Legislation and regulation	Use of laws to sanction or proscribe particular forms of behaviour. These are sometimes particular, such as licences to do certain things that are otherwise prohibited, and sometimes more general, such as the criminal law.
Administrative directions	Binding directions to public servants about how they must conduct themselves, or the services they are to provide.
Reporting	Mandatory requirements on corporations to report on aspects of operations and performance.
Taxation	Taxation can be used to direct private activity in particular directions, and to extract returns for government from particular forms of economic activity.

that must implement policies, and the risk that program objectives will be lost amid bureaucratic politics.

Incomplete specification

Policies are rarely complete, able to cover every contingency. They must allow some discretion to those who implement and operate the program. If policy objectives are too vague, however, agencies find them difficult to implement. The result may be a policy that pursues objectives not intended by cabinet, or that wastes resources because those responsible cannot be certain what was intended.

Table 10.2 Implementation choices: program delivery

Delivery mechanism	Characteristics	When appropriate	Example
Departmental program	• staffed by public servants	• when the service is too complex and interrelated with other services to be specified in a commercial contract	• policy advice
	• funded by consolidated revenue and fees	• when accountability and confidentiality requirements are essential	• contract monitoring of commercial suppliers
	• located in government offices	• when commercial suppliers are not available	• child protection services
		• when legal authority cannot be delegated	• administration of cash transfer program
Statutory	• program delegated to a statutory body, often with its own legislation	• regulatory bodies, and agencies that must make judicial or quasi-judicial decisions	• courts, regulatory authorities, commissions of inquiry
	• public sector employees	• when independence from ministerial control is required for public confidence	• Australian Broadcasting Corporation
	• funded by consolidated revenue or commercial income	• when independent advice is required	• environmental protection agencies
Government-owned enterprises	• commercial operations established under legislation	• for business units providing services for which commercial alternatives are available	• agencies supplying accommodation, vehicles and cleaning for government departments
	• government is sole owner through shareholding ministers	• for functions in transition to private ownership	• large utilities
	• not subject to taxation but pay equivalent dividends	• for testing internal provision against market costs	• organisations such as universities relying on public and private income
	• public sector workforce		
	• commercial accounting regimes		
	• subject to public sector accountability measures and equity targets		

Delivery mechanism	Characteristics	When appropriate	Example
Government-owned companies	• fully commercial operations in which government is a shareholder • established under corporations law • run by a board of directors • private sector workforce • subject to standard taxation and fiduciary arrangements	• becoming rare, but used when government has acquired an asset from private hands • when privatisation is inappropriate because of natural monopoly considerations • when competition is required in a market	• until recently, Telstra, Qantas, the Commonwealth Bank and Australian National Line were the best known national examples
Contracting	• government specifies product to be supplied, and awards contracts through a tender process • performance monitored by public service • may be on-off or a rolling contract	• when business or non-government organisations can supply goods at cheaper rates than the public sector • for short-term projects • when government does not wish to invest in necessary capital infrastructure • when necessary skills are in short supply	• computer services for government departments • case management for the unemployed • major building and road construction

The information required in cabinet submissions is designed to overcome incomplete specification. Nonetheless, often issues not contemplated by ministers arise during implementation, because matters of detail are rarely considered by cabinet but left to individual ministers and their departments to realise. Incomplete specification is especially critical for networked delivery arrangements. Governments cannot abrogate their responsibility by shifting implementation to an external organisation. Even if governments implicitly trust an external delivery agent, the chain of accountability demands that it ultimately remains responsible for program success or failure. This does not preclude, however, attempts to escape from the detailed responsibility that attaches to poor decisions or poor implementation. As Mulgan (2006:56) notes in relation to the Job Network program, 'Every attempt is being made to encourage private providers to act with the same

STUDIES IN FAILURE

The classic study in the field—*Implementation*, by Jeffrey Pressman and Aaron Wildavsky (1973)—offers a bleak view of government capacity.

Implementation stresses the difficulties of planning programs in the national capital for delivery in distant places. In this case, economic development and employment programs targeting inner-city, black residents of Oakland failed to deliver their desired outcomes. People did not get jobs. Minority businesses did not flourish. The abandoned streets of Oakland did not return to life.

Pressman and Wildavsky found two principal causes for this distressing result. First, the policy was flawed. Its assumptions about how and why businesses hire turned out to be wrong. Second, the program required close cooperation between a wide array of government and private agencies. Despite good intentions, this teamwork was not achieved.

Even under the best of circumstances, conclude the disappointed authors, successful implementation of public policies is 'exceedingly difficult'.
Pressman and Wildavsky (1973:xiii)

---

degree of professionalism as that expected from public servants... This is not to say that ministers or their senior officials never engage in buck-passing. Indeed, an increase in attempted blame-shifting and buck-passing has become a familiar feature of a more open and differentiated public sector.' The accountability dilemmas remain, even if their form shifts with the inclusion of new players. What is clear is that knowing and specifying exactly what the government wants is necessary if it—as a purchaser—is going to try to combat problems of moral hazard and adverse selection that characterise the principal-agent (or purchaser-provider) relationship (Althaus, 1997).

Inappropriate agency

The allocation of responsibility to a particular agency will affect the expertise available and the way a policy is delivered.

Government agencies have characteristic ways of running programs, often determined by the training and outlook of the core professional workforce (Taylor, 1993). A poor choice of agency can undermine policy objectives. Education departments, for example, are set up to teach on school premises within school hours. This makes sense for many child-based activities but may be inappropriate for particular needs, such as early intervention programs for young children with intellectual disabilities. A welfare department, on the other hand, is experienced in delivering home-based services and may be better suited to the task. Similarly, schools may not be the best environment for adults seeking to complete an interrupted schooling, but a TAFE college might be. Cabinet decisions must be clear about who is responsible—and will be held accountable for-implementation.

Conflicting objectives

All governments have multiple objectives, and these may be written into policy proposals. Australian Aid Abroad, for example, has humanitarian objectives, but also supports diplomatic efforts, promotes Australian technology and develops new markets. How should these be ranked and acted upon?

Usually the implementation agency must settle on operating principles. Conflicting objectives, however, can bring ministers and departments into dispute, as each stresses the objective they seek from the policy, potentially at the expense of overall coherence and effectiveness.

Incentive failures

Those in agencies have some discretion about which tasks to emphasise. Without sufficient incentive to implement carefully and thoroughly, policies can fail through neglect. Implementation requires a high priority from the agency, and strategies to communicate the benefits of a new policy direction. Failure is even more common when implementation is handed over to non-government bodies, whose private or community concerns may conflict with the government's public purpose.

Conflicting directives

Those who must implement a policy are often subject to conflicting instructions. Public servants, for example, may be told to cut budgets and staff numbers by cabinet, yet required to expand existing service delivery programs by clients and government. Policies are more likely to come to grief when the priorities of the agency are not clear to all involved.

Limited competence

Many political objectives do not sit comfortably with agency capacity. An instruction to stamp out prostitution, for example, is difficult for the police to implement, even if accompanied by additional resources. Studies observe that, when faced with an impossible policy objective, administrators tend to ignore official instructions and to pursue their own policy preferences.

Inadequate administrative resources

Cabinets sometimes announce new policies without providing adequate funds. Agencies must either find the money elsewhere (and so cripple some existing program), or doom the new policy to failure through insufficient funds or expertise. 'Don't allow yourself to accept responsibility for inadequately resourced initiatives' is sensible advice, but often not a practical course of action for administrators.

This discussion of obstacles to effective or successful policy action should not be viewed as a counsel of despair.

Many public policies and programs accomplish a great deal ... If few public problems are entirely resolved by governmental actions, many are at least partly solved or ameliorated.

James Anderson (2005:302–10)

Communication failures

Many policies rely on cooperation between government agencies and their clients. If the purpose of policy change is not explained carefully to the public sector workforce, and to those they serve, the policy is unlikely to achieve the necessary levels of commitment.

If any of these faults occurs, decision makers will not get the policy they want. Instead, agencies will be drawn into policy making, scaling down and redesigning the program. When cabinet makes symbolic gestures about a problem without providing precise instructions, a clear ranking of priorities or the right incentives and resources, it ensures implementation cannot succeed. When agencies allow too much discretion, a policy can be subverted from within, intentionally or by mistake. On the other hand, if discretion is too limited and instructions are too rigid, policies may be implemented literally but without sensitivity to objectives or context.

DESIGNING AN IMPLEMENTATION STRATEGY

Understanding why implementation succeeds or fails makes it possible to develop a strategy for implementation. While every cabinet decision is unique, there are common issues that require attention. A systematic approach to implementation improves the prospects of successful translation from cabinet minute to agency program.

Proper implementation of a complex policy will involve its own cycle, as problems are identified and analysed, options developed, consultation undertaken and decisions made.

The cycle will, for example, ensure new programs have appropriate administrative support to handle issues such as information flows, client consultation, reporting mechanisms, internal delegation appeals and approvals, and necessary publicity.

Implementation plans must now feature detailed marketing and media strategies. A complex array of techniques and institutional players factor in this aspect of policy implementation. Polling conducted by political parties will often inform ministerial consideration of particular policy preferences. This is not something that public officials do, but it flows into the political calculations of political advisers and politicians. Public opinion will sometimes be an implementation issue, and should be accommodated in communications plans for policy implementation.

More usually, however, the onus is on departments to develop and outline communications strategies to ensure successful implementation. While most departments now feature their own communications units, responsibility for advertising and public relations ultimately lies with a central agency, often the premier's or prime minister's department. It is their job to contain and control interaction with the media, provide a consistent and appropriate message, and avoid embarrassments.

The Government Communications Unit (GCU) was established in the Department of the Prime Minister and Cabinet in 1998. The role of the GCU is to provide advice and support on communications issues to the federal government and the Ministerial Committee on Government Communications (the approving authority for departmental media activity), and to manage the Central Advertising System (the contractual arm for communications strategies) (see Department of Prime Minister and Cabinet, 2006c).

Guidelines for Australian Government Information Activities specify the principles and procedures to be followed (Ministerial Committee on Government Information and Advertising, 1995). The GCU provides a range of 'how to' documents on its website (see www.gcu.gov.au/code/infodept/how_to.html), to inform policy makers of what is involved and required in compiling communications strategies.

Sometimes relationships with certain journalists are cultivated to promote interest in a particular policy initiative (Edwards, 2001:188). At other times, press conferences are used to open up debate or highlight a government's openness and transparency to inspire trust.

Queensland Premier Peter Beattie, for example, utilised this open-government approach to combat the scandal of the Shepherdson Inquiry rorts investigation (see Althaus, forthcoming).

But public relations and media interaction also takes place through public meetings, information sessions and advertising campaigns conducted through internet, television, print or radio

---

Why public policies may not have their intended effect:

- Inadequate resources may be provided for implementing a policy.
- Policies may be administered so as to lessen their potential effect.
- Public problems are often caused by a multitude of factors, but policy may be directed at only one or a few of them.
- People may respond or adapt to public policies in a manner that negates some of their influence.
- Policies may have incompatible goals that bring them into conflict with one another.
- Solutions for some problems may involve costs and consequences greater than people are willing to accept.
- Many public problems cannot be solved, at least not completely.
- New problems may arise that distract attention and action from a problem.
- In a federal system policies decided at one level of government may be implemented at another.

mediums. Middle level managers have to be as attuned to media demands and the sensitivities as their senior colleagues. Police officers have long relayed public information in the media on crime investigations. This media expertise is now routinely demanded in policy making, albeit senior officials operating under protocols through ministerial media advisers.

The expanding use of information and communications technology and the growth of 24-hour news media has placed huge pressures on governments to provide immediate responses to emerging issues. Governments today confront demands for ever-more transparency, openness and inclusiveness in decision making. Shergold (2004:5–6) painted the picture with the following observations. The Commonwealth Ombudsman has operated since 1976. Freedom of information (FOI) legislation has been in place since 1982 and requests have doubled from 20 000 in 1982 to 40 000 in 2003. A number of administrative law institutions and instruments are operational (Administrative Appeals Tribunal, Migration Review Tribunal, Social Security Appeals Tribunal) as is judicial review. The Auditor-General has substantial teeth to scrutinise government while there is now increased capacity on the part of parliament to directly interrogate public servants.

As a result of these pressures there is often a balancing act between timeliness and accuracy. In many ways, immediacy and media interactions help explain the growth in ministerial staff numbers and their greater involvement in the policy making process (see Edwards, 2002). Ministers use ministerial staff to help them cope with the seemingly voracious demands of the media. In turn ministerial staffers demand higher levels of responsiveness from public servants. This was evident in the 'children overboard' controversy. Inquiries into the incident found that the conduct and behaviour of the Minister for Defence's media adviser created a number of difficulties because of their frequent and sometimes aggressive interactions with often quite junior public servants (see Tiernan, 2007).

OPINION POLLING

Opinion polling, the process of gauging the views of the populace by sample surveys, is underused as an option in policy development in Australia.

Opinion polling is used politically, for example to gauge the level of support for political parties or for leaders or to identify political touchstone issues. The same techniques are used commercially to research retail products and consumer satisfaction with services.

Polling techniques have inherent problems and inaccuracies, such as sampling error, response bias and question bias. Policy makers should be wary of the risk of false leads from poorly conducted polling. And governments are sensitive to criticism about spending public funds on opinion polling given its widespread political use.

> Public sentiment is everything. With public sentiment, nothing can fail. Without it, nothing can succeed.
> *Abraham Lincoln*

Yet opinion polling clearly is a useful tool for policy makers seeking to identify issues better, and to understand which tools might enhance policy implementation. For example, opinion polling might show that fear of crime has a range of causes varying from place to place and across social groups (Standing Committee on Legal and Constitutional Affairs, 2004). A high incidence of violence in one community demands a different policy response from non-criminal anti-social behaviour or lack of knowledge that crime is actually reducing in their community. Differences between communities also highlight the desirability of a local policy focus rather than global approaches such as tougher penalties.

It is more common in Australia to use opinion polling in the implementation and evaluation stages of the policy cycle: service users might be surveyed about how useful a service is, how easy it is to access and so on. Examples of polling utilisation in the Australian context include the Department of Education, Science and Training survey on the new apprenticeship scheme (Higgins and Stern, 2005) and a survey of final year teacher education students (Department of Education, Science and Training, 2007).

CHECKLISTS

Appendix 1 offers a checklist of considerations to be kept in mind when implementing a policy decision, including the resources required for policy implementation.

Using checklists such as these provides a simple but systematic approach to implementation. Otherwise, implementation can prove the stumbling block for government. Great ideas may make hopeless programs.

The temptation for politicians is to blame program failure on the public service, but the fault more usually resides with poor policy design. Here ministers and their advisers are likely to share the fault. They can reduce the risk through a policy cycle that insists on systematic use of analysis, review and reconsideration.

Ideally, a policy will be based on a thoroughly tested model of cause and effect, with agreement about policy objectives; a central role for a single agency which is able to learn and adapt; consultation; staff commitment to the program; and regular evaluation.

Special complexity arises in a federal system. More players come into the field, each with their own reporting lines and agency objectives. The nature of policy design must change to reflect these circumstances. A bottom-up process of negotiation between interests, greater local participation, and a willingness to live with some inconsistency and overlap may be required (Sabatier, 1986). The success of implementation rests on the skill of policy makers, and their capacity to produce viable, realistic objectives which will translate into sustainable programs.

In this regard it is important to note the significance of pre-evaluation monitoring in the policy cycle. Ongoing monitoring of policy implementation is a helpful mechanism for policy makers to utilise to help keep a policy on track and to identify unplanned factors in order to develop redress mechanisms if needed. In Chapter 11 we discuss the formal stage of evaluation and there we stress the notion of continuous evaluation. Incorporating pre-evaluation monitoring into the policy process helps policy implementation to be conducted more smoothly and with greater efficacy. It aids evaluation by inculcating the policy process with lessons learned as implementation occurs.

Policies often become more effective over time because politicians, managers and agencies reflect on implementation. This is the process of 'policy learning'. It uses the lessons of implementation to reshape and refine a program (Majone and Wildavsky, 1984:170). As Lindblom (1980:65) perceptively observes, 'implementation always makes or changes policy in some degree'.

11 Evaluation

The policy cycle ends—and restarts—with evaluation. An issue has been identified, worked through, addressed in a policy proposal; a decision has been made and implemented, and is now the subject of a policy program. This turn of the cycle is almost complete.

The final step, evaluation, serves three purposes:

- It asks how well a policy, once implemented, meets its objectives.
- It holds officials accountable for the implementation of a policy.
- It provides important clues for future policy making.

Evaluation generates data for improved policy analysis and suggestions for making the program more effective. It assists policy learning. This is the end of the cycle and also the next beginning, the starting point for a new round of identification, analysis and decisions. Evaluation criteria should be built into the original program design.

In this context, evaluation is a tool for collecting and managing information about policies and programs. The former Commonwealth Department of Finance, now the Department of Finance and Administration (or Finance) (Department of Finance, 1994:3), suggested evaluation could assist decision makers and managers to:

- assess the continued relevance and priority of program objectives in the light of current circumstances, including government policy changes

SNAPSHOT
How do we know policy choices work? Is the government getting the outcomes it wanted? Do programs offer 'value for money'?

Evaluation is the point in the cycle when the utility of policy must be questioned, and a new cycle of analysis and adjustment, confirmation or abandonment begins.

Program evaluation can be defined as the systematic and objective assessment of a government program, or parts of a program, to assist the government and other decision makers to:

- assess the continued relevance and priority of program objectives in the light of current circumstances, including government policy changes (that is, appropriateness of the program)
- test whether the program outcomes achieve stated objectives (that is, its effectiveness)
- ascertain whether there are better ways of achieving these objectives (that is, its efficiency).

The objectives of program evaluation are to:

- provide a better information base to assist managers in improving program performance
- assist government decision making and setting priorities, particularly in the budget process
- contribute to improved accountability to the parliament and the public.

Australian National Audit Office (1999: Part Two, 1–2)

A performance audit is an independent review of the efficiency or administrative effectiveness of a program (or agency) but does not extend to assessing the policy merit of a program.

Ian McPhee (2006)

- test whether the program outcomes achieve stated objectives
- ascertain whether there are better ways of achieving these objectives
- assess the case for the establishment of new programs, or extensions to existing programs
- decide whether the resources for the program should continue at current levels, or be increased, reduced or discontinued.

The results should influence future policy advice and program design. A commitment to evaluation carries analytical rigour through the cycle, and emphasises that policy is iterative—an endless chain of experiments and rethinking, as policies and programs adjust to their changing circumstances.

EVALUATION AND THE POLICY CYCLE

Evaluation typically occurs when a policy has been implemented. The resulting program is tested for efficiency and effectiveness. Figure 11.1, developed from work by Waller (1996:11), suggests there is scope for evaluation at many points during the policy cycle.

In 2001 the ANAO conducted the performance audit 'Developing Policy Advice' to determine whether advice met expected standards for policy outputs. Policy advice is the foundation of programs; if the theory is flawed, implementation will fail. Yet interest in evaluating policy advice is surprisingly recent, and not yet systematic. A number of policy advice evaluations have been able to examine inputs, process, outputs and outcomes in much the same manner as a standard program evaluation.

Agencies can also evaluate their effectiveness in briefing ministers, preparing cabinet submissions and framing recommendations. Evaluation of policy formulation and decision making assess whether ministers and managers are receiving policy advice that 'meets fully the required standards of rigour, honesty, relevance and timeliness' (Waller, 1996:9). Like all evaluations, such exercises also keep policy advisers accountable for their work. The Department of Treasury and Finance in Victoria conducts peer reviews of policy briefs using a cross-divisional panel of experienced policy staff (ANAO, 2001:113).

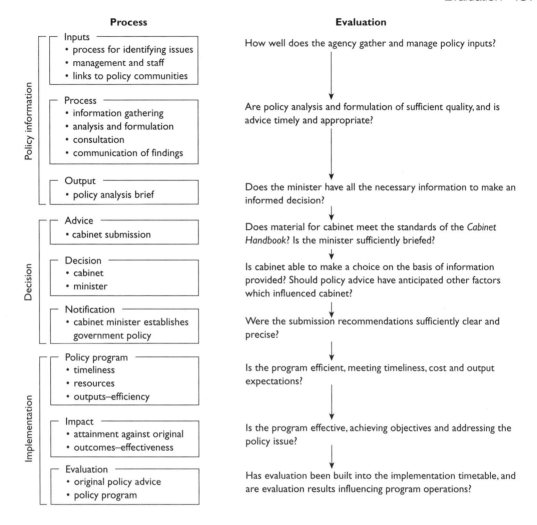

Figure 11.1 Opportunities for evaluation in policy formulation and implementation

Most evaluation work, however, focuses on the operational stage of policy implementation. There is now a substantial technical literature on evaluating programs, with specialist evaluation branches in many federal and state agencies. The Commonwealth requires agencies to evaluate their programs regularly, taking account of materiality, policy significance and risk. In addition to evaluation by individual agencies, separate evaluation and audit activity concerning indigenous programs is now undertaken by a division of Finance, the Office of

> I evaluated one programme that was pronounced dead by one arm of government in the very same month as funding for its evaluation had been raised from another.
> *Ray Pawson, talking about evaluation experience in the United States Government (2006:10)*

EVALUATION VERSUS PERFORMANCE AUDIT

Commonalities:

- Both are fundamental links in the accountability chain;
- Both contribute to better program management and performance accountability by commenting on 'value for money' albeit from different perspectives; and
- Both endeavour to identify better practice.

Differences:

- Evaluation focuses on policy and makes qualitative assessment of policy effectiveness whereas performance audit is focused on evaluating economy, efficiency, and effectiveness of public administration;
- Audit is independent whereas evaluation is not necessarily so; and
- Independent audit in the public sector is reported direct to parliament while evaluations are reported to relevant minister or agency head and are not always made public.

Ian McPhee (2006)

Evaluation and Audit (Indigenous Programs) which was established under the *Aboriginal and Torres Strait Islander Act 2005*.

The Australian government also has a strategic review process, linked to budget planning and decision making, that involves a centrally-coordinated evaluation of major initiatives. These evaluations are usually undertaken in large, complex, cross-agency and cross-program initiatives. The strategic reviews are coordinated by Finance.

TYPES OF EVALUATION

Various levels of evaluation are possible depending on the objective. Finance (Department of Finance, 1994:4) identifies four types of evaluation, each appropriate for a different step in the policy life-cycle.

- *Appropriateness evaluation* helps decision makers determine whether a new program is needed, or whether an existing program should be maintained. A key question in appropriateness evaluations is the delivery mechanism—should government, the private sector, or the third sector or community deliver the service?
- *Efficiency evaluation* examines how well inputs are used to obtain a given output. Is the program efficient in the way it uses public money for policy purposes?
- *Effectiveness evaluation* asks whether the program is producing worthwhile results. Do the outcomes justify the expense? Is the program meeting its objectives?
- Finally, *meta-evaluations* assess the evaluation process itself. Since agencies are required to evaluate programs, are their evaluation practices professional, sensitive to the social and physical environment of the program and producing reports which influence management choices (see Australian National Audit Office, 1999)?

Figure 11.2, developed by Martin and Amies (Department of Finance, 1994:8), captures the range of evaluation types, and the information required by an evaluation team to reach a judgment.

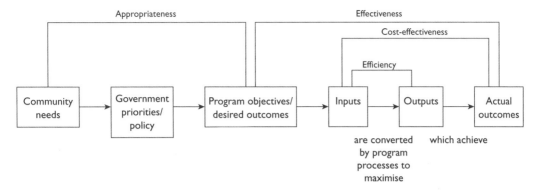

Figure 11.2 Evaluation types
(From Department of Finance, 1994:8)

Fischer (1995:20–1) notes that efficiency and effectiveness evaluations are more common than discussions of appropriateness, because asking about broader social interests and policy goals carries evaluation into the political realm. Even so, governments have techniques to evaluate politically sensitive policy areas, including external review committees and commissions of inquiry.

EVALUATION MEASURES

Each type of evaluation focuses on a different measure of policy success. These are:

- *inputs*—the raw materials and resources used to deliver a policy
- *process*—the way resources are transformed into service provision
- *outputs*—the products discharged from the system
- *outcomes*—results of policy implementation for the clients and others (Kettner and Martin, 1987).

Traditional auditing counts inputs and checks compliance with process rules. Evaluation stresses outputs and outcomes: the

> Value for money asks 'how much input achieves how much output or what outcome?'
>
> - How many hip replacements were achieved within the budget?
> - How much taxpayer subsidy went to each public transport trip?
> - How many cases can be managed by a rehabilitation case worker?

> The [United States] federal government spends over $2 trillion a year on approximately 1000 federal programs. In most cases, we do not know what we are getting for our money. This is simply unacceptable.
>
> *United States Office of Management and Budget, Executive Office of the President, 2003*

significance of a policy lies in its impact. Only when outputs are clear can value for money questions be asked.

Outputs can often be measured, but outcomes may be elusive. It can take years for the effects of a policy to become clear. Will a more modest target for reducing greenhouse gas emissions have serious environmental consequences? Will urban renewal strategies improve community safety? When hard data is not available, policy makers need to estimate likely outcomes.

The Commonwealth Department of Education, Science and Training has developed a useful working definition of evaluation objectives. It sees evaluation as the systematic assessment of performance of programs and policies in terms of whether:

- inputs are used to maximise outputs (*efficiency*)
- outcomes achieve stated objectives (*effectiveness*)
- objectives remain consistent with government priorities and these in turn continue to be consistent with community needs (*appropriateness*) (Crossfield and Byrne, 1994:4).

For some reviews, all three measures—efficiency, effectiveness and appropriateness—may need investigation. For other exercises with more limited objectives, a focus on just efficiency and effectiveness may be more appropriate. The subject matter at hand, and the purpose of the evaluation, should define the level of analysis.

METHOD

Evaluations can follow a standard format. Terms of reference are prepared for consideration by a steering committee and evaluation team. An evaluation strategy is prepared, specifying the questions to be tested and the approach to be taken. Data can then be collected, and consultation undertaken with clients, stakeholders and staff. The information gathered is analysed, leading to findings and recommendations.

Evaluation, however, is not always this simple (see O'Faircheallaigh, 2002). There is often a contest over what and whose goals should be used to evaluate a program. Is the evaluation intended for public use to merely satisfy external accountability requirements or is a more probing investigation desired? Who should be incorporated into the evaluation

> While performance monitoring is not the only tool that can lift public sector performance, it is a very important one. We, as servants of the public, have an obligation to the community to give value for money. This goes beyond the dollars and cents of budget papers and program costings. We need to have the courage to look critically at ourselves to review how we perform and find ways to do things better.
>
> *Bill Scales (1997:108)*

process? Are stakeholders or clients to be included in developing evaluation criteria? Will they participate in the evaluation process and, if so, are they willing and capable of participating? What comparisons, if any, will be used? Are causal relationships easily identifiable and commonly accepted or are they subject to debate that requires adjudication?

Evaluation can be as political as any other facet of the policy process. Figure 11.3 presents the 'conventional' approach to evaluation contrasted with an 'alternative' approach in Figure 11.4. They are taken from O'Faircheallaigh's assessment of evaluation undertaken in relation to mining agreements struck with indigenous Australians which highlights some of the complexity associated with evaluation exercises.

Figure 11.3 'Conventional' approach to evaluation

(O'Faircheallaigh, 2002:19; reprinted with the permission of Ashgate Publishing Ltd)

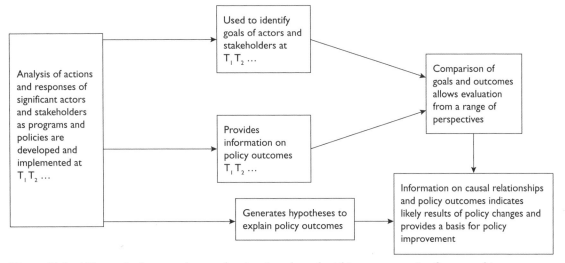

Figure 11.4 'Alternative' approach to evaluation (conducted within a comparative framework)

(O'Faircheallaigh, 2002:19; reprinted with the permission of Ashgate Publishing Ltd)

In short, the evaluation process mirrors the original cycle that produced the policy; the process is iterative and dynamic. Much depends on what kind of evaluation is intended or wanted.

The choice of evaluation team must be consistent with the goals of the project. An important decision will be to determine whether internal or external evaluation will be undertaken. Along with issues of timing and accountability, and other process requirements that might mandate selection of a particular evaluator, Conley-Tyler (2005) outlines the following list as factors that might influence the choice of evaluation method:

- Cost
- Availability
- Knowledge of program and operations
- Knowledge of context
- Ability to collect information
- Flexibility
- Specialist skills and expertise
- Perceived and real objectivity
- Accountability for use of government funds
- Willingness to criticise
- Utilisation of evaluation
- Dissemination of results
- Ethical issues
- Organisational investment.

Many program evaluations double as an internal management review. In an ideal situation, those involved with the program are also part of the evaluation, since they can be in the best position to draw lessons and implement findings.

To avoid conflicts of interest, agencies sometimes establish evaluation branches, seconding relevant staff for a given review. When a report is likely to be contentious, agencies may turn to external consultants. The 'disadvantage of turning evaluation over to outsiders is that they lack intimate knowledge of the program, lack the experience of having seen its difficulties and savoured its successes as they were achieved' (Corbett, 1996:181). Agencies need to assess their ongoing capacity to perform evaluation and the development of organisational culture that promotes evaluation as a routine part of the policy making process (Beere, 2005).

The precise method to be followed by the evaluation team should reflect the questions to be answered. Evaluators also need to accommodate the needs of *impact evaluations* which are retrospective in orientation and *proactive evaluation* which helps with future program design or redesign (Wyatt et al., 2005). For example, an evaluation was undertaken of the Supported Accommodation Assistance Program (SAAP IV), which is a joint initiative of Commonwealth and state governments for responding to homelessness in Australia. This program serves almost 100 000 people annually and is undertaken by more than 1200 non-government and community organisations with an annual budget of approximately $300 million. Evaluators included a strategic review of the program where impact was assessed according to changes in employment, housing and income status before and after periods of support. They also included an evaluation based on a 'homelessness futures' exercise, which provided more information for use in forward design purposes of social policy responses to the problem of homelessness (Wyatt et al., 2005).

While approaches vary, and Table 11.1 is not exclusive, it is possible to link some methods with particular levels of evaluation.

Terminating programs—those with a defined end date.

Lapsing programs—those where government commitment is expected to continue but the government has not yet provided on-going funding.
Ian McPhee (2006:12)

Table 11.1 Evaluation methods

Inputs (efficiency)	Process (technical efficiency)	Outputs (effectiveness)	Outcomes (appropriateness)
• examining accounts and invoices	• benchmarking to test efficiency of the production process	• interviews with participants and clients	• cost-benefit analysis
• comparing budget and actual production	• production measures such as wastage and down time	• historical and descriptive evaluation	• longitudinal research studies
• benchmarking with similar programs in other jurisdictions	• gap analysis and compliance audits	• calls for submissions from interested parties	• external policy review (such as royal commissions)
		• developing performance indicators	• long-term testing against performance objectives

One important instrument to assist in the process of evaluation is the performance indicator. Performance indicators have become an integral part of program design. Commonwealth practice requires that every new policy proposal include a plan of action for evaluation. Performance indicators can be developed for each level of analysis, from 'the agency will deliver the program nationally within a budget of $33 million' as a general efficiency test, through to sophisticated outcome measures about, for example, the expected reduction in road deaths following the adoption of new safety regulations and lower speed limits.

Despite its obvious benefits, there are predicaments created by the use of performance data. To start, there is often a lack of measurement consistency. Different jurisdictions often use different indicators; a real problem for federal systems such as Australia. Even if agreement on a consistent set of indicators is reached, over time this settlement can change and the time series may become hopelessly muddled and yield meaningless results for comparative purposes. For example, during the 1990s a Steering Committee of the Productivity Commission attempted to formulate a regime for national performance monitoring of government trading enterprises. The last publication of the so-called 'red book' series was released in 2002 and appears to have fallen out of use. The challenges of ongoing, cross-jurisdictional, time series data proved too much. Greater attention has been paid to social services policy areas in recent times and attempts to secure comparative data are continuing. The standard criticism of the frameworks, however, remain: they are usually geared to budgeting requirements rather than good policy outcomes (see for example Tilbury, 2006, commenting on child protection data collection).

There are also problems of data collection, aggregation and accountability. Performance frameworks are being utilised to monitor and manage policy delivery, funding arrangements, and the achievement of outputs and outcomes as well as due process. This is becoming more important with the growth of network and purchaser-provider arrangements. Incorporation of evaluation mechanisms into contracts and other network instruments is an essential 'must', even if it is often forgotten and involves a lot of resources and costs to include.

Performance indicators allow qualified rather than absolute judgments. Few programs are unambiguous successes or failures. The typical pattern is progress toward goals, rarely complete attainment. The language of absolutes is therefore of little help. If the target for a new police initiative is 'no street crime', failure is certain. If, on the other hand, performance indicators can demonstrate a reduction in street incidents, a lower rate of reported crimes or improved public perception about safety in public places, then the same program might well be judged a success. When 'goals are stated as absolutes ... anything less than complete success tends to be construed as failure. This reading masks the real accomplishments of many public policies' (Anderson, 2005:310).

FINDINGS

An evaluation must produce concise and defensible findings if it is to influence future policy design. Evaluation reports therefore resemble briefing papers offering policy analysis. They must specify the object under study, present the evidence, explore alternative explanations for the findings, and justify the particular recommendations presented.

Sometimes an evaluation process struggles to reach conclusions. Obstacles may include:

- uncertainty over policy goals
- difficulty in determining causality
- diffuse policy impacts
- difficulties in data acquisition
- resistance
- a limited time perspective (Anderson, 2005:271–5).

The fault may reside within the evaluation process, or reflect poor design in the program under scrutiny.

Studies of evaluation, though, argue that evaluation must live with ambiguity (Guba and Lincoln, 1989:253–6). Many social and political variables cannot be measured, yet they influence the effectiveness of government programs. Evaluation teams should see their work as collaborative exercises, a learning

> Evaluation is 'a form of practical deliberation concerned with the full range of empirical and normative issues that bear on policy judgment'.
> *Fischer (1995:2)*

opportunity for all involved. The lessons generated will change the program before the evaluation is complete.

Certainly, available time and methods constrain definitive judgments about much which government does; the short-term investigations of evaluation teams sit uncomfortably with the gradual accumulation of outcomes which characterises public sector activity. Still, evaluation findings remain an important moment for self-reflection—an opportunity, yet again, to begin the policy cycle.

EVALUATION

Integrating evaluation into policy design and implementation adds rigour, consistent with the idea of carefully considered decisions made by a well-informed, accountable decision maker. Evaluation can be the beginning, as well as the end, of the policy cycle.

Evaluation is essential if programs are to improve. Information generated through evaluation informs the next round of policy development and implementation.

Evaluation also helps keep programs adaptive and responsive. It provides a formal focus for policy learning, a way to record and share the lessons of program experience.

There are dilemmas for government in undertaking evaluation. Evaluations might show that a particular program is not achieving its goals or is no longer required. In the business sector the response would be to cut the program. Governments, however, operate under political constraints. Hospital, school or rail line closures are often not feasible options. The policy making process must accommodate and incorporate this political reality into evaluation studies. While public sector evaluations should not incorporate partisan analysis, intangibles should be acknowledged in the analysis of the success or failure, and the future of a particular policy.

It can be difficult to persuade those who offer policy advice or deliver services that evaluation is a positive. Few people enjoy close scrutiny, or suggestions from outsiders about how to improve their performance. It takes management skill, and a professional standard of evaluation report, to maintain the commitment and enthusiasm of those subject to review.

> Asked how many moves he considered before making a decision, chess master Bobby Fischer replied: 'one, the right one'.
> *Jones (1997:37)*

12 Managing the policy process

The Australian Policy Handbook provides tools for practitioners working within government. It suggests a sequence of steps in the form of a cycle to provide a sense of heuristic coherence to what happens in policy making and what might be possible. The cycle is neither static nor predictable but dynamic, iterative and organic; there is no one way of policy making and many parties contribute to the process in varied, often unpredictable ways. This cycle is but a map; a guide to help provide some semblance of order to a process that otherwise may appear random. Its purpose is to help insulate practitioners against gaps in their skills or knowledge or their blindspots by mapping the types of issues that might be considered in policy making. It is a representation, not a reproduction. A map may not always be to scale but the information it imparts can guide you to your destination. More importantly, it can save you from being directionless or being completely lost.

The desire to impose some sense of order on the complex world of policy making reflects the practical demands placed on practitioners: policy briefs must be developed; reforms must be attempted; evaluation should be undertaken; analysis must be conducted; implementation never stops; advice will be sought; decisions always have to be made.

The cognitive lens used by individuals to look at the policy system influences how practitioners respond to these demands and the way theorists attempt to explain the process. *The Australian Policy Handbook* starts with the tradition of rational authoritative choice, recognising that it provides merely an

SNAPSHOT
The policy process does not run itself. At each stage, ministers, their staff, policy professionals and administrators are responsible for the sequence of actions required to move policy from ideas to implementation and beyond.

Those managing policy development must deal with inherent complexity, scarce resources and skills, time pressures and conflicting roles.

This chapter:

- examines the importance of procedural integrity
- examines ethical considerations in policy work, and
- explores some of the management challenges in public policy and techniques available to meet them.

overlay on a complex, nuanced reality; having digested the material, one can move beyond the cycle and throw away the script. Nonetheless there is an ideal of policy making worth striving for. A better process has a chance of producing better policy. For those committed to promotion of the public interest, it is worth persisting in the efforts to secure better processes and better policies.

But experience is often the most useful guide to how policy happens. Learning from others' mistakes and successes is invaluable. Being open to innovation and creative alternatives is as important as paying careful attention to due process and minimisation of risk.

POLICY PROCESS MANAGEMENT

Public policy is the stuff of resourceful organisations: departments, community action groups, statutory authorities, NGOs, private corporations and entire governments. It is usually multidisciplinary, and always involves multiple players. Policy is made possible by the contribution and the interaction of those in the political, policy and administrative domains. Managing those interactions and the resources that develop, implement and evaluate policy proposals is a key challenge for both ministers and senior managers.

Policy proposals based on good quality analysis and consultation still require management. This task is necessarily divided among many officials. Policy development is not a single, continuous activity, but a set of related functions that sum to a policy cycle. At various stages, policy development may be in the hands of ministers and policy specialists (identifying a problem), line agencies and networked service delivery bodies (policy analysis, implementation), central agencies (coordination) or the cabinet (decision making). Each must ensure its part of the process is done well, and flows smoothly into the next step.

Managing the public policy process is not the responsibility of one person or institution but of many. The policy cycle depends on a shared commitment to procedural integrity and professional ethics, on clear and accessible procedures, on adequate resources and appropriate structures, on delineation of roles, and on capacity to plan and complete projects.

People who are prepared to devote themselves to the national interest in advising government, in administering it and in carrying out decision making, are people who should be recognised and admired, not constantly denigrated.
Peter Costello, November 2000

Public servants need to stand up and speak out for public service. We must be more willing to extol the relative efficiency of our processes and quality of our outcomes. We should be proud that the management of our public administration is recognised internationally as progressive and innovative.
Shergold (1997:124)

PROCEDURAL INTEGRITY

The substantive work of public policy—the technical, creative and intellectual rigour that makes policy—must be complemented by a rigorous approach to procedure that ensures each domain is afforded its proper role. The policy cycle is structured by detailed procedures. Many are reflected in the various cabinet handbooks and other procedure manuals. This documentation is important, because it is often the only authoritative guide to processes which otherwise can seem disconnected and overly rule-bound. It provides institutional memory that might otherwise be lost with staff changes.

Documentation is the basis of procedural integrity—a set of rules policy players can understand and implement. In the complex world of politics, procedural integrity is a source of consistency, a way to ensure, amid political excitement, that policy development remains methodical and systematic. These documents are in fact cabinet's instructions to the players about how they must conduct themselves.

Procedural integrity means respecting policy process rules, and living within their spirit. Line departments, central agencies and other arms of government all have their roles to play and it is vital that processes and records be accurate, detailed and honest.

Policy procedures must be kept up to date and all the players must be educated about cabinet and policy process requirements. In the age of networked partnerships and high involvement of third sector and private sector participants in the policy process, it is important for players external to government to understand and adhere to the principles of 'due process'. External agencies need to be educated and conformed to public sector rules of accountability and professional integrity. Sometimes this demands tight contract provisions and constant monitoring. At other times dilemmas remain in maintaining accountability while maximising the benefits of involving 'outsiders'.

Ministers are usually the ultimate decision makers. For them, procedural integrity relies on 'playing by the rules'—taking policy proposals to cabinet, presenting a detailed and balanced case, ensuring the passage of legislation or implementation and living with the decision. Ministers who leak information to the media to strengthen their hand in debate, or who insist on cabinet considering hasty and ill-prepared submissions, undermine the overall process. The breakdown of policy process rules is a reliable sign the government is divided and undisciplined.

The prime minister as chair of cabinet holds a pivotal position in the policy cycle. When prime ministers insist on procedural integrity, they signal a commitment to coherence and method in making policy choices. This comes at a cost, often offending senior ministers who expect to be excused from the burdensome demands made on others. It also requires self-restraint, avoiding the temptation to dominate all choices or to resist the scrutiny imposed on the submissions of others. Prime ministers who impose strict cabinet rules risk being seen as too focused on process, too bureaucratic and too domineering.

Yet, to be effective over the long run, government requires the consistency and coordination brought by procedural integrity to complement the technical expertise, though sometimes narrow focus, of line departments. Mike Codd (1990:10), a former Commonwealth cabinet secretary, notes the prime minister is 'guardian of the principles underlying the cabinet system'. Should cabinet processes cease to work properly, ministers become restless and the prime minister's authority is undermined.

The policy process is, of course, fallible. Clever operators get proposals into cabinet without appropriate scrutiny, citing urgency or pressing political concerns, or sometimes simply by asserting seniority. The crisis atmosphere of political life and the constant manoeuvring accentuate short-term expediency. Everyone expects, and can live with, occasional flexibility, but if the rules are broken regularly and without penalty, if routines apply to some but not others, procedural integrity is lost and the political costs accumulate.

ROLES AND ETHICS

Almost every decision taken by a public sector manager has an ethical dimension.
Corbett (1996:218)

The policy cycle depends on a division of labour to make sense of the complexity of government. Those involved within the formal government structures are:

- *political players*—ministers and their staff, who must consider the political implications of a policy proposal

- *the policy advisers*—central agency officials and policy specialists within departments who provide detailed advice on submissions, coordinate government action and manage the flow of business through government
- *administrators*—staff in agencies who must implement and evaluate cabinet decisions, providing material for the next iteration of the policy cycle.

Outside the formal structure of government the third sector, private sector participants, and citizen and community groups contribute through networks and contracted arrangements to all facets of the policy cycle. Engagement with these groups may be dedicated to the public interest, but their ultimate concern is usually about stakeholder, shareholder or member needs.

While good policy depends on close working relationships between these groups, the differing objectives of political staff and public officials must be respected. Australia's tradition of a professional and impartial public service defines the acceptable limits of involvement by policy advisers and administrators in the policy process—even if this tradition is under siege in some places.

The goals of network partners must also be acknowledged. Public officials cannot expect them to act with the same decorum or according to the same rules. In all likelihood their contribution is likely to be sought precisely because they are different and not bound to formal governmental rules and requirements! If they are to contribute in a formal manner to implementation or policy design, their role will need to conform to appropriate structures of accountability and process expected by the public yet not in a way that stifles their creativity.

There is an 'ethic of role' that governs behaviour in office (see Uhr, 2005; EARC, 1992:21–8). Ministers and their staff subject policy advice and implementation proposals to intense political scrutiny. They ask: 'Is this proposal a sensible move for the government? What are the implications for marginal electorates? Are there more politically sensitive ways to proceed?' These are legitimate questions to ask about policy—indeed, they are the political concerns ministers and their staff are employed to pursue. Policies are about political objectives.

It's your job to understand the political dimensions. Understand them—not to comment on them, not to participate in them and not to promote them. Because from the political considerations and all the other factors that are fed into the melting pot, government makes decisions. These decisions are the policy. You give effect to the decisions which is [sic] expressed as a policy. So you understand the policy. You are able to speak about it, but not to comment on its worth, its validity, its accuracy, its desirability. That's an issue for the public and the political level of leadership. That's always been the same.

Peter Cosgrove in conversation with Richard Fidler, The Conversation Hour, ABC Queensland, 2 November 2006

The ethic of political office also requires restraint. Ministers may reject advice on political grounds, but cannot demand that public servants do political work, such as writing speeches for party political events, giving political advice or surveying citizens for political opinions. Nor should ministers become involved in the internal administration of an agency, particularly on matters such as staff selection. The minister's political agenda is supported by the ministerial office, not by the department.

Officials too have an ethic of role. The landmark report on the conduct of public officials by Queensland's Electoral and Administrative Review Commission (1992:16) identifies the traditional roles expected of public officials when serving governments. These are an expectation of loyal and honest service, care not to undermine public confidence in the government or its members, responsiveness and accountability, integrity, diligence, economy and efficiency. Public officials are expected to abide by various requirements, codes of conduct and values often stated formally in public employment laws such as the Commonwealth *Public Service Act 1999*.

This ethic of role has important implications for policy officials. They must provide advice 'without fear or favour' and should avoid involvement in political deliberations within government. Policy officials must respect the confidentiality of cabinet deliberations, including those of previous governments, and protect the confidentiality of public information, upholding privacy, avoiding defamation, maintaining commercial-in-confidence information, and respecting freedom of information and other accountability demands. Above all, officials accept the right of elected ministers to make the final decision.

These distinct roles ensure continuity for the policy system. When ministers or governments change, public officials remain to provide advice and administrative support to the new team. A policy cycle based on recognition of different contributions can thus endure, offering each government an opportunity for discipline and coherence in decision making.

FRANK AND FEARLESS ADVICE

Ministers and chief executives need the benefit of advice offered 'without fear or favour'—advice which is tough-minded, objective and, if necessary, unpalatable.

If the advice is not taken, officials should ensure the warning has been heard, then respect the right of ministers to make the final choice.

As one official said of working with Commonwealth ministers, 'to object once is obligatory, twice is necessary, three times is suicidal'.

Quoted in Weller and Grattan (1981:83)

POLITICISATION, PROFESSIONALISATION AND DEMOCRATISATION

The demands on policy makers are intense, multi-layered and sometimes paradoxical. They must be servants as well as leaders, media-savvy yet independent, managers as well as operators and advisers, apolitical yet politically responsive, respectful of tradition yet embracing of change, innovators as well as stabilisers, specialists as well as generalists. In many ways, while the modern environment is unique and complex, many traditional debates continue in the contemporary era. Tinged though they might be with new flavours, they reflect enduring dilemmas of the policy process.

'Claims of politicisation go back as far as federation' according to Briggs (2005a). The debate peaks every now and again; sometimes because governments are in power for long periods, at other times because governments change quickly, bringing in staff of their own liking. Politicisation can be use of the public service for partisan purposes or it can refer to personnel or staffing decisions made on the basis of party political influence rather than neutrality and independence (see Mulgan, 1998). In reverse, politicisation refers to whether public servants are being impartial and are able to provide loyal service to whatever government is elected. Wesley (2006) frames this in the context of intelligence agency independence: 'A government that turns its intelligence agencies into policy cheerleaders is depriving itself of its most important warning mechanism.'

A merit-based career public service is the aim in the Australian system but within that framework there are many possibilities. For example, does security of tenure contribute to the provision of independent advice? This is especially pertinent in an age of contract-based employment and partnership arrangements. The 'diminution of the role and independence of the central personnel agency' according to Hawkes (2006) has resulted in an 'all-powerful' function of the Prime Minister's or Premier's Department which overtook the shared responsibility model for the public sector between the Public Service Commissioner, head of the Prime Minister's (Premier's) Department and the head of Treasury.

When a government creates a bureaucracy peopled by its own supporters, or by staff who are intimidated into providing politically palatable advice, the government is effectively deprived of the opportunity to consider the full range of relevant factors (including but not confined to political considerations) in making decisions.
Fitzgerald (1989:130)

FORTUNE VERSUS PLANNING
I am disposed to hold that fortune is the arbiter of half our actions, but that it lets us control roughly the other half.

I compare fortune to one of those dangerous rivers that, when they become enraged, flood the plains, destroy trees and buildings, move earth from one place and deposit it in another. Everyone flees before it, everyone gives way to its thrust, without being able to halt it in any way. But this does not mean that, when the river is not in flood, men are unable to take precautions, by means of dykes and dams, so that when it rises next time, it will either not overflow its banks or, if it does, its forces will not be so uncontrolled or damaging.
Machiavelli ([1513], 1988:85)

Policy makers have to contend with another balancing act. On the one hand, their purpose is to serve democratically elected officials and facilitate the implementation of the political agenda, being responsive to the objectives of the government of the day. At the same time, the democratic system requires impartiality on the part of the policy makers, demanding that they have a certain loyalty to the preservation of the public interest and to act as a check against the decision making power of elected politicians (see Barker, 2007).

Through initiatives like participatory governance, community engagement, deliberative democracy and e-democracy, public servants are contributing to the development of democracy within communities. A certain 'democratisation' of the public service is also occurring as some policy makers cultivate democratic governance. This trend raises interesting ethical, personal and accountability issues concerning how far public servants should go in directly promoting democratic practice (see Bogason and Musso, 2006; Sørensen and Torfing, 2006). If programs are approved by government and supported by ministers, the public service contribution is non-controversial. But there is a certain delicacy if consultation brings, results in or builds relationships that might conflict with the objectives of the government of the day.

But it is the minister, not the public servant, who is responsible for deciding what is accepted. 'Rarely is the "frankness" of policy advice delivered through heated confrontation. More typically the public servant will seek to persuade the Minister through argument, persistence and guile. In my experience the most effective quality of advice is not that it is "fearless" but that it is convincing' (Shergold, 2006). Management of the policy process, in other words, involves an application of sharpened skills that mix policy substance with democratic sensibilities and political sensitivity.

This skill mix highlights the growing tendency towards professionalisation of the policy making occupation. A profession is '. . . a disciplined group of individuals who adhere to ethical standards and uphold themselves to, and are accepted by, the public as possessing special knowledge and skills in a widely recognised body of learning derived from research, education and training at a high level, and who are prepared to exercise this knowledge and these skills in the interest of others' (Professions Australia, 2006). The public service 'can be regarded as a profession to the degree its members possess specialist expertise, professional ethics, ideals of public service, a degree of collegiality and some autonomy. It differs from a full profession though inasmuch as there is no relatively definite and teachable skill, no prescribed course of training for entrants, no standard and indispensable qualifications for admission and minimal control exercised by means of peer review and recommendation' (Matheson, 1998:22).

Many agencies have a strong professional workforce—engineers, scientists, nurses, school teachers, social workers—with skills essential for program delivery. Harnessing their expertise in policy development is a management challenge because of the potential for conflict between governmental and professional agendas. Will professionals be on tap, or on top?

Good policy process avoids this difficulty by insisting on coordination. When proposals are developed against 'whole of government' objectives, and tested with sceptical central agencies, the possibility of professional bias is reduced. The 1987 amalgamation of Commonwealth agencies into 'megadepartments' was designed in part to ensure policy proposals were considered from a range of perspectives. Combining foreign affairs and trade, for example, provides a dialogue between foreign policy and Australia's trade interests.

Properly managed, the policy cycle brings together political, policy and administrative players in government. Professionals are an important part of the equation. Their role—like that of other advisers—is to be part of a wider process, and to accept that policy balances professional rationality with political need and administrative practicality.

A range of specialist and generalist skills are needed in policy making. This mirrors the trends in the range of elected politicians who occupy parliament, although Jones (2006:652) estimates that as at 2005, some 38 per cent of Australian Commonwealth parliamentarians 'could be defined as belonging to a class of professional politicians'. Essentially, there is no one qualification or background that is going to make a person

> The challenge lies in the ability of officials to respond to political reality. The truth is that Governments rarely capitulate on big decisions. But they rely on high quality advice from public servants to help form the decision. Inability to change or to respond to shifting political demands can pre-empt political decision making because Ministers' options have been cut off. At its worst this can become like an episode of *Yes Minister*.
>
> Peter Bridgman (quoted in Malone, 2006:18)

better or worse at the policy making game. Learning from experience, both one's own and that of others, is essential, as is the application of this learning to new cases. 'Like parliamentarians themselves, their staff should possess indefinable qualities to do an indescribable job' (Jones, 2006:648).

PLANNING PROJECTS

Planning for public policy is partly structured by the cabinet process, partly by annual budgets and partly by the ebb and flow of the electoral cycle. The information required for a cabinet submission, along with consultation rounds, central agency negotiation, cabinet's decision and then implementation, provides a regular sequence to policy making. The budgetary process 'sets the framework for the conduct of fiscal policy and establishes policy priorities and strategies for the nation's governance' (Smith, 2005). Departments adjust their budget proposals in line with continual direction given through established review and committee processes that incorporate the perspectives of politicians and central agencies, taking into account shifting agendas and resource constraints. Meanwhile, the cycle of elections every three or four years ensures politicians have only a particular window in which to decide and implement an agenda. Margo Kingston (2001) from the *Sydney Morning Herald* somewhat cynically observes that: 'The first year you take the risks. The second year you bed down your risks. And the third year you give away all the money you saved in the first two years. It's suck-simple, it's just pathetic really.'

Despite the rhythm of these procedural requirements, managers responsible for policy development are inevitably rushing between projects. Priorities compete for attention. Ministers need information now. 'Urgent' takes precedence over 'important'. The pressures are emerging from the greater complexity of modern life. The electoral cycle now resembles a continuous campaign. Ministers typically engage in continuous media and image management in order to stay on top of the popularity stakes (see Young, 2004; 't Hart and Wille, 2006). 'Governments employ the same techniques used in election campaigning to make people aware of information that assists in attaining policy objectives . . .' (Stockwell, 2005:206).

Managers develop routines for each step of the cycle to keep things moving. These 'routines within routines' evoke a familiar, systematic approach for every new policy problem, allowing a degree of standardisation of the unfamiliar. Managers stay in control by learning to plan projects according to a standard, proven methodology.

Across the policy cycle, managers seek to identify the task at hand, the resources and time required, and the sequence to be followed. The objective is not elaborate plans, but simple and regular processes ensuring proper consideration at each stage of the policy cycle.

Planning is important throughout the policy cycle, and managers should become familiar with the range of standard planning tools. Among the most familiar is a Gantt chart, used to sequence activities, allocate resources and budget time, as in Figure 12.1. Key achievement points ('milestones') mark completion of significant sub-tasks, allowing a complex project to be divided into attainable portions.

The 'critical path method' also helps budget time, but is more sophisticated. This method recognises that a complex sequence may be required, with some tasks completed simultaneously before the next can begin. Managers can estimate 'float' or flexible times. The critical path is the sequence of steps requiring most time to complete, and therefore likely to delay other sub-tasks. Figure 12.2 shows a sample critical path chart. The upper line is estimated to take 28 weeks (identify issues, policy analysis, policy instruments, coordination, decision and implementation). The lower line is estimated to take 36 weeks (identify issues, consultation, coordination,

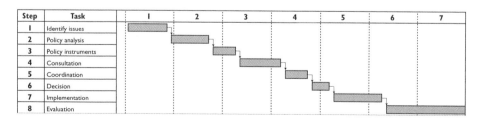

Figure 12.1   A sample Gantt chart

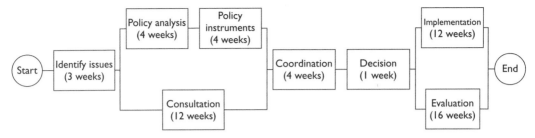

Figure 12.2 A sample critical path chart

decision and evaluation). This is the 'critical path' because the combined tasks take more time than the non-critical (upper) path, which is said to have 'float' or tolerance in the timing of its tasks.

Managers must make judgments about the required level of data, the resources to be dedicated to the task, and the available time lines for the project in order to plan properly. In general, the more urgent the policy task, the greater the resources required for a quality result. The methods described here are no substitute for professionalism and experience.

TIMING

One of the key judgments required of policy professionals is setting aside sufficient time for each step of the process. This will vary depending on the urgency of the matter, its complexity and size. The range of players interested in the decision is a major determinant of complexity. In a few urgent cases, cabinet submissions are prepared, discussed and approved in a short space of time. When problems emerge—for example, following a court ruling on tax laws—new legislation can sometimes be drafted and presented to the parliament in a matter of days.

Most government activities, though, proceed at a slower pace. This is necessary if each step of the policy cycle is to receive the attention required, and to be completed to a satisfactory standard.

Each step in the policy cycle, for a typical policy issue that becomes the subject of a cabinet submission, is illustrated in Table 12.1. While these time lines are illustrative only, the typical

---

> It is an inevitable defect, that bureaucrats will care more for routines than for results: or, as Burke put it, 'that they will think the substance of the business not to be much more important than the forms of it.' Their whole education and all the habit of their lives makes them do so.
>
> Bagehot (1867:195)

Table 12.1 Indicative timetable for a policy cycle

Policy step	Process	Indicative times Short	Indicative times Long
Identifying issues	• a briefing paper is prepared • minister and agency agree a policy problem exists • work is commissioned	3 weeks	2 months
Policy analysis	• data collected about the problem • agency seeks information on responses in other jurisdictions • a policy paper is prepared and considered by the agency and minister	4 weeks	4 months
Policy instruments	• potential policy instruments considered, compared, and a choice made • if necessary, draft legislation prepared for consultation	2 weeks	5 months (drafting legislation can take longer)
Consultation	• discussion with relevant government agencies • discussion with external interest groups • intra- and inter-governmental negotiations • may be undertaken concurrently with other tasks	4 weeks	3 months
Coordination	• analysis by central agencies • links to budget and legislative program established • negotiation over cabinet submission • clearance for inclusion on cabinet agenda	2 weeks	3 months
Decision	• consideration by cabinet • decision issued as a cabinet minute	2 weeks	1 month
Implementation	• agency secures resources to act • necessary legislation passed by parliament and given assent (parliamentary times depend on available sittings and are not included) • subordinate legislation developed and promulgated • program established and operational	5 weeks	6 months
Evaluation	• program review, report and modifications	26 weeks	1 year
Timing range	• assumes legislation takes no longer than six months to prepare, and excludes parliamentary stages	48 weeks	3 years

policy cycle takes from four months to nearly two years between recognition of a problem and program implementation. Long-standing policies may go through the cycle many times, being reviewed and modified while assumptions remain unchanged.

MANAGEMENT AND THE POLICY PROCESS

From the perspective of a policy manager in a line department, many people have a stake in the policy cycle:

- ministers and their political advisers
- the agency's chief executive
- the heads of the policy unit and relevant division
- the staff working on the policy issue
- the agency's cabinet liaison staff
- network partners and implementation agencies, including those from the third sector and the private sector
- the community or clients associated with the policy
- the general public.

All expect to be consulted during the course of policy deliberations. Policy officers are likely to receive calls from:

- central agencies, particularly the PM&C and Treasury
- other line agencies interested in the policy area
- groups likely to be affected by any policy change
- external groups such as lobbyists, consultants, think tanks, and even the media.

Managing the policy process requires significant judgment and people skills. John Wanna and his colleagues (1994:1.2.4) suggest policy managers must learn to manage up, across, down and out.

When *managing up*, the policy officer recognises the needs of the minister and chief executive. These people are unlikely to become involved in the detailed drafting of policy, but their views must be taken into consideration. Ultimately, it is the minister who owns, and must argue for, a cabinet submission. The skill of managing up is to recognise how the world looks from various standpoints. Public servants properly put great stress on operational questions, but a minister and chief executive must deal with a bigger picture—not just whether a policy can be implemented, but how it fits into the wider mosaic of government priorities. Understanding the particular concerns

---

One of the key lessons I learnt as a public servant was pay attention all the time on a day-to-day basis to the process, who you're involving, why you're involving them, what structures you're going to use, what stages you're going to go through in developing the policy.
Meredith Edwards, August 2002, Corridors of Power, *ABC*

Policy is the means by which the lives of individuals, families and communities are shaped. It is the means by which we shape the character and future of the nation. It is the purpose of political life, the only worthwhile measure of political success, and by far the most significant measure of the worth of politicians and political parties.
Paul Keating

of those in command is important; as the saying goes, 'where you stand depends on where you sit'.

In *managing across*, policy officers deal with their peers in their own and other line agencies, with similarly placed officers in the central agencies, and across jurisdictions and the various non-government sectors that form part of particular policy networks and communities. Managing across is part of coordination in government, the endless task of letting others know what is proposed and giving them an opportunity to comment and participate in the process. It means circulating drafts of policy documents, organising meetings to discuss proposals, and obtaining and negotiating input into the development, implementation and evaluation of policy ideas. Equally, managing across requires policy officers to respond to the requests of others for comment and ideas. In a world of networks, managing across is assuming increasing importance. Even if the network is only connected to a 'virtual' community of peers through electronic mail and fax machines, policy managers should work to keep the network active, while also challenging and encouraging network members.

Policy managers often supervise staff. *Managing down* is not just commanding, but expressing and cultivating empathy, encouragement and appreciation of the others' contributions. General Patton was fond of saying: 'Never tell people how to do things. Tell them what you want to achieve, and they will surprise you with their ingenuity' (Gore, 1993:12). Policy development typically requires teamwork. A skilful manager builds team morale and competence, delegates, and sets goals and time lines for the work team.

Finally, in a policy context, *managing out* means dealing with clients likely to be affected by policy change—community members and groups and those within the public sector responsible for delivering the program. Their cooperation may be essential to the policy achieving its objectives. Managing out often involves informing and advising about policy choices; sometimes it means organising formal consultation sessions and ensuring feedback influences policy design.

All facets of managing the policy process require sensitivity to political demands: '... ministers expect officials to correctly anticipate the political ramifications of any given issue and policy proposal' ('t Hart and Wille, 2006:131). Discreet attention must be paid to anticipating the potential political risks and ramifications of plans, the potential to generate 'package deals' with stakeholders, the tradeoffs that might spill over into unrest or adverse media attention. It is a challenging assignment. Ministers and political advisers are keen to protect their own turf and do not want public officials second-guessing politics. At the same time, they do not want policy advice tainted by political naivety.

Balancing all of these tasks is a formidable undertaking. The key skills required are shown in Table 12.2.

Table 12.2 Management skills for policy officers

Task	Skills
Managing up	• recognise expectations of ministers and senior officers
	• anticipate requirements of ministers and senior officers
Managing across	• recognise extent of interest in, and impact of, issues across agencies
	• encourage and be receptive to coordination
Managing down	• implement programs
	• support and maintain personnel
Managing out	• respond sensitively to client needs

(From Wanna et al., 1994:1.2.4)

The way public policy is managed can be vitally important. It can impact heavily on the choices that are available as we move around the policy cycle.

Government's capacity to manage its internal affairs is also a measure of how well government manages generally.

There is no 'correct' organisation for every circumstance. Organisational choices must change from time to time to suit the needs of the government, the relevant minister, the relevant agency and changing circumstances.

ORGANISING FOR PUBLIC POLICY: MACHINERY OF GOVERNMENT

The public sector is generally effective at organising, yet strangely pays little attention to organising specifically for public policy. Effective public policy requires resources, and a commitment to outcomes. This is true for both specific projects and the durable infrastructure of departments.

Failure to organise may have high costs. Therefore, organising is an investment in the integrity of the systems that support ministers and chief executives as they carry out their broad and complex responsibilities as policy decision makers. Good organisation design is likely to pay dividends because policy lessons and effort will survive even fundamental changes such as those in personnel, practice, policy direction, the architecture of government, and the political complexion of the ministry. Criteria that the World Bank suggest are important to consider in making machinery of government decisions are outlined in Figure 12.3.

The overall architecture of government is the starting point for policy organisation. Machinery of government decisions are an important prerogative, and are usually jealously guarded by the prime minister or premier, who will consult only with close allies and advisers before negotiating on the details with other ministers and chief executives.

Jurisdictional limits

The Commonwealth's main focus is on policy services rather than service delivery (with some notable exceptions), so many Commonwealth agencies have elaborate and well-resourced policy capacity. States and territories are more focused on services. The vast bulk of their resources are committed to public officials who deliver services to the community rather than policy services to the government of the day. In smaller jurisdictions, it is even more likely that resources are directed to program delivery rather than policy support.

ORGANISING CONSUMES RESOURCES

The second law of thermodynamics describes an important constraint on organisation and structure in the physical world—any process in a closed system will have a cost in 'wasted' energy or, put another way, energy input from outside is needed to bring order and to make systems work.

Running government involves expenditure on structures, systems and the other 'overheads' of organising. Even the best designed system takes energy to maintain and develop, reducing the energy available to other ends of government.

Well-run systems cost money or, as Seife (2000) puts the second law of thermodynamics, 'there is no such thing as a free lunch'.

---

1. Mandates, responsibilities and accountabilities should be clearly allocated, grouping like activities while avoiding ambiguity, duplication and overlap.
2. The structure should be simple and robust. Principles on which the structure is based should be clear to all sets of stakeholders. In most cases, the key is that each minister's set of portfolios should be related in some important way.
3. The structure should provide ministers with an appropriate span of control.
4. Strategic policy coordination should be centralised within a few central agencies, with sectoral policy formulation shifted to ministers, supported by small line ministries and responsible for broad policy portfolios rather than narrow tasks.
5. The structure should promote a strong client orientation, and be based on a rough delineation between policy formulation and implementation responsibilities.
6. The structure should seek to avoid potential conflicts of interest.
7. Ministries are not intended to last indefinitely, and at any one time the structure should reflect priority issues facing the country and facilitate achievement of the government's key medium-term priorities.
8. The structure should provide for maximum possible decentralisation of service delivery responsibilities to regions and local governments; but decentralisation is set within an appropriate and robust accountability framework.

Figure 12.3 World Bank criteria for machinery of government decisions
(World Bank, 2002)

This size principle is also applicable within governments. Bigger agencies, like health, education and transport, can afford to meet the organisational cost of strong policy support. Smaller agencies may struggle to meet these 'overheads', as the chief executive of any smaller line agency in a state will readily confess.

CONSTRAINTS

Some aspects of public policy organisation are relatively stable and others more open to change. An organisation that supports policy effort will build on the strengths, and accommodate the weaknesses, of what cannot readily be changed by working with the things that are easier to manipulate.

Things that are harder to change constrain choices. Constraints are the more stable features of the policy landscape, and more resistant to change by a player. But a different, more powerful player may be able to manipulate things that constrain others. Part of the policy adviser's art is to identify who can change what, and under what constraints.

Constraints are described here under four headings: the minister; ministerial staff, the chief executive; and the system of government.

The minister

Ministerial tenure may be political, but their presence during that tenure should be assumed—only a foolhardy bureaucrat would work to hasten a minister's demise! Along with the office comes the person, with unique interests and skills, deficits that need to be recognised and managed, relative authority in the cabinet and political aspirations. Chief executives and policy advisers do not decide these things, but must accept the decision made by others about who is the minister. While departmental officers might applaud and express sighs of relief due to the skills of certain ministers, the inadequacies of other ministers are something beyond the control of policy makers—policy staff will need to use their skills to work harder or in more creative ways to make up for a perceived deficit, and explore ways to use a minister's strengths.

In the Australian system of government, ministers traditionally confine their efforts (outside cabinet) to their portfolio

> When asked to name the chief qualification a politician should have: 'It's the ability to foretell what will happen tomorrow, next month, and next year—and to explain afterward why it didn't happen.'
> Sir Winston Churchill

responsibilities. Portfolio allocation is therefore a major constraint on a minister.

The machinery of government and portfolio allocation decisions made by the prime minister delineate a minister's responsibilities and describe the policy matters that require attention. The more diverse the portfolio, the more complex the skills needed both by the minister and by public servants and the greater the investment required in policy effort and organisation.

The prime minister can manipulate the machinery of government, granting or removing responsibilities and dictating key relationships. Thus machinery of government constrains ministers and bureaucrats, but may be operated on by the prime minister. Deciding the architecture of government is important in shaping a government's agenda.

Even a prime minister is constrained by the real politic of governing, including factors such as: the power of other players; the resources available; the skills and personalities of ministers and chief executives; the need to balance divergent political groupings within the governing party; and the political flux. Even small practicalities like the physical location of offices may influence portfolio allocation and the development of governmental synergies.

The King himself ought not to be subject to man, but subject to God and the law.
Lord Chancellor Henry of Bracton
c. 1210–1268, De Legibus Et Consuetudinibus Angliæ (On the Laws and Customs of England)

Ministerial staff

Ministerial office staff are selected by varying processes; the first minister, usually through their chief of staff, may seek to complement ministers with suitable staff. This can be an important influence on ministers' management of their portfolios: policy officers will often deal with the relevant minister through political staff in the ministerial office. Understanding of the policy process by political staff may be excellent and facilitate outcomes, but it may equally be poor and retard the smooth progress around the policy cycle. The political staff are responsible for connecting the minister's political program with departmental priorities, and for managing the minister's interface with portfolio stakeholders. This responsibility may diverge from the role of the policy officer, adding complexity to the demands placed on the policy organisation.

The chief executive

The chief executive must deliver policy and executive support to the minister, and manage the agency overall. Chief executives are usually expected to contribute actively to whole of government or cross-portfolio outcomes rather than building an empire separate from other government objectives. Thus government priorities and directions also constrain a chief executive.

The minister's capacity, style and interests are constraints on the chief executive. Ministers may have strong views about the role of the public service, requiring well-established departmental practices to be changed to accommodate those views. For example, a minister who believes that public servants do not 'make policy' would probably not accept a large working group called a Policy Division, staffed by policy officers. Nonetheless, quality advice must still be developed and analysis prepared for the minister's consideration.

The system of government

Government is a complex set of organisations with many constraints and possibilities. Ministers and chief executives who strive to organise effectively for policy must work within the constraints and still explore the possibilities to suit their own needs and the constellation of issues and staff available to them. The demands of the political and administrative domains, which are overlaid with separate legislative, executive and judicial authority, provide a certain organisational rhythm.

The system of government limits choice of organisational form to that which is governmental (as opposed to, say, commercial, industrial, familial or communitarian). Any chosen organisation must serve the purposes of government, and not be antagonistic in form or action.

The structures must acknowledge and serve the minister's place in the political domain, and be manageable by the departmental head.

This does not mean novel organisational elements or patterns are forbidden. Networks, virtual networks, matrices and other collaborative forms are all available and are increasingly used in modern policy making.

The law

Government is unique in its organisational form because it is subject to constitutional constraints and the rule of law, while it also has the law as a policy instrument.

The federal constitution distributes power among the Commonwealth and the states, and state laws distribute authority in turn to local government and state related entities.

Governments are creatures of the law and can do only what the law authorises. Much power and many resources are entrusted to ministers and public officials. It is fundamental that power is exercised and resources managed honestly and lawfully. Courts have a special role in overseeing the lawfulness of decisions made by officials through judicial review and other administrative law remedies.

Specific laws apply in every jurisdiction to the architecture of government and management of staff, money and other resources. These include the *Public Service Acts* and financial management and audit laws.

There are also Acts governing non-discriminatory treatment of people, workplace health and safety and industrial practices, remuneration and other entitlements and, increasingly, clearly articulated ethical standards about the conduct of public employees.

Accountability framework

Governments require the public sector to be accountable. Complex obligations vary among jurisdictions, with key components often driven not only by a principled approach, but also by landmark political events, such as 'WA Inc' in Western Australia, and inquiries into police corruption in New South Wales and Queensland.

Accountability is not solely about corruption. Planning and reporting, and accounting using professional standards, have been borrowed from the commercial world. Budgeting practices provide links between the administrative and political domains. Internal and external auditors scrutinise systems and activities.

Many laws describe the bounds of proper conduct, and provide mechanisms for officials to be called to account. The

---

DECLARATION OF ETHICS PRINCIPLES

4.(1) The ethics principles mentioned in subsection (2) are declared to be fundamental to good public administration.

(2) The 'ethics principles' for public officials are:

- respect for the law and the system of government
- respect for persons
- integrity
- diligence
- economy and efficiency.

Public Sector Ethics Act 1994 (Qld)

most significant of these are the administrative laws: judicial review, administrative appeals, freedom of information. A range of fair treatment laws affect organisational accountability, including laws preventing discrimination, bullying or other inappropriate workplace behaviour, and ensuring equal opportunity, merit protection and workplace health and safety.

Cabinet processes

Every government expects its most important decisions to be made in an orderly way. Cabinet, as the primary political decision-making body, makes rules about how matters are brought into this forum. Those rules will drive certain choices about organisation. For example, an agency must provide properly for the staff, equipment and other resources to prepare cabinet submissions in the expected way, and to manage document security.

Resource constraints

Government resources are finite, and distributed through formal budgeting processes. This imposes serious constraints on agencies that must nonetheless provide sufficient support to the minister and chief executives to ensure that government processes are managed properly and policy outcomes managed effectively through the policy cycle.

As noted earlier, smaller agencies may struggle to meet the 'overheads' of dedicated staff for cabinet processes and policy analysis, development, implementation and evaluation.

ORGANISATIONAL CHOICES

Despite the many constraints, decision makers can make choices in organising for public policy. This section explores some of the choices, and offers guidance to decision makers for building the most effective organisation for their needs.

There are some threshold considerations for decision makers. Should their policy organisation be:

- central or distributed (proximity to chief executive and minister)
- functional, sectoral, methodological or networked in character

- inclusive or targeted
- constant or ad hoc (employed and stable or contracted-in and flexible)
- built into the agency's cost base?

Above all, form should follow function, and a sustainable skills base should be developed.

SOME PRINCIPLES FOR WELL-ORGANISED PUBLIC POLICY

There are no fixed formulas for building policy organisations, but there are some useful principles to keep in mind when making choices about these elements and their interactions.

1. *Policy advice and development is a public service activity.* The public service is the major conduit of policy information to ministers and the cabinet. It manages the flow of documents, ensures the coherence and integrity of the systems that support the policy cycle, and is uniquely positioned to provide government with an insider's view of issues.

    External advisers are often used to inform policy development and analysis, bringing specialised skills and knowledge, and a remoteness from government that may sometimes assist stakeholder engagement. But external advisers rarely possess the process knowledge or skills to manage an issue through the entire policy cycle. The overhead costs inherent in a system rigorous enough for cabinet processes may be non-commercial, and in many governments external service providers will not build the necessary relationship of trust with ministers.

    Departments also need to serve ministers' need for advice on the operations and policy relating to independent bodies within the portfolio. Examples include independent auditors, police, quasi-judicial bodies and service agencies or licensing and regulatory authorities established to keep issues at arm's length. Such bodies should not be responsible for developing policy proposals, because that could destroy their independence. Naturally these bodies should be consulted on policy developments affecting them, but it is

PRINCIPLES FOR POLICY ORGANISATION

1. Keep public policy public
2. Embed contestability
3. Capture but do not be captured
4. Be flexible
5. Be proactive
6. Enhance policy skills
7. Build networks.

the responsible department that should offer independent, contestable advice to the minister.
2. *Embed contestability.* The institutionalised contestability provided by the Department of Prime Minister and Cabinet should be replicated in other agencies. Knowing that another set of critical eyes will read, analyse and report is a useful check on front-line advisers. Chief executives and ministers should be provided with the best analysis, and that means more than one perspective has been used in its development. This may be as simple as economic and legal analysis being applied routinely; or more sophisticated, with tight controls and multiple pathways.
3. *Capture information without being captured.* The opposite of contestable advice could well be 'capture' of policy staff by vested interests. Staff naturally form strong relationships with stakeholders and develop deep understanding of issues. It is their job to find out, and reflect, the views of stakeholders, but to do so objectively. Timely advice usually requires specialist and detailed knowledge. Capturing that knowledge without being captured by interest groups and stakeholders is a challenge.
4. *Be flexible—build capacity to respond.* Policy challenges may arise suddenly. If staff are heavily committed on pre-planned projects, there will be little capacity to respond to emerging issues without other priorities falling behind. A culture of responsiveness is also important.

The skill base of the agency needs to be sustainable, implying that more than one person can provide a service, and some consideration needs to be given to succession planning in the event of a key individual's departure.
5. *Be proactive—build capacity to forecast.* Of course it is better to predict than respond. A habit of exploring possibilities will position agencies to manage the unexpected as well as the expected. Staff need to keep abreast of developments in other jurisdictions, as well as national and international trends in the substantive policy areas, and to be aware of academic and journalistic opinion.
6. *Enhance the policy skills of others.* Inherent in contestability is the idea that other people understand how to make a

contribution. Policy effort is best shared among many rather than kept exclusively, even if there are tight controls and rigorous process to maintain high standards. Encouraging and building a learning organisation will improve the quality of policy work, enhance the connection between service delivery and government direction, and assist in broadening the vision of staff who may visit policy effort only occasionally.

7. *Build networks from the centre to the edge*. Size is not everything. Small, well-structured policy units can be very potent by marshalling the resources around them.

Trust and relationships are important elements of a fully functioning policy area. Ministers and chief executives must know that advice offered is able to be trusted, and that the people can do the job well, with discretion. In turn, policy officers should be able to build effective relationships with stakeholders, other staff, counterparts in other agencies (external and internal to government) and ministerial advisers.

MEASURING POLICY ADVICE PERFORMANCE

Policy advice is inherently difficult to measure because of the subjective and political overlays in the decision making process. A precisely drafted and technically excellent brief may be discarded because political considerations dictate other directions. Emerging events may overtake the careful work of the most diligent policy officer.

The objective measures of performance for policy advice are few:

- count (e.g. how many briefs prepared in a given period)
- time (e.g. finalised by required time; number of days to turnaround an issue)
- form (e.g. conformity with *Cabinet Handbook* requirements; length; readability; grammar and expression)
- reported satisfaction.

Under the Commonwealth outcome and outputs framework, agencies are required to report on policy advice provision as an

THE SEVEN PRINCIPLES OF PUBLIC LIFE

Selflessness: Holders of public office should take decisions solely in terms of the public interest. They should not do so in order to gain financial or other material benefits for themselves, their family, or their friends.

Integrity: Holders of public office should not place themselves under any financial or other obligation to outside individuals or organisations that might influence them in the performance of their official duties.

Objectivity: In carrying out public business, including making public appointments, awarding contracts, or recommending individuals for rewards and benefits, holders of public office should make choices on merit.

Accountability: Holders of public office are accountable for their decisions and actions to the public and must submit themselves to whatever scrutiny is appropriate to their office.

Openness: Holders of public office should be as open as possible about all the decisions and actions that they take. They should give reasons for their decisions and restrict information only when the wider public interest clearly demands.

Honesty: Holders of public office have a duty to declare any private interests relating to their public duties and to take steps to resolve any conflicts arising in a way that protects the public interest.

Leadership: Holders of public office should promote and support these principles by leadership and example.

United Kingdom Committee on Standards in Public Life (2005)

output. This is a challenging task. Specification is often loose (what is counted as policy advice), and linkage between the output of policy advice to outcomes is difficult to identify and measure and inevitably involves political judgment. There is a question of what is being measured. Is it the policy advice itself or the process of its provision? Somehow policy advice needs to be separated from other factors impacting on outcomes. The identity of the client is hotly contested too. Is it the minister, the ministerial office, cabinet, parliament (see Di Francesco, 1999)?

Various attempts have been made to assess policy advice performance. A common occurrence involves departments across Australian jurisdictions asking ministers and ministerial offices to rate such things as the quality of their briefing notes, submissions and correspondence. For example, the Commonwealth Department of Finance and Administration used a reported satisfaction indicator that showed a high level of

Table 12.3 Quality standards for policy advice

Quality standard	Advice for managers
Purpose	Aim of the advice is clearly set and addresses any question set
Logic	Assumptions upon which the advice is based are clearly stated Argument is supported by evidence
Accuracy	Evidence used is accurate and reliable All material facts are included
Options	An adequate range of options is presented Benefits, costs and consequences of each option to both the government and the community are identified
Responsiveness	Advice is aware of current realities Advice anticipates developments
Consultation	Evidence of appropriate consultation with other government agencies and affected interests
Presentation and Concision	Format meets specified presentation standards Advice is presented in a clear and concise manner
Practicality and Relevance	Recommendations take account of anticipated problems of implementation, feasibility, timing and whole-of-government policy consistency
Timeliness	Advice complied with deadlines or response times specified by the government

(Department of Finance and Administration, 2002, www.finance.gov.au)

satisfaction with briefings and responses, but indicated scope for further improvement. Specifically, June 1998 data showed 38 per cent of ministerial responses and 27 per cent of briefs were rated as excellent (Department of Finance and Administration, 1998: part 4, 20).

Meanwhile, the Victorian Auditor-General's Office (2004) conducted a performance audit of the policy advice performance across eight policies in three Victorian agencies. The audit focused on policy development only and not on government decision making, the merits of the advice or its implementation. It found that consultation was variable. There was poor use of disciplined project management methodologies, especially in the area of risk management where there was a failure to provide clear statements of risks associated with recommendations leading to either ill-informed ministers or departments making risk-averse recommendations. All departments were facing challenges in developing and maintaining staff skills in the area of policy advice.

These types of measures are mostly feedback mechanisms, and hence managerial in nature. Experience suggests that the primary indicator of 'quality' advice rests in a relationship of trust between the officer and the minister. A trusted officer's advice will be seen as of higher quality than that from an unknown or mistrusted source, regardless of the integrity and excellence of the actual words and presentation.

POLICY CAPACITY

The audit experience in Victoria suggests a skill shortage in policy advice, and this seems to be a trend across Australia. All jurisdictions must grapple with a perceived deficit in policy capacity that might pose alarming problems for the policy process.

Painter and Pierre (2005:2) describe policy capacity as 'the ability to marshal the necessary resources to make intelligent collective choices about and set strategic directions for the allocation of scarce resources to public ends'. The perceived decline in policy capacity is emerging from political leaders and from public service executives. Accusations from prime ministers and premiers of 'lack of vision', 'lack of follow-through on

> The quality of any government is dependent, in large part, upon the quality of advice it receives... Australia must be assured that its governments, of whatever political persuasion, will be guided by considered, honest advice based on rigorous analysis, sound knowledge of administrative practice and sensible precedent.
>
> *John Howard, June 2001*

> When ministers succeed, there is usually a small army of public servants who have turned an embryonic idea into something which can make a difference to the way people live. When ministers stumble, there is often at least one public servant whose warnings were ignored. The world beats a path to politicians' doors. The lobbies are crowded with people to speak for industries, institutions, regions, mates, causes. But ministers are supposed to speak for the nation and can't do so without public servants to cast a discerning but unsentimental eye on everyone's pet projects.
>
> *Tony Abbott, May 2002*

decisions', and lack of 'strategic thinking' imply a range of faults. Possible causes for this decline include: a loss in analysis, advice, responsiveness and alignment with government priorities; a deficit in skills-base due to poor workforce planning; or poor coordination and collaboration across the sector (Tiernan and Wanna, 2006).

The policy capacity argument links policy process performance to internal abilities as well as government performance. It is not just an administrative and management dilemma but a political imperative. Policy managers must somehow match the structures, routines and resources of the policy machine with the bigger picture of political pragmatism. Statecraft is fundamental in policy process: governments are necessarily concerned with their ability to make decisions and implement their priorities.

Policy capacity can be distinguished from policy capability. Capacity implies structural and physical attributes. Capability is about the intellectual dimension of policy making which includes determination and desire as well as intelligence and creativity (Tiernan and Wanna, 2006). Both elements must be attended to by policy managers.

Networked governance poses fascinating challenges for policy capacity. Access to the process as well as prioritisation of roles and responsibilities of the various players shifts and shakes throughout the cycle. Sometimes communities or influential individuals will dictate the terms of engagement. At other times, politicians will impose their will on the system. Business stakeholders and the media might stir the policy cauldron. But sometimes, the policy machine will be left to the steerage of public officials through the labyrinth of government.

Policy making can be a kaleidoscopic affair. Conventions of the standard policy cycle remain valid but more open to variation and fluid interpretation. Policy makers must pay attention to their own skills and aptitudes as well as the systemic priorities and deficiencies of the day.

In many ways, the debates over policy capacity point to a need to be strategic in thinking and operation. Being conscious of the defects and shortcomings of policy making is as important as knowing its strengths and advantages. Bringing together all the pieces and ensuring that they are operational and working to peak is as much a part of policy making as the substantive analysis of a particular problem or the development of technical criteria for its evaluation. Successful policy making involves integration of complex information, processes and relationships; negotiation and arbitration of these same complexities using political, policy and administrative skills; and practical appreciation that policy making is not technically pure or perfect but realistically pragmatic and political. It is essential to grasp the processes and procedures and work with them while at the same time questioning traditional assumptions and critically evaluating what is 'given' (see Briggs, 2005b).

There is always a risk that a consensus among professionals will crowd out other, non-professional, views. As Frank Fischer (1995:12) notes, the 'rational person' seems the one 'who agrees to submit to the properly derived technical and administrative knowledge of the scientific expert. The authority of the expert, from this perspective, ultimately takes precedence over the democratic exchange of opinions.'

MANAGING THE POLICY PROCESS

The policy cycle is a form of coordination, a way to sequence the various tasks and skills necessary for making, delivering and evaluating public policy.

To work effectively, this cycle requires procedural integrity, acceptance of differing roles, careful planning, and policy officers able to manage complexity and ambiguity, so keeping the process focused.

These skills must be widely shared across government, and procedures documented. The policy cycle is not a smooth loop of assigned tasks, but a quite disjointed process with each step belonging to different players. Continuity is provided by the routines of decision making, and the commitment of dedicated people working for better processes and better policy.

Policy making is a daunting task—Godlike even—for in attempting to change a society we are, for better or worse, helping to create new kinds of human beings with new values.
David Donnison (1994:29)

APPENDIX 1
Checklists for policy development

SNAPSHOT
This chapter provides a summary of the policy cycle, and systematic checklists of actions required to make public policy choices.

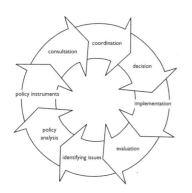

The Australian Policy Handbook is based on a policy cycle, and is designed to encourage a systematic approach to decision making. Good process cannot guarantee good policy, but it does encourage rigour and prevent elementary mistakes.

Policy making is political and hence unpredictable. Few decisions are afforded sufficient time or resources for every step in the policy cycle; most are rushed, and the pressure for ad hoc work remains great. Reality tempers the ideal of systematic policy development.

Over time, policy cycle routines and role prescriptions foster policy skills. Policy makers learn to recognise the interplay of politics, policy and administration. They become proficient at designing and testing policy options. They become sensitive to the responses of others. Preparing concise, informative briefing notes and cabinet submissions becomes a familiar activity, as do consultation and evaluation. Ministers and their advisers become familiar with the rhythms of cabinet process, the format of key documents, and the data needed for informed decisions.

Such policy skills, widely dispersed, are essential for good government. They assist a professional approach to decision making. Policy participants who value thoughtful, well-argued and properly evaluated policy proposals reduce the risk of foolish choices, and of bringing government into disrepute.

Policy making is a cooperative venture between political operatives, public servants, and a number of players from within civic society. Each domain plays to its strengths, yet they maintain separate roles. It does not help the policy process if public servants become politicised. Equally, ministers are not well served if their advisers become bureaucrats, more concerned about the technical detail than the government's political objectives. Nor can third sector or private sector operators assume the authority—and carte blanche its associated chain of accountability—that is granted to elected officials.

Policy making must meld different perspectives into viable cabinet submissions and programs. These balance politics with policy, and good ideas with sound administration. Issues move back and forward across the players on their long journey from ideas to implementation.

The routines of cabinet provide some structure for the policy process, but significant discretion remains for departments and other policy players and domains to establish their own procedures. Thus, within government, each agency or policy domain develops unique characteristic ways of making policy. Some stress documentation of each step. Others are more informal, relying on the skills and experience of policy officers and policy community practitioners to carry policy development through the cycle.

These differences in operating procedure do not matter if policy outputs are of high and consistent quality, and policy outcomes achieve the changes required. They may even add diversity, and with it the potential for creativity within the strictures of process.

We offer the following summary and policy checklists, knowing that even experienced policy specialists need occasionally to refresh their skills and knowledge. The Australian National Audit Office used this checklist approach in its 2001 Guide on *Some Better Practice Principles for Developing Policy Advice*, and much of our material was incorporated into their guide.

Table 13.1 provides a summary of the policy process, which is then expanded in a series of checklists for developing policy

Table 13.1 Summary of the policy process

Policy cycle step	Political domain	Policy domain	Administrative domain
Identifying issues	• search for ideas • regular discussion with sources of policy advice • sensitivity to emerging policy concerns	• regular advice to government about current and emerging issues	• data capture and flow
Policy analysis	• specification of policy issues and the range of choices government might consider	• briefs on policy issues and their consequences • technical analysis	• data and technical support
Policy instruments	• indication of ministerial preference	• policy instrument options • advice on legal issues	• data and technical support
Consultation	• stakeholder identification • political level consultation	• agency stakeholder identification • policy community consultation	• process support
Coordination	• ministerial office negotiations • clearance of cabinet submission	• preparation of policy submission • negotiations with central agencies • document quality control	• financial, administrative and personnel data for the cabinet submission
Decision	• determination by cabinet	• preparation of cabinet minutes and further briefs	• action planning on basis of cabinet minute
Implementation	• minister kept informed on progress	• resource identification • legal document preparation	• resource allocation and utilisation
Evaluation	• request for information • political analysis of results • decision about continuation	• monitoring performance • analysis of data from evaluation • identification of issues for next turn of the cycle	• regular evaluation, reporting of results, adjustments to program

objectives, offering policy advice and managing the policy cycle.

Finally, Table 13.2 provides a guide to implementing new policies. The focus here is on translating policy decisions into viable government actions. This interplay of good ideas and well-designed actions, of plausible theories and thoughtful programs, is the core of good public policy.

POLICY OBJECTIVES CHECKLIST

Does a policy statement express a considered response to an issue? ❏
Is the policy consistent with, and expressive of, government philosophy? ❏
Is the policy a clear and authoritative statement of intent? ❏
Does the policy provide sufficient detail to allow implementation?
 —implementation responsibility assigned ❏
 —resources identified ❏
 —implementation plan prepared ❏
 —implementation project team identified and available ❏
 —drafting instructions for legislative changes ❏
Are the goals sufficiently precise and detailed to allow later evaluation?
 —costs and benefits articulated ❏
 —benchmarks identified ❏
 —performance criteria stated and agreed ❏
Are resources available to implement the policy?
 —operating costs ❏
 —capital costs and set up costs ❏
Is someone else required to contribute financially or in kind?
 —staff ❏
 —staff training program ❏
 —office space in appropriate centres ❏
 —office equipment and requisites ❏
 —plant and equipment ❏
 —contractors ❏
 —support services ❏
 —communication plan ❏
Is the policy enforceable?
 —legally sustainable ❏
 —enforcement resources identified and available ❏
 —enforcement procedures identified ❏
 —timely enforcement practical and achievable ❏
 —sanctions and rewards relate to desired behaviour change ❏

POLICY ADVICE OBJECTIVES CHECKLIST

Will the decision maker hear about relevant issues in a timely manner? ☐
Is the decision maker informed about contending opinion on the matter? ☐
Are clear, different options available and presented honestly to the decision maker? ☐
Does the decision maker have sufficient information to make a decision?
—budget information ☐
—staff and other resource requirements ☐
—legal implications ☐
—social, environmental, political and other impacts ☐
—technical data ☐
—consultation and its results ☐
Can the decision be tested by evaluating program performance?
—performance criteria developed ☐
—benchmarks established ☐
—measurement instruments ☐
—reporting requirements established ☐

MANAGING THE POLICY CYCLE CHECKLIST

Are there procedure manuals to guide the policy process? ☐
Are staff allocated responsibility for coordinating policy responses within the agency and across government or external networks as necessary? ☐
Are adequate skills available for well rounded analysis? ☐
Is there appropriate project planning? ☐
Is the need for procedural integrity, and the separation of political and policy roles, understood and built into the policy development process? ☐
Is the project timetable realistic? ☐
Does the project manager understand the need to manage up, across, out and down? ☐
Have the perspectives of professionals been included in policy advice?
Have communication and evaluation and interaction with the ministerial office been sufficiently clarified and streamlined? ☐

POLICY CYCLE OBJECTIVES CHECKLIST

Issue identification
—Is there agreement on the nature of the problem? ☐
—Are there feasible solutions to the problem? ☐
—Is this an appropriate issue for government? ☐
—For whom in government is this a problem? ☐
—For whom in the community is this a problem? ☐

Policy analysis
- —Has the issue been accurately formulated? ☐
- —Are objectives and goals explicit and clear? ☐
- —Has the search for alternatives, both in terms of different options as well as experiences to be gained from policy learning, been thorough? ☐
- —Have the appropriate analytical tools been used for the issue? ☐
- —Have resource constraints, legal requirements and external accountability been taken into account in any policy advice? ☐
- —Is there a superior alternative? ☐
- —Have implementation and evaluation been considered in policy design? ☐

Policy instruments
- —Is advocacy, money, direct government action or law the best approach to this problem? ☐
- —Is this a reasonable way of proceeding in this policy area? ☐
- —Will the preferred instrument be cost-effective? ☐
- —Can this instrument get the job done? ☐
- —Is the instrument simple and robust, and can it be implemented? ☐
- —What evaluation tools are available for this instrument? ☐

Consultation
- —Are the objectives of the consultation process clear? ☐
- —What existing partnerships and networks exist and are they appropriate forums for the policy or should new or other parties be included? ☐
- —What level of participation is wanted for this policy? ☐
- —Has an appropriate information, consultation, partnership, delegation or control strategy been developed? ☐
- —Does the timetable allow sufficient scope for meaningful input and consideration? ☐
- —Are the resources to be committed commensurate with the importance of the problem? ☐
- —Have all relevant stakeholders been identified and included? ☐
- —Is there information available, and appropriate access to the consultation process? ☐
- —Have contributions been acknowledged? ☐
- —Has feedback from consultation been incorporated into policy advice? ☐

Coordination
- —Is the required money properly targeted and fully budgeted? ☐
- —Have the employment, industrial, equity and fairness consequences of a proposal been worked through? ☐
- —Have other factors which might influence attainment of policy objectives been identified? ☐

—Are proposals logical, well considered and consistent with other government initiatives? ❏
—Does this policy require whole-of-government instruments? ❏
—What parties and relationships are required to ensure enactment of the policy? ❏

Decision
—Should this matter go to cabinet? ❏
—Is the submission in the appropriate format? ❏
—Do the recommendations provide an adequate basis for a cabinet minute? ❏
—Has an implementation timetable been indicated in the submission? ❏
—Have the minister and ministerial office been briefed on likely objections? ❏
—Does cabinet have sufficient information to understand the consequences of its choice? ❏

Political dimensions
—What level of political involvement is required in the policy process from ministers or the prime minister/premier? ❏
—Is a political champion required for this policy? ❏
—What level of political involvement is required from the ministerial office in this policy process to secure goals and ensure smooth process? ❏
—How consistent is this policy with government objectives and priorities? ❏
—How relevant is this policy to the community and broader concerns beyond the government mandate? ❏
—What level and type of inter-agency and cross-sector partner relationships is necessary to give effect to the policy and what instruments should be used to facilitate the smooth operation of the policy within political confines? ❏
—What kind of political approvals are necessary as opposed to second-guessing political desires or intentions? ❏
—Is the policy likely to appear in media coverage and, if so, what kind of coverage would it receive? ❏
—Is there any aspect of this policy that is likely to cause political embarrassment to the minister? ❏

Implementation
—Is the objective clear and the underlying causal model reliable and tested? ❏
—Is a top-down or bottom-up approach most appropriate to the issue? ❏
—Is the assigned agency the most appropriate to implement the policy? ❏
—Can implementation steps and players be kept to a minimum? ❏
—Is there an agreed project leader and a clear chain of accountability? ❏
—Have 'street level bureaucrats' been involved in implementation design? ❏
—Has an evaluation strategy been included in the implementation plan? ❏
—Is legislation necessary, and used only as a 'last resort'? ❏
—How will the policy's effect be communicated to staff and clients? ❏

—Has consideration been given to the needs of special audiences? ❑
—Are there any implementation risks and have they been addressed? ❑
—Is the policy enforceable? (see Policy Objectives Checklist) ❑
—Will implementation meet the desired objective and achieve the desired results? ❑

Evaluation
—Is the appropriate measurement of policy success evaluation of inputs, process, outputs or outcomes? ❑
—Given the nature of the policy problem, has an appropriate level and type of evaluation been identified? ❑
—Can performance indicators be developed for the program? ❑
—Have evaluation findings informed the next cycle of policy advice? ❑
—Should the program be continued, modified or terminated? ❑

Table 13.2 Designing a new program

Issue	Action
Clarify objective	• Is it listed in cabinet submission? • Conflicting criteria must be recognised and ranked. • Specification of the objective is crucial, since it will form the basis of later evaluation.
Agree on an appropriate process	• Implementation can proceed through top-down or bottom-up approaches. The process should be guided by the objectives and the nature of the policy issue. • Use a project planning methodology to map out time frames, resource requirements, milestones and reporting dates.
Identify an implementation team	• Cabinet minutes assign implementation responsibility to a minister and agency. • Within the agency those managers with implementation responsibility are identified and assigned tasks. • To ensure accountability, implementation requires a team leader with appropriate authority to ensure follow-through.
Create a reporting mechanism	• To monitor implementation, a sequence of regular reports is important. • Reports should indicate progress against timetable and budget, feedback from those involved, and assessment of pending problems or opportunities.
Identify policy instruments	• The cabinet submission will indicate the preferred policy instruments, but re-evaluation is often necessary, especially if cabinet alters the proposed recommendation. • The implementation team must reflect on the proposed course of action, and confirm or modify the choice of instruments.

Issue	Action
Identify required resources	• The original cabinet submission should include costings for the policy and identification of available resources. • Resources should be matched with milestones, so that cash flow requirements (or other inputs) can be calculated and planned.
Agree on a timetable and milestones	• Cabinet may provide a timetable for implementation, but this is often left to the discretion of the agency. • Time lines are crucial for project planning. • Once an end date for implementation is settled, project planning should include 'milestones'—points along the way when specific actions must be completed. • Reporting dates should be agreed in advance with the minister and department.
Information systems	• Identify the information necessary for this program to run, and the information technology equipment required. • Plan information system installation to match implementation timetable.
Plant and equipment	• If delivered within government, a program will need appropriate accommodation, equipment and consumables. • Internal responsibility for procuring and maintaining these assets must be established, with appropriate reporting and monitoring systems.
Delegations	• If run in-house, the program will need staff and resource delegations, preferably devolved to the lowest available unit. • Delegations and approval systems should be supported by procedure manuals and appropriate accountability documentation.
Prepare communication plan	• Implementation relies on understanding by staff and clients. • A new policy will therefore need a communication plan, which explains the rationale and the process for implementation. • This may include meetings with staff and customers, printed material, even advertising. • Consider any special communication needs for remote areas or widely distributed staff, and for staff or clients with special communication needs (e.g. languages other than English).
Consultation	• The communications plan should include opportunities for feedback so that the implementation team can gauge reaction to the policy, and identify possible problem areas.
Mark the completion of implementation	• To communicate that implementation has been completed, to acknowledge the work of the team, and to build commitment to the new program, it is often useful to mark the completion of implementation.
Evaluation	• The implementation timetable should include an evaluation phase. • Evaluation should be conducted by people outside the implementation team, and should test the program against the original policy objectives and budget.

APPENDIX 2
Internet research tools for public policy

Disclaimer: This appendix is a resource. We do not necessarily endorse the material contained on these sites.

AUSTRALIAN GOVERNMENT SITES

Australian Government Entry Point
www.australia.gov.au

Australian Government Information Management Office—Government Access Point
www.agimo.gov.au/information/access

Australian Local Government Sites
www.alga.asn.au/links/obc.php

Australian Local Government Association
www.alga.asn.au

National Library Australian Government Page
www.nla.gov.au/oz/gov

Connected Government
www.connected.gov.au/

Australian Government and Politics Database
www.elections.uwa.edu.au/

EXECUTIVE GOVERNMENTS

Australian Commonwealth
www.australia.gov.au

New South Wales
www.nsw.gov.au

Victoria
www.vic.gov.au

Queensland
www.qld.gov.au

Western Australia
www.wa.gov.au

South Australia
www.sa.gov.au

Tasmania
www.tas.gov.au

Australian Capital Territory
www.act.gov.au

Northern Territory
www.nt.gov.au

Norfolk Island
www.pitcairners.org

AUSTRALIAN PARLIAMENTS

Parliament of Australia
www.aph.gov.au

Parliament of New South Wales
www.parliament.nsw.gov.au

Parliament of Victoria
www.parliament.vic.gov.au

Parliament of Queensland
www.parliament.qld.gov.au

Parliament of Western Australia
www.parliament.wa.gov.au

Parliament of South Australia
www.parliament.sa.gov.au

Parliament of Tasmania
www.parliament.tas.gov.au

ACT Legislative Assembly
www.legassembly.act.gov.au

Northern Territory Legislative Assembly
www.nt.gov.au/lant

AUSTRALIAN POLITICAL PARTIES

Australian Democrats
www.democrats.org.au

Australian Labor Party
www.alp.org.au

Australian Greens
www.greens.org.au

The Liberal Party of Australia
www.liberal.org.au

National Party of Australia
www.nationals.org.au/

One Nation
www.onenation.com.au

Christian Democratic Party
www.christiandemocratic.org.au/

Country Liberal Party
www.clp.org.au/

Democratic Labor Party
www.dlp.org.au/

Democratic Socialist Party
www.dsp.org.au/site

Socialist Party Australia
www.socialistpartyaustralia.org/

Family First
www.familyfirst.org.au/

AUSTRALIAN POLITICAL PAGES

Australian Politics Resources
www.geocities.com/CapitolHill/3860/links.html

Australian Policy Online
www.apo.org.au/

Democratic Audit of Australia
http://democratic.audit.anu.edu.au/

VCEpolitics.com
http://vcepolitics.com

Political Science in Australia
www.anu.edu.au/polsci/austpol/aust/frame.htm

Elections: Voting with Mumble
www.mumble.com.au

Australian Conservative Politics
www.geocities.com/CapitolHill/4975

Australian Libertarian Society
www.libertarian.org.au/

Yahoo! Australian Government and Politics Page
http://dir.yahoo.com/regional/countries/australia/government/

Australian Review of Public Affairs (published by the School of Economics and Political Science, University of Sydney)
www.econ.usyd.edu.au/drawingboard

AUSTRALIAN PUBLIC POLICY PROFESSIONAL ORGANISATIONS

Australia and New Zealand School of Government
www.anzsog.edu.au/

Australasian Political Studies Association
http://auspsa.anu.edu.au/

Institute of Public Administration Australia
www.ipaa.org.au/

National Institute for Governance
http://governance.canberra.edu.au

AUSTRALIAN INTEREST GROUPS, LOBBIES AND THINK TANKS

Australasian Political Studies Association—Listing of Australian NGO and Interest Groups
http://auspsa.anu.edu.au/www/Australia_NGO.htm

The Australia Institute
www.tai.org.au/

Australian Council of Social Services
www.acoss.org.au

Australian Council of Trade Unions
www.actu.asn.au

Australian Conservation Foundation
www.acfonline.org.au

The Australian Republican Movement
www.republic.org.au

Council for Aboriginal Reconciliation
www.austlii.edu.au/au/orgs/car

Evatt Foundation Web
www.evatt.labor.net.au

National Farmers Federation
www.nff.org.au

National Women's Justice Coalition (NWJC) Australia
www.nwjc.org.au

Women's Electoral Lobby (WEL) Australia
www.wel.org.au

Business Council of Australia Web Page
www.bca.com.au

Australian Chamber of Commerce and Industry (ACCI)
www.acci.asn.au

For a listing of Australian and international philanthropic sites see:

www.partnerships.gov.au/links/links_philanthropy.shtml

www.ozco.gov.au/news_and_hot_topics/hot_topics/artsupport_australia/

www.abaf.org.au/site_tools/links.html#Philanthropy

AUSTRALIAN LEGAL SITES

Australasian Legal Information Institute
www.austlii.edu.au

SCALEplus
www.scaleplus.law.gov.au

Law and Justice Foundation of New South Wales
www.lawfoundation.net.au

AUSTRALIAN NEWS RESOURCES

Australian Broadcasting Corporation (for news, radio and television)
www.abc.net.au/

Australian Financial Review
www.afr.com

Canberra Times
www.canberratimes.com.au

Crikey
www.crikey.com.au

News Limited Newspapers
www.news.com.au

Nine-msn
news.ninemsn.com.au

The Age
www.theage.com.au

The Sydney Morning Herald
www.smh.com.au

The Chaser
www.chaser.com.au

Yahoo! News
au.yahoo.com

Local Government Focus—Australia's National Local Government Newspaper Online
www.loc-gov-focus.aus.net/

INTERNATIONAL PUBLIC POLICY RESOURCES (INCLUDING INTEREST GROUPS, LOBBIES AND THINK TANKS)

Brookings Institution
www.brookings.edu

Policy Hub
www.policyhub.gov.uk/

Demos
www.demos.co.uk

Electronic Policy Network
http://movingideas.org

GovLeaders.org
www.govleaders.org

Harvard's John F. Kennedy School of Government
www.ksg.harvard.edu

Hubert H. Humphrey Institute of Public Affairs
www.hhh.umn.edu

Institute for Public Policy & Social Research, Michigan State University
www.ippsr.msu.edu

International Centre for Policy Studies, Kiev
www.icps.com.ua/eng/index.html

Jay's Leftist and 'Progressive' Internet Resources Directory
www.neravt.com/left

National Centre for Policy Analysis
www.ncpa.org

Policy Library
www.policylibrary.com

Policy Network
www.policy-network.net

Progressive Challenge
www.netprogress.org

Public Policy Institute of New York State
www.ppinys.org

Reason Foundation
www.rppi.org

FUTURES ORGANISATIONS

World Futures Studies Federation
www.wfsf.org/index.shtml

World Future Society
www.wfs.org/

Millennium Project
www.acunu.org/

The Australia Foresight Institute
www.swin.edu.au/afi/

FOREIGN GOVERNMENTS

Canadian Government
http://canada.gc.ca

New Zealand Government Online
www.govt.nz

British Monarchy
www.royal.gov.uk

United Nations Home Page
www.un.org

United Kingdom Government Information Service
www.direct.gov.uk/Homepage/fs/en

UK Houses of Parliament
www.parliament.uk

White House
www.whitehouse.gov

Library of Congress List of US Federal Agency Home Pages
www.loc.gov/rr/news/fedgov.html

US Government Official Web Portal
www.firstgov.gov

FedWorld—Search US Govt Web Space
www.fedworld.gov

FOREIGN MEDIA

ABCNEWS.com
www.abcnews.go.com

Asia Pacific News
www.asiapacificnews.com/

Asia Times Online
www.atimes.com

BBC News
http://news.bbc.co.uk

CNN
www.cnn.com

The Onion
www.theonion.com

The Guardian
www.guardian.co.uk

Pravda
www.pravda.ru

New York Times
www.nytimes.com

EuroNews
www.euronews.net

Fox News
www.foxnews.com

NewsTrawler
www.newstrawler.com

1stHeadlines
www.1stheadlines.com

PUBLIC POLICY EMAIL LISTS

e-network, the email news service of the Canadian Policy Research Networks
www.cprn.org/en/e-network.cfm

The daily newsletter for US federal executives, managers and employees
www.govexec.com/email

Number 10 Downing Street email news site
www.pm.gov.uk/output/Page36.asp

CITIZEN AND COMMUNITY ENGAGEMENT: INTERNET SITES

Institute for Citizen-Centred Service
www.iccs-isac.org

Australian Universities Community Engagement Alliance Inc. (AUCEA)
www.aucea.net.au

Eidos Institute
www.eidos.org.au

Social Ventures Australia
www.socialventures.com.au/

New South Wales Community Builders
www.communitybuilders.nsw.gov.au

Bank of I.D.E.A.S.
www.bankofideas.com.au/

E-DEMOCRACY/E-GOVERNANCE: INTERNET SITES

Australian Government Information Management Office
www.agimo.gov.au/

Australian e-Democracy
http://democracy.nationalforum.com.au/

Multimedia Victoria's E-government Resource Centre
www.egov.vic.gov.au
www.mmv.vic.gov.au

Victorian government site with extensive links to sites relating to e-democracy
www.go.vic.gov.au/Research/ElectronicDemocracy/voting.htm

Queensland Government e-democracy site
www.getinvolved.qld.gov.au

Fibreculture, a forum for Australian net culture and research, encouraging critical and speculative interventions in the debates concerning information technology and policy
www.fibreculture.org/publications.html

E-DEMOCRACY DIRECTORIES/LINKS

Politics online—extensive list of e-democracy resources
www.politicsonline.com/content/main/resources/

E-Democracy resources
www.publicus.net/articles/edemresources.doc

VoxPolitics
www.voxpolitics.com/

GLOSSARY

A common language is prerequisite to shared policy understanding. This glossary is offered to facilitate that common language.

act
law made by parliament; that is, a bill passed by parliament and given assent
See also: legislation
Compare: bill; regulation

administrator
head of state for the Northern Territory
See also: head of state
Compare: governor; governor-general

agency; government agency
a department or other entity, usually formed under an act, that discharges government functions
Compare: department of state

amendment
an alteration to a bill or act

appropriations; annual appropriation
1. acts that appropriate money for the government to spend on its activities. 2. parliament's authority to a government to spend monies from consolidated funds or loan funds for specified purposes
See also: budget

assent; royal assent
approval of a bill by the governor-general or governor, making it law. The final stage of parliament's legislative action, making a bill into an act
See also: commencement

aye
word used for voting 'yes' in parliament

backbench
1. members of parliament who are not ministers or shadow ministers, and who hold no other special office (e.g. speaker or president). 2. the seats at the back of a

legislative chamber, occupied by those members
See also: member

ballot-paper
a piece of paper listing the names of those putting themselves forward for election, on which voters mark the person, or people in order of preference, they want elected

bicameral system
a parliamentary system with two houses of parliament. The Commonwealth and all state parliaments, with the exception of Queensland, are bicameral. Literally, two rooms
See also: house of parliament
Compare: unicameral system

bill
proposed act introduced to parliament, but not yet passed and given assent
See also: assent
Compare: act; subordinate legislation

bipartisan
support or membership of two political parties or factions

budget
government's annual plan of revenue and expenditure. The budget is a major statement of policy intentions, and takes the form of appropriation bills, various budget statements and the treasurer's budget speech (the second reading speech on the appropriation bills)
See also: appropriations

by-election
an election to fill a seat left vacant because a member has resigned or died, or is otherwise ineligible to sit as a member
Compare: general election

cabinet
1. a group of senior ministers, responsible for a government's major policy decisions. In some states and the territories, all ministers are in the cabinet. 2. a meeting of ministers called as cabinet

cabinet bag
See: cabinet folder

cabinet committee
a group of cabinet ministers formed to discuss a particular policy issue or group of policy issues and make recommendations to the full cabinet

cabinet folder
a collection of cabinet papers, delivered in an envelope and usually kept in a locked briefcase. The folder contains the agenda and submissions for a cabinet meeting

cabinet submission
a document prepared for cabinet's consideration on a policy matter

campaign
1. period before an election in which parliamentary candidates and parties seek to win the support of voters. 2. Contest between rival candidates or parties seeking political office

central agency
a department or office within a department responsible for policy, economic or personnel coordination across government. Central policy agencies are usually those supporting the head of government
Compare: line department

chamber
the room in which a house of parliament meets

chief minister
the leader of a territory's government
Compare: prime minister; premier

[to] christmas tree
An informal term from the United States Congress describing legislation adorned by a large number of unrelated amendments, often providing special benefits to special interest groups

COAG
Council of Australian Governments, comprising the prime minister, premiers and chief ministers
See also: Council for the Australian Federation; ministerial council

coalition
combination of two or more political parties to form a government or an opposition

collective responsibility
doctrine that ministers must publicly support cabinet's decisions, or alternatively resign

commencement
the starting date for an act. Acts commence on assent, unless stated otherwise. The alternative is for the act to commence by a proclamation made by the executive council, usually done to allow other implementation to take place after the act is passed, such as subordinate legislation

Commonwealth
1. the national entity of Australia, called 'the Commonwealth of Australia'. 2. the national level of government within the federation. 3. short name for the Commonwealth of Nations, mostly consisting of member states once British colonies
See also: federation; state

confidence
1. the measure of the lower house of parliament's support for a government. Success of a motion of 'no confidence' or 'want of confidence' normally results in a government resigning, and another government being formed, or an election being called. 2. a measure of the support of a house of parliament in a minister

conscience vote
vote in which members of parliament are not bound by party discipline, commonly used where issues of morality are debated, such as euthanasia or sexual preference

consolidated fund; consolidated revenue fund
the fund created to receive revenue raised by, or granted to, the Commonwealth or a state or territory government and which requires parliamentary authorisation to be expended

constitution
1. the legal foundation of the nation, a state or territory, consisting of constitutional laws and practice. 2. the act of parliament that defines the role and power of the parliament

consultation
a structured process to seek, and respond to, views about a policy issue from relevant interest groups or individuals, or the community generally

coordination
the act of ensuring that politics, policy and administration work together

Council for the Australian Federation
forum of the state premiers and territory chief ministers designed to improve service delivery and coordination of governments
Compare: COAG

cross the floor
to vote in parliament against party policy position

crossbench
seats in the chamber occupied by independents or members of minor parties that form neither government nor opposition
Compare: backbench; frontbench

crown
1. the Queen as head of state, represented by the governor-general for the Commonwealth and the governors for the states. 2. the legal entity of the Commonwealth or the states (as in 'the Crown in the right of the Commonwealth')
See also: executive government

debate
formal discussion of an issue in parliament, conducted in accordance with standing orders

decision
1. a formal resolution of cabinet 2. choices made by government

delegated legislation
See: subordinate legislation

department of state; government department
organisational structure within government, staffed by public servants. Ministers are responsible for one or more departments, although a department may have several ministers, especially large Commonwealth departments

discussion paper
document released by government seeking public comment on a matter, traditionally printed on green paper
See also: green paper
Compare: policy paper; white paper

dissolution of parliament
termination of parliament by issue of writs for a general election. Usually called by the Queen's representative either on the advice of the leader of the government, or when a government loses parliament's confidence

division
a formal vote in parliament in which a detailed record of members' votes is taken

double dissolution
a simultaneous election for both houses of parliament
Compare: general election

electorate
1. the area that a Member of Parliament represents 2. all of the people who live in an area represented by a Member of Parliament. 3. for the Senate, the state or territory for a senator

estimates
expenditure plans for departments or programs
See also: budget

evaluation
a process for examining the worth of a program, by measuring outputs and outcomes, and comparing these with targets

executive council
the body that advises the head of state in the discharge of the government's formal functions. Ministers are members of the executive council
Compare: cabinet

executive government
that part of government concerned with policy choices and the delivery of public services, in contrast to the legislature and the judiciary
See also: separation of powers

federation
1. the creation in 1901 of the Commonwealth of Australia from the colonies that became the states. 2. the federated states and the Commonwealth government
See also: Commonwealth

first reading
the stage in parliamentary proceedings introducing a bill to a house, and ordering the bill be printed. The first reading is immediately followed by the second reading speech (qv)

franchise
the right to vote in an election

frontbench
1. the senior members of the government, being the ministers, and the opposition, the shadow ministers. 2. the seats at the front of a chamber, occupied by those members
Compare: backbench; crossbench

fundamental legislative principles
requirements that ensure legislation has sufficient regard to the rights and liberties of individuals and the institution of parliament, thereby supporting the system of parliamentary democracy based on the rule of law

general election
an election for all members of the lower house
Compare: by-election; double dissolution

governance
1. the distribution of authority to make decisions and the systems of accountability for exercising that authority. 2. processes, systems and controls for the effective management of an organisation. 3. processes, institutions and relationships through which citizens articulate their interests and exercise their rights to government. 4. the obligations of fairness, transparency and accountability imposed on the leaders of a government or corporate entity

government
the party or parties in coalition that have the confidence of the lower house, and from whose number ministers are appointed
Compare: governance; opposition

government department
See: department of state

government legislation
bills prepared under authority of the government and introduced by a minister
Compare: private member's bill

government of the day
1. the executive branch of government. 2. the government holding office at any one time, used as such to describe government as a stable institution, independent from political notions of a party group winning power and becoming the government

governor
the Queen's representative in a state, and the head of state for that jurisdiction
See also: administrator; governor-general; head of state

governor in council
the executive council of a state
See also: governor-general in council

governor-general
the Queen's representative in Australia and head of state for the Commonwealth
See also: administrator; governor; head of state

governor-general in council
the executive council of the Commonwealth

green paper
a discussion paper, so called because it was at Westminster traditionally printed on green paper
See also: discussion paper
Compare: white paper

Hansard
written, largely verbatim records of parliamentary debate
Compare: votes and proceedings

head of government
the prime minister of the Commonwealth, the premier of a state, and the chief minister of a territory
See also: COAG; Council for the Australian Federation
Compare: head of state; senior officials

head of power
authority given in an act for a body other than parliament to make subordinate legislation or make a certain decision. If there is no head of power, the subordinate legislation or decision is unlawful

head of state
the Queen, represented in the Commonwealth by the governor-general, and in the states by governors
See also: administrator; governor; governor-general
Compare: crown; head of government

house of assembly
the lower house of parliament in South Australia and Tasmania
See also: legislative assembly

house of parliament
1. the building in which parliament meets.
2. each house in a bicameral system (e.g. House of Representatives and the Senate for the Commonwealth; Legislative Assembly and Legislative Council for most states) and the one house in a unicameral system (in Australia, the Legislative Assemblies of the Australian Capital Territory, the Northern Territory and Queensland)
See also: parliament

House of Representatives
the lower house of the Commonwealth parliament

implementation
the process of converting a policy decision into action

issues
the subject matter of politics, expressed as key topics of public debate and policy deliberation

leader of government business
the member responsible for the conduct of the government's business through a house of parliament, usually a minister
Compare: whip

leader of the opposition
the leader of the party or group of parties forming the parliamentary opposition

legislation
law made by parliament, or by another person or body under a delegation by parliament
See also: act; head of power; regulation; subordinate legislation

legislative assembly
the lower house in the states. For Queensland and the territories, the only house of parliament
See also: house of assembly
Compare: House of Representatives; Senate

legislative council
the upper house in the states, except Queensland

line department
a department responsible for delivery of specific services to the community on behalf of the executive government
Compare: central agency

Loan Council
a ministerial council comprising the Commonwealth and state and territory treasurers that meets annually to coordinate public sector borrowing levels for the new financial year

lobby
1. the area immediately outside the chamber reserved for use by members, where they meet journalists, policy advisers or 'lobbyists'.
2. attempt to influence opinions or policy decisions of government

lower house
the house of parliament from which the government of the day derives. For the Commonwealth, the House of Representatives, and for the bicameral states, the Legislative Assembly or House of Assembly

machinery of government
the structure of executive government departments, determined by the head of the government in allocating portfolio responsibilities to ministers

mandate
support claimed by a government for its policies from its most recent electoral victory

member; MHR; MHA; MLA; MLC; MP
1. a person elected to a seat in a house of parliament. 2. a member of a lower house: MHR for Member of the House of Representatives; MHA for Member of the House of Assembly (South Australia and Tasmania); MLA for Member of the Legislative Assembly; MLC for Member of the Legislative Council. Many state assemblies use the abbreviation MP for Member of Parliament

minister
a member of the government responsible for administering a portfolio, including the prime minister, premier and chief minister of a jurisdiction. Ministers are members of the executive council. The cabinet is made up of some or all ministers
See also: ministerial responsibility; responsible government

ministerial council
a meeting of Commonwealth, state and territory ministers responsible for a certain policy area. New Zealand and Papua New Guinea's ministers sometimes participate
See also: COAG; Council for the Australian Federation; Loan Council

ministerial responsibility
a doctrine that holds ministers responsible for their government's policies and for the actions of public servants in their departments, including the cabinet documents prepared in the minister's name
See also: responsible government; Westminster system

natural justice
legal rules requiring decision makers to act fairly and in good faith, without bias (pre-judgment or interest in a matter), to provide details of any matters affecting individuals, and to ensure a fair hearing

non-government legislation
See: private member's bill
Compare: government legislation

opposition
the main political party or coalition of parties that is not the government
Compare: government

order in council
a form of subordinate legislation made by the executive council
See also: subordinate legislation

outcome
impacts on, or consequences for, a community of government activity that are sought or expected in a given policy area and that give the rationale for government interventions

output
goods or services provided by government agencies or programs to citizens or clients to achieve outcomes

parliament
1. the legislative arm of government. For the Commonwealth, the Queen, represented by the governor-general, the Senate and the House of Representatives. Generally, the head of state and each house of parliament. 2. the period between general elections (for example the 15th Commonwealth Parliament, from 1937 to 1940)

parliamentary committee
a group of members assigned a task of investigating and reporting to the parliament or a house of parliament on a particular matter

parliamentary counsel
specialists in drafting legislation

peak body
pressure group representing interests of many other groups with related interests
See also: lobby; pressure group

petition
document presented in a required form to a house of parliament by a person or group of people asking for action on a particular subject

plain English
content, language, presentation, structure and style aimed at making material readable and understandable by the target audience. Often contrasted with legalese. Also contrasted with simply poorly written material. Complex ideas may still require complex language, even in plain English

platform
the electoral promises of a political party

policy
a statement of government intent, and its implementation through the use of policy instruments

policy analysis
1. analysis of a policy problem, designed to state the nature of the problem, leading to options for addressing the issue. 2. analysis of government's action, designed to discern the underlying policy choices of that government

policy analyst
See: policy professional

policy instrument
the means by which a policy is put into effect

policy paper
statement of a government's policy intention in a particular area. Also called a 'white paper'

because it is traditionally printed on white bond paper
Compare: *discussion paper; green paper*

policy professional
an adviser with expertise and skills in a substantive policy area. Also called 'policy analyst'. The terms are used only rarely in Australia

portfolio
the responsibilities of a minister, made up of the acts the minister administers, the organisations accountable to the minister and other functions of the minister. Portfolios are assigned by the prime minister, premier or chief minister

PPP
public-private partnership, a risk sharing relationship between government and the private sector for delivery of major infrastructure or services. The types of partnership include BOT (build-own-transfer), BOO (build-own-operate) and BOOT (build-own-operate-transfer) schemes, PFI (private financing of infrastructure) models, and PFPs (privately financed projects)

premier
the leader of a state government
Compare: *prime minister; chief minister*

president
the presiding officer of the Senate
Compare: *speaker*

press gallery
1. journalists accredited to report on parliamentary proceedings 2. special galleries in a house of parliament where accredited journalists sit to observe parliamentary debates, and in which they may make notes, an activity prohibited by the general public in the gallery

pressure group
group that attempts to influence opinions or decisions of government or opposition without themselves seeking election to parliament
See also: *lobby*

prime minister
the leader of the Commonwealth government
Compare: *chief minister; premier*

principal-agent theory
economic theory that analyses the relationship between an agent and the principal on whose behalf the agent acts, a significant purpose being to structure incentives so the agent acts to benefit the principal. In the public sector, used to analyse government as an agent for society or institutions as agent for government

private member's bill
a bill introduced by a member other than a minister
Compare: *government legislation*

prorogation
termination of a parliamentary session by the governor-general or governor without a general election
Compare: *dissolution of parliament*

public policy
1. intentions and deeds of a government.
2. description of principles governing the way decisions are made

public servant
employee of government under a *Public Service Act*, usually in a department of government. Compare employees in statutory authorities, or staff employed under specific acts, such as police officers

question time
an allotted time in each house of parliament when ministers are asked questions by members of parliament about their areas of responsibility

red tape
pejorative term for official forms and procedures, especially those that are complex and time-consuming, that are required to gain approval for something. The expression alludes to the former British custom of tying up official documents with red ribbon

referendum
a vote by all voters on a particular question. In Australia it is nearly always used in relation to proposed laws to change the Constitution

regulation
form of subordinate legislation made by executive council, usually describing detailed administrative or technical matters

representative government
form of government in which franchise holders elect a person to represent their interests in parliament

reserve powers
powers reserved to the head of state, including, for example, power to dismiss a government

responsible government
system of government in which the executive must be supported by parliament, and answerable to the people through an electoral process. Sometimes called the Westminster system, reflecting its origins in the British parliament located in the Palace of Westminster
See also: representative government

retrospective operation
application of laws before the day the law comes into effect, a device usually considered repugnant because people cannot obey a law that did not exist at the relevant time. Sometimes used to implement taxation changes from the date the policy was announced to prevent tax avoidance in the interim

royal assent
See: assent

second reading speech
speech made by the member introducing a bill into parliament, stating the policy of the bill. These speeches are admissible evidence in court of the intention of the law. For government legislation, this speech is made by the relevant minister

Senate
The upper house of the Commonwealth parliament
Compare: House of Representatives

senator
a member of the Senate
Compare: member

senior officials
a regular meeting of heads of central policy agencies from the Commonwealth, states and territories to prepare position papers for COAG

separation of powers
doctrine holding that the legislative, judicial and executive arms of government should be separate and, in particular, that the executive should not seek to direct the work of the judiciary or to misuse for political purposes the discretionary authority of the police service

shadow cabinet
meeting of shadow ministers

shadow minister
member of the opposition responsible for nominated policy area, and said to 'shadow' the relevant minister

Sir Humphrey
a senior public servant who maintains the status quo or stifles reform by using a treasure trove of baffling phrases, paradoxical reasoning and enigmatic explanations. Taken from the popular British comedy *Yes Minister*
See also: red tape

sitting days
days on which a house of parliament meets

speaker
the presiding officer of the lower house of parliament

standing orders
rules about the conduct of debate and business in a house of parliament

state
1. the legal entity of a nation at international law, for example, the Commonwealth of Australia. 2. one of the six states within the federation. 3. the legal entity of a jurisdiction (e.g. Commonwealth of Australia; state of New South Wales; Australian Capital Territory). 4. geographical area of one of the six states. 5. the body politic
See also: Commonwealth; federation; territory

statutory authority
an agency of the government, created under an act
Compare: department of state

subordinate legislation
legislation made under an act, by a person other than parliament. Regulations, made by executive council, are the most common. Also called delegated legislation because it is made under parliament's delegation

supply
budget allocation that allows government to fund its programs, including salaries to public servants
See also: appropriations; budget

territory
Australian Capital Territory and Northern Territory, each of which has self-government under Commonwealth acts. Territories are represented in the Senate, but by fewer senators than for the states
Compare: state

triple bottom line
a framework for measuring and reporting on performance according to economic, social and environmental measures

unicameral system
a parliamentary system with one house of parliament. This system prevails in Queensland and the territories. New Zealand's parliament is also unicameral

uniform legislation
legislation that applies uniformly throughout the federation because each jurisdiction has made or adopted the law. Compare Commonwealth legislation that applies throughout the federation and overrides any incompatible state or territory law

upper house
one of two houses in bicameral systems. The Senate for the Commonwealth; the legislative council for a state
Compare: *lower house*

votes and proceedings
official record of parliamentary business
See also: *Hansard*

Westminster system
See: *responsible government*

whip
the member of a party responsible for keeping the party members informed about parliament's business, especially if a vote is expected. The whip and deputy whip are usually not ministers
Compare: *leader of government business*

white paper
See: *policy paper*
Compare: *discussion paper; green paper*

REFERENCES

The Age 2001. 'Policy Backflips Carry a Cost', *The Age*, 12 March.

Alcorn, G. 1995. 'Marshall Law', *The Age*, 24 May.

Alford, J. and O'Neill, D. 1994. *The Contract State: Public Management and the Kennett Government*, Geelong, Victoria: Deakin University, Centre for Applied Social Research.

Alinsky, S.D. 1989. *Rules for Radicals: A Pragmatic Primer for the Realistic Radical*, New York: Vintage Books.

The Allen Consulting Group 2006. *Stakeholder Engagement and Consultative Arrangements in Government: A Collaborative Study*. Melbourne: The Allen Consulting Group.

Althaus, C. 1997. 'The Application of Agency Theory to Public Sector Management' in G. Davis, B. Sullivan and A. Yeatman (eds), *The New Contractualism*, South Melbourne: MacMillan Education Australia: 137–53.

——forthcoming. *Political Risk Calculation*, Sydney: University of New South Wales Press.

ANAO (Australian National Audit Office) 1998. *Audit Report: New Submarine Project*. Audit Report no. 34, Canberra: Commonwealth of Australia.

——1999. *Audit Report No. 3 1999–2000: Program Evaluation in the Australian Public Service*, Canberra: Australian National Audit Office.

——2001a. *Developing Policy Advice*, Audit Report No. 21, Performance Audit, DETYA, DEWRSB, DFCS.

——2001b. *Some Better Practice Principles for Developing Policy Advice*, Canberra: Commonwealth of Australia.

Anderson, J.E. 2005. *Public Policymaking: An Introduction*, 6th revised edition, Boston: Houghton Mifflin.

Atkinson, M.M. and Nigol, R.A. 1989. 'Selecting Policy Instruments: Neo-institutional and Rational choice Interpretations of Automobile Insurance in Ontario', *Canadian Journal of Political Science*, 22, 1:107–35.

Aucoin, P. 1986. 'Organizational Change in the Canadian Machinery of Government: From Rational Management to Brokerage Politics', *Canadian Journal of Political Science*, 19, 1:3–27.

The Australian 2002. 'All bets off for Costello', *The Australian*, 21 March.

Bachrach, P. and Baratz, M.S. 1963. 'Decisions and Nondecisions: An Analytical Framework', *American Political Science Review*, 57, 3:632–42.

Bagehot, W. 1867. *The English Constitution*, reprinted 1963, Ithaca: Cornell University Press.

Bardach, E. 2000. *A Practical Guide for Policy Analysis*, New York: Chatham House.

Barker, G. 2007. 'The public service', in C. Hamilton and S. Maddison (eds), *Silencing Dissent: How the*

Australian Government is Controlling Public Opinion and Stifling Debate, Crows Nest: Allen & Unwin: 124–47.

Barrett, P. 2003. *Governance and Joined-up Government—Some Issues and Early Successes*, speech to Australasian Council of Auditors—General Conference, Melbourne, 6 February, www.anao.gov.au/WebSite.nsf/Publications/BA41A52A3DD5F25B4A256CC900254178, [20 November 2006].

Bashford, G. 2000. 'The New Interface between Government and the Community in Social Service Delivery, Centrelink: Is It Working as Hoped?', *Canberra Bulletin of Public Administration*, 96 (June 2000):22–33.

Beck, U. 1992. *Risk Society: Towards a New Modernity*, New Delhi: Sage.

Beere, D. 2005. 'Evaluation capacity-building: a tale of value-adding', *Evaluation Journal of Australasia*, 5, 2:41–47.

Benkler, Y. 2006. *The Wealth of Networks: How Social Production Transforms Markets and Freedom*, New Haven: Yale University Press.

Berlin, I. 1996. 'On Political Judgment', *New York Review of Books*, 3 October: 26–30.

Birkland, T.A. 2005. *An Introduction to the Policy Process: Theories, Concepts and Models of Public Policy Making*, Armonk: ME Sharpe.

Bogason, P. and Musso, J.A. 2006. 'The Democratic Prospects of Network Governance', *American Review of Public Administration*, 36, 1:3–18.

Boin, A., 't Hart, P., Stern, E. and Sundelius, B. 2005. *The Politics of Crisis Management: Public Leadership under Pressure*, Cambridge: Cambridge University Press.

Boston, J. 1995. *The State Under Contract*, Wellington: Bridget Williams Books.

——1999. 'Public Sector Management, Electoral Reform and the Future of the Contract State in New Zealand', *Australian Journal of Public Administration*, 57, 4:32–43.

Boston, J., Martin, J., Pallot, J. and Walsh, P. 1996. *Political Management: The New Zealand Model*, Auckland: Oxford University Press.

Botsman, P. and Latham, M. (eds) 2001. *The Enabling State: People before Bureaucracy*, Annandale, NSW: Pluto Press.

Brandreth, G. 2002. 'A Closed Book Opens', *Sunday Telegraph*, 23 June.

Brewer, G. and deLeon, P. 1983. *The Foundations of Policy Analysis*, Homewood, Ill.: Dorsey Press.

Bridgman, P. and Davis, G. 2003. 'What Use is a Policy Cycle? Plenty, if the aim is clear', *Australian Journal of Public Administration*, 62, 3:98–102.

Briggs, L. 2005a. 'Public Service Reform', Senior Executive Service Breakfast Speech, 12 May, Canberra.

——2005b. 'Thinking and Acting Strategically: Building the Strategic Capability of the Australian Public Service', speech for the Australian Strategic Policy Institute, 8 December.

Burch, M. and Wood, B. 1989. *Public Policy in Britain*, Oxford: Blackwell.

Burgess, J. 2003. 'Reviewing the Model Behind the Job Network', *Australian Journal of Labour Economics*, 6, 2:227–40.

Burton, P. 2006. 'Modernising the Policy Process? Making Policy Research More Significant', *Policy Studies*, 27, 3:173–95.

Business Council of Australia 2002. *Towards Prosperity: Submission to the Dawson Review of the Trade Practices Act 1974 and its Administration*, Melbourne: Business Council of Australia, www.bca.com.au/Content.aspx?ContentID=87572, [7 May 2007].

Byrne, J. and Davis, G. 1998. *Participation and the NSW Policy Process*, Sydney: The Cabinet Office, NSW.

Cameron, J. and Grant-Smith, D. 2005. 'Building Citizens: Participatory Planning Practice and a Transformative Politics of Difference', *Urban Policy and Research*, 23, 1:21–36.

Carson, L. and Hartz-Karp, J. 2005. 'Adapting and Combining Deliberative Designs: Juries, Polls, and Forums', in J. Gastil and P. Levine (eds), *The Deliberative Democracy Handbook: Strategies for Effective Civic Engagement in the Twenty-First Century*, San Francisco: Jossey-Bass.

Chalmers, J. and Davis, G. 2001. 'Rediscovering Implementation: Public Sector Contracting and Human Services', *Australian Journal of Public Administration*, 60, 2:74–85.

Cobb, R.W. and Elder, C.D. 1972. *Participation in American Politics: The Dynamics of Agenda-building*, Baltimore: Johns Hopkins University Press.

Codd, M. 1990. 'Cabinet Operations of the Australian Government', in B. Galligan, J.R. Nethercote and C. Walsh (eds), *The Cabinet and Budget Process*, Canberra: Centre for Research on Federal Financial Relations: 1–22.

Colebatch, H.K. 1993. 'Policy-Making and Volatility: What is the Problem?', in A. Hede and S. Prasser (eds), *Policy-Making in Volatile Times*, Sydney: Hale and Iremonger.

——1998. *Policy*, Buckingham: Open University Press.
Colebatch, H.K. (ed.) 2005. *The Work of Policy: An International Survey*, Lanham: Lexington.
——2006. *Beyond the Policy Cycle: The Policy Process in Australia*, Sydney: Allen & Unwin.
Commonwealth Department of Family and Community Services 2005. *Giving Australia: Research on Philanthropy in Australia*, Canberra: Commonwealth of Australia.
Conley-Tyler, M. 2005. 'A fundamental choice: internal or external evaluation?', *Evaluation Journal of Australasia*, 4, 1&2:3–11.
Considine, M. 1994. *Public Policy: A Critical Approach*, Melbourne: Macmillan.
——1998. 'Making Up the Government's Mind: Agenda Setting in a Parliamentary System', *Governance*, 11, 3:297–317.
——2005. *Making Public Policy: Institutions, Actors, Strategies*, Cambridge: Polity.
Constitution Commission of Victoria 2002. *A House for our Future*, Melbourne: Constitution Commission of Victoria.
Cook, T.E. 1998. *Governing With the News: The News Media as a Political Institution*, Chicago: University of Chicago Press.
Corbett, D. 1996. *Australian Public Sector Management*, 2nd edn, Sydney: Allen & Unwin.
——1997. 'Serving the Public: Six Issues to Consider', in G.L. Clark, E. Prior Jonson and W. Caldow (eds), *Accountability and Corruption: Public Sector Ethics*, St Leonards, Allen & Unwin.
Cox, E. 1995. *A Truly Civil Society* (The 1995 Boyer Lectures), Sydney: ABC Books.
Crase, L, Dollery, B. and Wallis, J. 2005. 'Community Consultation in Public Policy: The Case of the Murray-Darling Basin of Australia', *Australian Journal of Political Science*, 40, 2:221–37.
Crossfield, L. and Byrne, A. 1994. *Review of the Evaluation Function in DEET*, Department of Employment, Education and Training, Canberra: AGPS.
Crosweller, A. 2002. 'Movement at the Station', *The Australian*, 20 April.
Cupps, S.D. 1977. 'Emerging Problems of Citizen Participation', *Public Administration Review*, 37, 5:478–87.
Daley, P. 2001. 'A Note of Chaos Heralds New Currency', *The Age*, 25 December.
Damgaard, B. 2006. 'Do Policy Networks Lead to Network Governing?', *Public Administration*, 84, 3:673–91.
Dart, B. 2002. 'Senator Tips a Bucket on the Stars with Politics in Their Eyes', *Sydney Morning Herald*, 8 June.
Davis, G. 1990. 'The Politics of Traffic Lights: Professionals in Public Bureaucracy', *Australian Journal of Public Administration*, 49, 1:63–74.
——1995. *A Government of Routines: Executive Coordination in an Australian State*, Melbourne: Macmillan.
——1996. *Consultation, Public Participation, and the Integration of Multiple Interests into Policy Making*, report prepared for the Organisation for Economic Cooperation and Development, Paris, May.
Davis, G., Wanna, J., Warhurst, J. and Weller, P. 1993. *Public Policy in Australia*, 2nd edn, Sydney: Allen & Unwin.
Davis, G. and Weller, P. 1987. 'Negotiated Policy or Metanonsense? A Response to the Policy Prescriptions of Murray Frazer', *Australian Journal of Public Administration*, 46, 4:380–7.
——1993. *Strategic Management in the Public Sector: Managing the Coastal Zone*, report prepared for the Resources Assessment Commission, Brisbane: Griffith University.
Department of Education, Science and Training 2007. *Survey of Former Teacher Education Students: A Follow-up to the Survey of Final Year Teacher Education Students*, Canberra: Commonwealth of Australia, www.dest.gov.au/sectors/research_sector/publications_resources/profiles/survey_of_former_teacher_education_students.htm, [15 March 2007].
Department of Finance n.d. *Reasons Why Evaluation Should Be Done and Why Finance Should be Involved*, Canberra: Department of Finance.
——1994. *Doing Evaluations: A Practical Guide*, Canberra: Department of Finance.
Department of Finance and Administration 1998. *Annual Report 1997–1998*, Canberra: Department of Finance and Administration.
——1999. *Outputs and Aims*, www.dofa.gov.au/scripts/outcomes_and_ outputs.asp, [7 May 2007].
Department of Premier and Cabinet 1999. *Cabinet Office*, www.dpc.vic.gov.au, [7 May 2007].
Department of Prime Minister and Cabinet 1999. *Portfolio Budget Statement 1999–2000*, Canberra: Department of Prime Minister and Cabinet.
——2001. *Annual Report 2000–01*, Canberra: Commonwealth of Australia, www.dpmc.gov.au/annual_reports/2000-01/report.pdf, [7 May 2007].

———2004. *Cabinet Handbook*, fifth edn, Canberra: AGPS.

———2006a. *The Role of the Department of the Prime Minister and Cabinet*, www.dpmc.gov.au/about_pmc/index.cfm

———2006b. *About PM&C. What we do and how we do it*, Canberra: Commonwealth of Australia, http://www.dpmc.gov.au/about_pmc/docs/about_pmc.pdf, [8 January 2007].

———2006c. *About the GCU*, www.gcu.gov.au/code/about/index.html, [7 May 2007].

Dery, D. 1984. *Problem Definition in Policy Analysis*, Lawrence: University of Kansas Press.

DEST 2002. *Higher Education at the Crossroads*: A Review of Australian Higher Education, www.backingaustraliasfuture.gov.au/publications/crossroads/default.htm, [7 May 2007].

Di Francesco, M. 1999. 'Measuring Performance in Policy Advice Output: Australian Developments', *International Journal of Public Sector Management*, 12, 5:420–31.

Doherty, T. and Horne, T. 2002. *Managing Public Services—Implementing Changes: A Thoughtful Approach to the Practice of Management*, London: Routledge.

Downs, A. 1972. 'Up and Down with Ecology—the "issue–attention cycle"', *The Public Interest*, 28, Summer: 38–50.

EARC 1992. *Report on Codes of Conduct for Public Officials*, Brisbane: Electoral and Administrative Review Commission.

The Economist 2001. 'Despair and Anger', 360, 32–4.

Edward A. Clark Centre for Australian Studies 1999. *Yacker* Newsletter No. 20, University of Texas, Austin, www.utexas.edu/depts/cas/fall99.html, [26 June 2007].

Edwards, M. (with C. Howard and R. Miller) 2001. *Social Policy, Public Policy: From Problem to Practice*, Crows Nest: Allen & Unwin.

Edwards, M. 2002. 'Ministerial advisers and the search for accountability', *Canberra Bulletin of Public Administration*, 105, September:16–19.

Emy, H.V. 1976. *Public Policy: Problems and Paradoxes*, Melbourne: Macmillan.

Emy, H.V. and Hughes, O. 1991. *Australian Politics: Realities in Conflict*, 2nd edn, Melbourne: Macmillan.

Eyestone, R. 1978. *From Social Issues to Public Policy*, New York: Wiley.

Fallon, L.D. and Kriwoken, L.K. 2003. 'Community involvement in tourism infrastructure—the case of the Strahan Visitor Centre, Tasmania', *Tourism Management*, 24:289–308.

Fenna, A. 1998. *Introduction to Australian Public Policy*, Melbourne: Longman.

———2004. *Australian Public Policy*, 2nd edn, Frenchs Forest: Pearson Longman.

Fischer, F. 1995. *Evaluating Public Policy*, Chicago: Nelson-Hall.

———2003. *Reframing Public Policy: Discursive Politics and Deliberative Practices*, Oxford: Oxford University Press.

Fishkin, J.S., Luskin, R.C. and Jowell, R. 2000. 'Deliberative Polling and Public Consultation', *Parliamentary Affairs*, 53, 4:657–66.

Fitzgerald, J. 2006. *You Can't Expect Anything to Change if You Don't Speak Up: Lobbying in Australia*, Dural: Rosenberg Publishing.

Fitzgerald, T. 1989. *Report of a Commission of Inquiry Pursuant to Orders in Council*, Brisbane: Government Printer.

Franklin, N.E. 1992. 'Initiative and Referendum: Participatory Democracy or Rolling Back the State?', in M. Munro-Clark (ed.), *Citizen Participation in Government*, Sydney: Hale and Iremonger: 55–68.

Frantz, J.E. and Sato, H. 2005. 'The Fertile Soil for Policy Learning', *Policy Sciences*, 38: 159–76.

Freebain, J. 1998. 'Where and Why Government Should be Funded—A Perspective from Economics', *Australian Journal of Public Administration*, 57, 4:66–74.

Gallop, G. 2006. 'Strategic Planning: Is it the New Model?', address to the Institute of Public Administration (NSW), Sydney, 13 November.

Garratt, B. 2000. *The Learning Organization: Developing Democracy at Work*, London: HarperCollinsBusiness.

Geva-May, I. (ed.) 2005. *Thinking Like a Policy Analyst: Policy Analysis as a Clinical Profession*, New York: Palgrave Macmillan.

Giddens, A. 1990. *The Consequences of Modernity*, Cambridge: Polity Press.

Goldsmith, S. and Eggers, W.D. 2004. *Governing by Network: The New Shape of the Public Sector*, Washington DC: Brookings Institution Press.

Gore, A. 1993. *Creating a Government That Works Better and Costs Less: The Gore Report on Reinventing Government*, New York: Times Books.

Guba, E.G. and Lincoln, Y.S. 1987. *Effective Evaluation*, San Francisco: Jossey-Bass.
——1989. *Fourth Generation Evaluation*, Newbury Park: Sage.
Gunn, L.A. 1978. 'Why is Implementation so Difficult?', *Management Services in Government*, 33:169–76.
Hajer, M.A. and Wagenaar, H. (eds) 2003. *Deliberative Policy Analysis: Understanding Governance in the Network Society*, Cambridge: Cambridge University Press.
Hasluck, P. 1968. *The Public Servant and Politics*, Robert Garran Memorial Oration, Canberra: Royal Institution of Public Administration Australia.
Hawkes, D. 2006. 'Politicisation from another perspective', *Public Interest* (Newsletter of the Institute of Public Administration Australia—Queensland Division), June:32–3.
Hayes, M.T. 1992. *Incrementalism and Public Policy*, New York: Longman.
Hendriks, C. 2002. 'Institutions of Deliberative Democratic Processes and Interest Groups: Roles, Tensions and Incentives', *Australian Journal of Public Administration*, 61, 1:64–75.
Higgins, T. and Stern, S. 2005. *An Analysis of Survey Data on the New Apprenticeships Scheme*, Canberra: Commonwealth of Australia, www.dest.gov.au/sectors/research_sector/publications_resources/profiles/analysis_survey_data_new_apps.htm [7 May 2007].
Hogwood, B.W. and Gunn, L.A. 1990. *Policy Analysis for the Real World*, Oxford: Oxford University Press.
Holden, A. and O'Faircheallaigh, C. 1995. *Economic and Social Impact of Silica Mining at Cape Flattery*, Aboriginal Politics and Public Sector Management, Research Monograph No. 1, Brisbane: Centre for Australian Public Sector Management, Griffith University, November.
Holland, I. 2002. 'Consultation, Constraints and Norms: The Case of Nuclear Waste', *Australian Journal of Public Administration*, 61, 1:76–86, March.
Hollander, R. 2006. 'National Competition Policy, Regulatory Reform and Australian Federalism', *Australian Journal of Public Administration*, 65, 2: 33–47.
Hood, C. 1983. *The Tools of Government*, London: Macmillan.
Howard, J. 1998. *A Guide on Key Elements of Ministerial Responsibility*, Canberra: Department of Prime Minister and Cabinet.
Howlett, M. 1991. 'Policy Instruments, Policy Styles, and Policy Implementation: National Approaches to Theories of Instrument Choice', *Policy Studies Journal*, 19, 2:1–21.
Howlett, M. and Ramesh, M. 1995. *Studying Public Policy: Policy Cycles and Policy Subsystems*, Don Mills, Ontario: Oxford University Press.
——2003. *Studying Public Policy: Policy Cycles and Policy Subsystems*, 2nd edition, Don Mills, Ontario: Oxford University Press.
Ingraham, P.W. 2005. 'You Talking to Me?', *Accountability and the Modern Public Service*, PS: Political Science & Politics, 38, 1:17–21.
Ingram, H. 1990. 'Implementation: A Review and Suggested Framework', in N.B. Lynn and A. Wildavsky (eds), *Public Administration: The State of the Discipline*, New Jersey: Chatham House.
Irvin, R.A. and Stansbury, J. 2004. 'Citizen Participation in Decision Making: Is it Worth the Effort?', *Public Administration Review*, 64, 1:55–65.
Jones, K. 2006. 'One Step at a Time: Australian Parliamentarians, Professionalism and the Need for Staff', *Parliamentary Affairs*, 59, 4:638–53.
Jones, T. 1997. 'Diary', *London Review of Books*, 5 June: 37.
Jones, B.D. and Baumgartner, F.R. 2005. *The Politics of Attention: How Government Prioritizes Problems*, Chicago: University of Chicago Press.
Kane, J. 2001. *The Politics of Moral Capital*, Cambridge: Cambridge University Press.
Kay, A. 2006. *The Dynamics of Public Policy: Theory and Evidence*, Cheltenham UK: Edward Elgar.
Keating, M. 1996. 'Defining the Policy Advising Function', in J. Uhr and K. Mackay (eds), *Evaluating Policy Advice*, Canberra: Federalism Research Centre and the Department of Finance: 61–7.
——1999. 'The Public Service: Independence, Responsibility and Responsiveness', *Australian Journal of Public Administration*, 58, 1:39–47.
Keating, M. and Weller, P. 2000. 'Cabinet Government: An Institution Under Pressure', in M. Keating, J. Wanna and P. Weller (eds), *Institutions on the Edge? Capacity for Governance*, Sydney: Allen & Unwin.
Kettner, P.M. and Martin, L.L. 1987. *Purchase of Service Contracting: A Sage Human Services Guide*, Newbury Park: Sage.
Kimber, M. and Maddox, G. 2003. 'The Australian Public Service Under the Keating: Government: A Case of Weakened Accountability?', *International Journal of Public Sector Management*, 16, 1:61–74.

Kingdon, J. 2003. *Agendas, Alternatives, and Public Policies*, 2nd edn, New York: Longman.

Kingston, M. 2001. Personal interview, 11 December, Sydney.

Kjaer, A. 2004. *Governance*, Malden MA: Policy Press.

Krumholz, N. and Forster, J. 1990. *Making Equity Planning Work: Leadership in the Public Sector*, Philadelphia: Temple University Press.

Lasswell, H. 1951. 'The Policy Orientation', in D. Lerner and H. Lasswell (eds), *The Policy Sciences*, Stanford: Stanford University Press.

Leeder, S. 2002. 'The "Health Insurance" Furphy That the Public Can't Afford', *Sydney Morning Herald*, 11 March.

Levi-Faur, D. and Vigoda-Gadot, E. 2006. 'New Public Policy, New Policy Transfers: Some Characteristics of a New Order in the Making', *International Journal of Public Administration*, 29 (4–6):247–62.

Levine, P., Fung, A. and Gastil, J. 2005. 'Future Directions for Public Deliberation', in J. Gastil and P. Levine (eds), *The Deliberative Democracy Handbook: Strategies for Effective Civic Engagement in the Twenty-First Century*, San Francisco: Jossey-Bass.

Lindblom, C.E. 1959. 'The Science of "Muddling Through"', *Public Administration Review*, 19, 2:79–88.

——1965. *The Intelligence of Democracy*, New York: Free Press.

——1979. *Politics and Markets*, New York: Basic Books.

——1980. *The Policy-Making Process*, 2nd edn, New Jersey: Prentice Hall.

Linder, S.H. and Peters, B.G. 1989. 'Instruments of Government: Perceptions and Contexts', *Journal of Public Policy*, 9, 1:35–58.

Ling, T. 2002. *Delivering Joined-Up Government in The UK: Dimensions, Issues and Problems*, Public Administration, 80, 4:615–42.

Lipsky, M. 1983. *Street Level Bureaucracy: Dilemmas of the Individual in Public Services*, New York: Russell Sage Foundation.

Lovell, D.W., McAllister, I., Maley, W. and Kukathas, C. 1998. *The Australian Political System*, 2nd edn, South Melbourne: Longman.

Lucy, R. 1993. *The Australian Form of Government: Models in Dispute*, 2nd edn, South Melbourne: Macmillan Education Australia.

Lunde, T.K. 1996. 'Client Consultation and Participation: Consumers and Public Services', in OECD (ed.), *Responsive Government: Service Quality Initiatives*, PUMA Public Management Service, OECD, Paris: 71–83.

Lunn, S. 1999. '... So You Should Be, Says New MP', *The Australian*, 23 September.

Lyons, M. 2001. *Third Sector: The Contribution of Nonprofit and Cooperative Enterprise in Australia*, Crows Nest: Allen & Unwin.

Lyons, M. and Passey, A. 2006. 'Need Public Policy Ignore the Third Sector? Government Policy in Australia and the United Kingdom', *Australian Journal of Public Administration*, 65, 3:90–102.

MAB-MIAC 1992. *The Australian Public Service Reformed: An Evaluation of the Decade of Management Reform*, Taskforce on Management Improvement Prepared for the Commonwealth Government Management Advisory Board with Guidance from the Management Improvement Advisory Committee, Canberra: AGPS.

MAC 2004. *Connecting Government: Whole of Government Responses to Australia's Priority Challenges*, Report of the Management Advisory Committee, Canberra: Commonwealth of Australia.

Machiavelli, N. [1513] 1988. *The Prince* (eds Q. Skinner and R. Price), Cambridge: Cambridge University Press.

MacIntyre, A. 1983. 'The Indispensability of Political Theory', in D. Miller and L. Siedentop (eds), *The Nature of Political Theory*, Oxford: Clarendon Press.

Mackay, K. 1996. *The Institutional Framework for Evaluation in the Australian Government*, paper presented to a World Bank Seminar on Australia's Program and Policy Evaluation Framework, Washington DC, 30 April.

Majone, G. and Wildavsky, A. 1984. 'Implementation as Evolution', in A. Pressman and A. Wildavsky (eds), *Implementation*, 3rd edn, Berkeley: University of California Press.

Malone, N. 2006. 'Interview with Peter Bridgman', *The Public Interest*, Brisbane: Institute of Public Administration Australia (Queensland), September.

March, J. and Olsen, J. 1989. *Rediscovering Institutions: The Organisational Basis of Politics*, New York: Free Press.

Marston, G and Watts, R. 2003. *Tampering with the Evidence: A Critical Appraisal of Evidence-Based Policy-Making*, The Drawing Board: An Australian Review of Public Affairs, 3, 3:146–63.

Matheson, C. 1998. 'Is the Higher Public Service a Profession?', *Australian Journal of Public Administration*, 57, 3:15–27.

—— 2000. 'Policy Formulation in Australian Government: Vertical and Horizontal Axes', *Australian Journal of Public Administration*, 59, 2:44–55.

May, P., Sapotichne, J. and Workman, S. 2006. 'Policy Coherence and Policy Domains', *The Policy Studies Journal*, 34, 3: 381–403.

McAlpine, (Lord) 1993. *The Servant*, London: Faber and Faber.

McClean, S.L, Schultz, D.A. and Steger, M.B. (eds) 2002. *Social Capital: Critical Perspectives on Community and 'Bowling Alone'*, New York: New York University Press.

McKeown, D. and Lundie, R. 2002. *Free Votes in Australian and some Overseas Parliaments*, Parliamentary Library Current Issues Brief no. 1 2002–03, on-line, www.aph.gov.au/library/pubs/cib/2002-03/03cib01.htm [23 January 2007].

—— 2007. Personal communication regarding free vote calculation in the Australian Parliament, 31 January.

McLaughlin, M. 2005. 'Commonwealth goes it alone on waste dump', *The 7.30 Report*, shown 7 November, Australian Broadcasting Corporation.

McNutt, K. 2006. 'Research Note: Do Virtual Policy Networks Matter? Tracing Network Structure Online', *Canadian Journal of Political Science*, 39, 2:391–405.

McPhee, I. 2006. 'Evaluation and Performance Audit: Close cousins—or distant relatives?', speech presented by the Auditor-General, Australian National Audit Office, to the Canberra Evaluation Forum, Canberra, 16 February.

Meseguer, C. 2005. 'Policy Learning, Policy Diffusion, and the Making of a New Order', *The Annals of the American Academy of Political and Social Science*, 598, March:67–82.

Ministerial Committee on Government Information and Advertising. 1995. *Guidelines for Australian Government Information Activities: Principles and Procedures*, Canberra: Commonwealth of Australia.

Miragliotta, N. 2002. 'Poll Driven Government: A Review of Public Administration in 2001', *Australian Journal of Public Administration*, 61, 1:120–7.

Miser, H.J. and Quade, E.S. 1988. 'Toward Quality Control', in H.J. Miser and E.S. Quade (eds), *Handbook of Systems Analysis: Craft Issues and Procedural Choices*, Chichester: Wiley.

Moore, M.H. 1997. *Creating Public Value: Strategic Management in Government*, Cambridge MA: Harvard University Press.

Mulgan, G. 2003. 'Government, Knowledge and the Business of Policy-Making', *Canberra Bulletin of Public Administration*, 108, June:1–5.

Mulgan, R. 1998. 'Politicisation of Senior Appointments in the Australian Public Service', *Australian Journal of Public Administration*, 57, 3:3–14.

—— 2006. 'Government Accountability for Outsourced Services', *Australian Journal of Public Administration*, 65, 2:48–58.

Muller, D. and Headey, B. 1996. 'Agenda-Setters and Policy Influentials: Results from the Victoria Agendas Project', *Australian Journal of Political Science*, 31, 2:135–52.

Munro-Clarke, M. (ed.) 1992. *Citizen Participation in Government*, Sydney: Hale and Iremonger.

Murphy, K. 2002. 'BCA Spells Out Its Regulatory Wishlist', *Australian Financial Review*, 10 July.

Nagel, S.S. 1998. *Public Policy Evaluation: Making Super-Optimum Decisions*, Aldershot: Ashgate.

Nagel, S.S. (ed.) 2000. *Handbook of Global Political Policy*, New York: Marcel Dekker Inc.

National Institute for Governance. 2004. *Public Service Leadership: Emerging Issues*, A Report for the Australian Public Service Commission, Canberra: Australian Public Service Commission.

Norton, A. 1998. 'The welfare state: depreciating Australia's social capital', *Policy*, St Leonards: Centre for Independent Studies.

Nutley, S., Walter, I. and Davies, H.T.O. 2003. 'From Knowing to Doing: A Framework for Understanding the Evidence–into–Practice Agenda', *Evaluation*, 9, 2:125–48.

OECD 1994a. *Country Study on Public Consultation: Canada*, paper prepared for the Meeting on Public Consultation in Regulatory Development, Paris, August.

—— 1994b. *Public Consultation in Regulatory Development: Practices and Experiences in Ten OECD Countries*, paper prepared for the PUMA OECD Meeting on Public Consultation in Regulatory Development, Paris, October.

—— 1996. *Responsive Government: Service Quality Initiatives*, PUMA, Organisation for Economic Co-operation and Development, Paris.

—— 1997. *Managing Government Ethics*, PUMA Public Management Service, Organisation for Economic Co-operation and Development, Paris, February.

O'Faircheallaigh, C. 2002. *A New Approach to Policy Evaluation: Mining and Indigenous People*, Aldershot: Ashgate.

O'Faircheallaigh, C., Wanna, J. and Weller, P. 1999. *Public Sector Management in Australia: New Challenges, New Directions*, 2nd edn, Melbourne: Macmillan.

Office of the Cabinet 1992. *Queensland Cabinet Handbook*, Brisbane: Goprint.

——1993. *Consultation: A Resource Document for the Queensland Public Sector*, Brisbane: Goprint.

——1995. *Queensland Cabinet Handbook*, 2nd edn, Brisbane: Goprint.

——1996. *Queensland Policy Handbook*, Brisbane: Goprint.

Osborne, M. 2004. 'Making the Most of the Best: Formulating a Knowledge Management Strategy for a Government Advisory Body', *Australian Journal of Public Administration*, 63, 3:43–52.

Painter, M. 1981. 'Central Agencies and the Coordination Principle', *Australian Journal of Public Administration*, 40, 4:265–80.

——1987. *Steering the Modern State: Changes in Central Coordination in Three Australian State Governments*, Sydney: University of Sydney Press.

——1992. 'Participation and Power', in M. Munro-Clarke (ed.), *Citizen Participation in Government*, Sydney: Hale and Iremonger: 21–36.

Painter, M. and Pierre, J. (eds) 2005. *Challenges to State Policy Capacity: Global Trends and Comparative Perspectives*, Basingstoke: Palgrave Macmillan.

Pal, L.A. 2006. *Beyond Policy Analysis: Public Issue Management in Turbulent Times*, 3rd edn, Toronto: Thomson Nelson.

Parsons, W. 2002. 'From Muddling Through to Muddling Up: Evidence Based Policy-Making and the Modernisation of British Government', *Public Policy and Administration Journal*, 17, 3:43–60.

Patton, C.V. and Sawicki, D.S. 1993. *Basic Methods of Policy Analysis and Planning*, 2nd edn, Englewood Cliffs: Prentice Hall.

Pawson, R. 2006. *Evidence-based Policy: A Realist Perspective*, London: Sage Publications.

Perri 6, Raab, C. and Bellamy, C. 2005. 'Joined-Up Government and Privacy in the United Kingdom: Managing Tensions between Data Protection and Social Policy Part II', *Public Administration*, 83, 2:393–415.

Perrow, C. 1984. *Normal Accidents: Living with High Risk Technologies*, New York: Basic Books.

Podger, A. 2002. 'Whole of Government Innovations and Challenges', Keynote Address to 'Innovations and Impacts' Seminar, IPAA National Conference, Adelaide, 16 November, www.apsc.gov.au/media/podger161102.htm [7 May 2007].

Pressman, J. and Wildavsky, A. 1973. *Implementation: How Great Expectations in Washington are Dashed in Oakland; or, Why it's Amazing that Federal Programs Work at All*, Berkeley: University of California Press.

Productivity Commission 2003. *Social Capital: Reviewing the Concept and its Policy Implications*, Melbourne: Productivity Commission Research Paper.

Professions Australia 2006. 'About Professions Australia—Definition of a Profession' (adopted at Annual General Meeting, 26 May 1997, www.professions.com.au/defineprofession.html, [23 January 2007].

PSMC 1993. 'Policy Development and Advice', Executive Development Program, Senior Executive Service, Public Sector Management Commission (John Wanna et al. (eds)), kits 1–4, Brisbane: PSMC.

Public Service and Merit Protection Commission 1996. 'About our Values, Mission, Role and Goals', 19 March, www.psmpc.gov.au/about/mission.htm.

Putnam, R.D. 1995. 'Tuning In, Tuning Out: The Strange Disappearance of Social Capital in America', *PS: Political Science and Politics*, 2, 4:664–83.

——2000. *Bowling Alone: The Collapse and Revival of American Community*, New York: Touchstone.

Quade, E.S. 1982. *Analysis for Public Decisions*, 2nd edn, New York: North Holland.

Queensland Electoral and Administrative Review Commission 1992. *Report on the review of codes of conduct for public officials*, Brisbane: Queensland Electoral and Administrative Review Commission.

Queensland Government 2006. *2006 Premier's Awards for Excellence in Public Sector Management*, Brisbane: Queensland Government.

Quiggin, J. 2006. 'From Working Nation to Work Choices', *Parity*, 19, 4:23.

Quinten, C. 2002, 'Count to 12 and See the euro pay', *Sunday Times* (Perth), 24 March.

Radin, B. 2000. *Beyond Machiavelli, Policy Analysis Comes of Age*, Washington DC: Georgetown University Press.

Republican Advisory Committee 1993. *The Options—the Report*, The Report of the Republican Advisory Committee, Canberra: AGPS.

Rhodes, R.A.W. 1997. *Understanding Governance: Policy Networks*, Governance, Reflexivity and Accountability, Buckingham: Open University Press.

Rittel, H.W.J. and Weber, M.W. 1973. 'Dilemmas in a General Theory of Planning', *Policy Sciences*, 4:155–69.

Roberts, N. 2004. 'Public Deliberation in an Age of Direct Citizen Participation', *American Review of Public Administration*, 34, 1:315–53.

Robinson, M. and Metherall, M. 2001. 'Healthy Private Sector Fails to Help Hospitals', *Sydney Morning Herald*, 22 August.

Rose, R. 1993. *Lesson-Drawing in Public Policy: A Guide to Learning across Time and Space*, Chatham, NJ: Chatham House.

Rydin, Y. and Pennington, M. 2000. 'Public Participation and Local Environmental Planning: The Collective Action Problem and the Potential of Social Capital', *Local Environment*, 5, 2:153–69.

Sabatier, P. 1982. 'Regulating Coastal Land Use in California, 1973–75', *Policy Studies Journal*, 11: 88–102.

——1986. 'Top-Down and Bottom-Up Approaches to Implementation Research', *Journal of Public Policy*, 6:21–48.

——1988. 'An Advocacy Coalition Framework of Policy Change and the Role of Policy-Orientated Learning Therein', *Policy Sciences*, 21:129–69.

Sabatier, P.A. (ed.) 1999. *Theories of the Policy Process: Theoretical Lenses on Public Policy*, Boulder: Westview Press.

Sabatier, P.A. and Jenkins-Smith, H.C. (eds) 1993. *Policy Change and Learning*, Boulder: Westview Press.

Saint-Martin, D. 1998. 'Management Consultants, the State, and the Politics of Administrative Reform in Britain and Canada', *Administration and Society*, 30, 5:533–68.

Sanderson, I. 2006. 'Complexity, "Practical Rationality" and Evidence-based Policy Making', *Policy and Politics*, 34, 1:115–32.

Saunders, H.H. 2005. *Politics is about Relationship: A Blueprint for the Citizens' Century*, New York: Palgrave Macmillan.

Scales, B. 1997. 'Performance Monitoring Public Services in Australia', *Australian Journal of Public Administration*, 56, 1:100–109.

Schattschneider, E.E. 1960. *The Semi-Sovereign People*, New York: Holt, Rinehart and Winston.

Schneider, A. and Ingram, H. 1988. 'Systematically Pinching Ideas: A Comparative Approach to Public Policy', *Journal of Public Policy*, 8, 1:61–80.

Schultz, J. 1998. *Reviving the Fourth Estate: Democracy, Accountability and the Media*, Cambridge: Cambridge University Press.

Schwartzenberg, R. 1980. *The Superstar Show of Government*, New York: Barron's.

Sebald, W.G. 1995. *The Rings of Saturn*, London: The Harvill Press.

Seife, C. 2000. *Zero: The Biography of a Dangerous Idea*, London: Souvenir.

Shand, D. and Arnberg, M. 1996. 'Background Paper', in OECD, *Responsive Government*, PUMA Public Management Service, OECD, Paris: 15–38.

Sharkansky, I. 1970. *The Routines of Politics*, New York: Van Nostrand Reinhold.

Shergold, P. 1997. 'Ethics and the Changing Nature of Public Service', *Australian Journal of Public Administration*, 56, 1:119–24.

——2004. '"Lackies, careerists, political stooges"? Personal reflections on the current state of public service leadership', *Australian Journal of Public Administration*, 63, 4:3–13.

——2006. 'Pride in Public Service', speech to the National Press Club, 15 February, Canberra.

Sheridan, W. and Riley, T.B. 2006. *Comparing e-Government vs e-Governance*, Commonwealth Centre for e-Governance Research Paper, Canada, 21 June, available at: www.rileyis.com/publications/research_papers/SheridanRileyCompar/SheridanRileyComparEgov.html, [7 May 2007].

Simeon, R. 1976. 'Studying Public Policy', *Canadian Journal of Public Administration*, 9, 4:540–80.

Simon, H.A. 1973. 'The Structure of Ill-Structured Problems', *Artificial Intelligence*, 4:181–201.

Smith, G. and Wales, C. 2000. 'Citizens' Juries and Deliberative Democracy', *Political Studies*, 48: 51–65.

Smith, R. 2005. 'Budget doesn't come just once a year', *Defence Magazine*, March.

Smyth, P., Reddel, T. and Jones, A. (eds) 2005. *Community and Local Governance in Australia*, Sydney: University of New South Wales Press.

Sørensen, E. and Torfing, J. (eds) 2006. *Theories of Democratic Governance*, Basingstoke: Palgrave Macmillan.

Standing Committee on Legal and Constitutional Affairs (2004). *Inquiry into crime in the community: victims, offenders, and fear of crime*, www.aph.gov.au/house/committee/laca/crimeinthecommunity report.htm, [15 March 2007].

Stockwell, S. 2005. *Political Campaign Strategy: Doing Democracy in the 21st Century*, Melbourne: Australian Scholarly.

Stoker, G. 2006. *Why Politics Matters: Making Democracy Work*, Basingstoke: Palgrave Macmillan.

Stone, D. 1996. *Capturing the Political Imagination: Think Tanks and the Policy Process*, London: Frank Cass.

Sturgess, G. 1996. 'Virtual Government: What Will Remain Inside the Public Sector?', *Australian Journal of Public Administration*, 55, 3:59–73.

Sundakov, A. and Yeabsley, J. 1999. *Risk and the Institutions of Government*, Wellington: Institute of Policy Studies.

Sylvan, L. 2002. 'Opinion—BCA proposals will emasculate regulator', *Australian Financial Review*, 17 July.

't Hart, P. and Wille, A. 2006. 'Ministers and Top Officials in the Dutch Core Executive: Living Together, Growing Apart?', *Public Administration*, 84, 1:121–46.

Taylor, J. 1993. 'Interpreting Disorder Within a Transaction Cost Framework: A Case Study of the Delivery of Early Intervention Services in Three Australian States', doctoral dissertation, Griffith University, Brisbane.

The Telegraph 2002. 'A Closed Book Opens', 28 June, London.

Thomas, J.C. 1990. 'Public Involvement in Public Management: Adapting and Testing a Borrowed Theory', *Public Administration Review*, 50, 4:435–45.

——1993. 'Public Involvement and Governmental Effectiveness: A Decision-making Model for Public Managers', *Administrative Science and Society*, 24, 4:444–69.

Thompson, E. and Tillotsen, G. 1999. 'Caught in the Act: The Smoking Gun View of Ministerial Responsibility', *Australian Journal of Public Administration*, 58, 1:48–57.

Tiernan, A. 2006. 'Working With the Stock We Have: The Evolving Role of Queensland's Implementation Unit', *Journal of Comparative Policy Analysis: Research and Practice*, 8, 4:371–92.

——2007. *Power without Responsibility? Ministerial Staffers in Australian Governments from Whitlam to Howard*, Sydney: University of New South Wales Press.

Tiernan, A. and Wanna, J. 2006. *Competence, Capacity, Capability: Towards Conceptual Clarity in the Discourse of Declining Policy Skills*, paper presented to the International Comparative Policy Analysis Workshop, Australian National University, 28 November, Canberra.

Tilbury, C. 2006. 'Accountability via Performance Measurement: The Case of Child Protection Services', *Australian Journal of Public Administration*, 65, 3:48–61.

Uhr, J. 1998. *Deliberative Democracy in Australia: The Changing Place of Parliament*, Melbourne: Cambridge University Press.

——2005. *Terms of Trust: Arguments over Ethics in Australian Government*, Sydney: University of New South Wales Press.

Uhr, J. and Mackay, K. (eds) 1996. *Evaluating Policy Advice: Learning from Commonwealth Experience*, Canberra: Federalism Research Centre and the Department of Finance.

Vardon, S. 2000. 'We're from the Government and We're Here to Help—Centrelink's Story', *Australian Journal of Public Administration*, 59, 2:3–10.

Victorian Auditor-General 2004. *Report on Public Sector Agencies: Results of Special Reviews and Other Studies*, August, Victoria: Government Printer.

Waller, M. 1996. 'Framework for Policy Evaluation', in J. Uhr and K. Mackay (eds), *Evaluating Policy Advice: Learning from Commonwealth experience*, Canberra: Federalism Research Centre and the Department of Finance: 9–20.

Walter, J. 1992. 'Prime Ministers and their Staff', in P. Weller (ed.), *From Menzies to Keating: The Development of the Australian Prime Ministership*, Carlton: Melbourne University Press: 28–63.

——2006. 'Ministers, Minders and Public Servants: Changing Parameters of Responsibility in Australia', *Australian Journal of Public Administration*, 65, 3:22–27.

Walters, M. 2005. 'Cops and Consultation: Police Accountability Community Teams in New South Wales', *Alternative Law Journal*, 30, 3: 112–15, 148.

Wanna, J. 2006. 'From Afterthought to Afterburner: Australia's Cabinet Implementation Unit', *Journal of Comparative Policy Analysis: Research and Practice*, 8, 4:347–70.

Wanna, J., Davis, G., Weller, P. and Robinson, M. 1994. *Policy Development and Advice: Executive Development Program*, Senior Executive Service, Brisbane: Public Sector Management Commission.

Wanna, J., Kelly, J. and Forster, J. 2000. *Managing Public Expenditure in Australia*, St Leonards: Allen & Unwin.

Wanna, J., O'Faircheallaigh, C. and Weller, P. 1992. *Public Sector Management in Australia*, Melbourne: Macmillan.

Ward, I. 1995. *Politics of the Media*, Melbourne: Macmillan.

Weiksner, G.M. 2005. 'e-thepeople.org: Large-Scale, Ongoing Deliberation', in J. Gastil and P. Levine (eds), *The Deliberative Democracy Handbook: Strategies for Effective Civic Engagement in the Twenty-First Century*, San Francisco: Jossey-Bass.

Weimer, D.L. and Vining, A.R. 1992. *Policy Analysis: Concepts and Practice*, 2nd edn, Englewood Cliffs: Prentice Hall.

——2005. *Policy Analysis: Concepts and Practice*, 4th edn, Upper Saddle River NJ: Pearson Prentice Hall.

Weller, P. 1990. 'Cabinet and the Prime Minister', in J. Summers, D. Woodward and A. Parkin (eds), *Government, Politics and Power in Australia*, 4th edn, Melbourne: Longman Cheshire: 28–42.

——1992. 'Prime Ministers and Cabinet', in P. Weller (ed.), *Menzies to Keating: The Development of the Australian Prime Ministership*, Carlton: Melbourne University Press: 5–27.

Weller, P. (ed.) 1994. *Royal Commissions and the Making of Public Policy*, Melbourne: Macmillan.

Weller, P. 2007. *Cabinet Government in Australia 1901–2006*, Sydney: University of New South Wales Press.

Weller, P. and Grattan, M. 1981. *Can Ministers Cope? Australian Federal Ministers at Work*, Melbourne: Hutchinson.

Wesley, M. 2006. 'Have our Intelligence Agencies been Politicised?', unpublished paper, Griffith Asia Institute/Centre for Governance and Public Policy Research Seminar Series, 17 March, Brisbane.

Wildavsky, A. 1973. 'If Planning is Everything, Maybe it's Nothing', *Policy Sciences*, 4:127–53.

——1987. *Speaking Truth to Power: The Art and Craft of Policy Analysis*, New Brunswick: Transaction Books.

Willcox, I. and Alcorn, G. 1996a. 'Leaders Unite to Oppose Death Law', *The Age*, 28 June.

——1996b. 'PM Signals Challenge to Euthanasia', *The Age*, 26 June.

Wilson, S. 2005. 'Any Attention is Bad Attention? Public Opinion Toward the Howard Government's Industrial Relations Reforms in 2005', *Journal of Australian Political Economy*, 56: 284–98.

Winter, I. (ed.) 2000. *Social Capital and Public Policy in Australia*, Melbourne: Australian Institute of Family Studies.

World Bank 2002. http://web.worldbank.org/WBSITE/EXTERNAL/TOPICS/EXTPUBLICSECTORANGOVERANCE/EXTADMINISTRATIVEANCIVILSERVICEREFORM/0,,contentMDK:20132487~menuPK:191941~pagePK:210058~biPK:210062~theSitePK:286367,00.html, [23 January 2007].

Wyatt, T., Carbines, R. and Robb, L. 2005. 'Managing stakeholder relations in multi-site, multi-layered evaluations', *Evaluation Journal of Australasia*, 5, 1:33–41.

Yeatman, A. 1998. *Activism and the Policy Process*, Sydney: Allen & Unwin.

Young, S. 2004. *The Persuaders: Inside the Hidden Machine of Political Advertising*, North Melbourne: Pluto Press.

Young, S. (ed.) 2007. *Government Communication in Australia*, New York: Cambridge University Press.

INDEX

access (social justice principles) 78
administration 20, 23–6
administrators 195
advisory committee 110
advocacy 86, 89–90
agencies, central 22, 24, 26, 127, 129–38, 141, 143, 147, 192, 205
    personnel 135–6
    and professionals 199
agenda metaphor 44
Alinsky, Saul 55
alternative approach to evaluation 185
annual budget 24–5
appropriateness evaluation 182, 184
architecture of government 23–4, 38, 206–7, 209, 211
assessment studies 112
Atkinson, M.M. & Nigol, R.A. 87, 88
Attorney-General's Department 135
Australian Constitution 107, 155
Australian National Audit Office (ANAO) 65, 180, 221
Australian policy cycle 37–40
Australian policy instruments 88–9
Australian Public Service Commission 135
Australian system of government 12–13
authority to introduce submission 152
authority to prepare submission 152

Bachrach, P. & Baratz, M.S. 54
Be Strong, Be Heard 114–15
bills 5
biodiversity 78
board model 140
budget, annual 24–5
Burch, M. & Wood, B. 34, 37

cabinet 14–16, 156–7
    conventions and procedures 149
    decision 144–58
    executive council 155–6
    recommendations to 154
    recording decisions 154–5
    routines 146–9
    submissions 146, 150–2, 157–8
Cabinet Handbook 25, 28, 135, 137, 146, 147, 149, 150, 151, 153, 157
Cabinet Policy Unit (CPU) 25
CABNET 147
Cameron, J. & Grant-Smith, D. 99
Carson, Lyn & Hartz-Karp, Janette 103
case management 140
central agencies 22, 24, 26, 127, 129–38, 141, 143, 147, 192, 205
central personnel agencies 135–6
Centrelink 139–40, 162
chief executive 210

child protection 138–9
circulation of proposals 109
citizen participation 100, 116–17, 144
citizens' forums 101–2
Cobb, R.W. & Elder, C.D. 48, 50
commercialisation 75
commission of inquiry 107
committee model 140
committee reports 151
Commonwealth Department of Finance and Administration 134, 135, 179, 216
Commonwealth powers 88
Commonwealth–State Consultative Committee 109
communication failures 174
community engagement 102, 113–16, 237–8
competitive neutrality 75
Competitive Service Delivery (CSD) 75
Conley-Tyler, M. 186
connected government 139–40, 229
Constitution, the 14, 79, 88, 107, 112–13, 155–6, 211
consultation 38–9, 97–123
   advantages of 104–5
   continuum 106
   coordination and efficiency 128–30
   defined 106
   diamond 105
   e-consultation 116–19
   instruments 107–13
   key contacts 108–9
   objectives 108
   and participation 122–3
   and policy 38–9, 97–123
   problems of 104–5
   process design 119–22
   role of 97–100
   and social capital 113–16
   types of 106–7
control of policy issues 107, 112–13
conventional approach to evaluation 185
coordination 39, 124–43
   coherence 125–7
   comments 137
   consistency 128
   consultation and efficiency 128–30
   in departments 137–8
   network governance 125
   policy alignment 138–42
   and politics 141–2
   routines 28–31
   systems 143
cost-benefit analysis 72–4, 99
cost-effectiveness analysis 73–4
Council for the Australian Federation 129
Council of Australian Governments (COAG) 129, 152
Creative Democracy—Homelessness 115
critical path method 201–2

debt redemption 75
decision 39–40, 144–58
delegation 107, 111–12
deliberation 103, 119
deliberative democracy 100–3
deliberative polling 103–4
democracy 71, 80, 97, 111
   deliberative 100–3, 115, 198
   liberal 12
Department of Prime Minister and Cabinet (PM&C) 22, 132–4, 151, 152, 154, 157, 175, 214
dialogue 119
Dialogue with the City 102–3
documentation 193
Downs, Anthony 50
due process 34, 70, 104, 125, 188, 192, 193

ecological sustainability 78
economic framework and policy analysis 72–7
e-consultation 116–19
e-democracy 118, 198, 238
Edwards, Meredith xi, 167, 204
effectiveness evaluation 182, 184
efficiency evaluation 182, 184
e-governance 118, 238
e-government 118
election platforms 5
Emy, Hugh 12, 13
environmental framework and policy analysis 72, 78
environmental impact study (EIS) 78, 109, 112
environmental policy 35–6, 78, 111
environmental quality 78
equity (social justice principles) 77
ethic of role 195–6
ethics 70–1, 85, 194–6, 198–9, 211
evaluation 40, 179–90
   alternative approach 185
   conventional approach 185
   defined 180
   findings 189–90

and implementation 181
  measures 183–4
  methods 184–9
  objectives 180
  and the policy cycle 180–2
  types of 182–3
  versus performance audit 182
evidence-based policy 67–71
executive arm of government 13–14
Executive Council Handbook 156
Executive Council Minutes 152
Expenditure Review Committee (ERC) 24–5, 158
external issue drivers 46–7

Federal Executive Council 155–6
focus group research 108
fourth estate *see* media

Gantt chart 201
garbage can approach 35
governance network *see* network governance
government
  action and policy instruments 86, 89, 92–4
  as administration 23–8
  architecture of 23–4, 38, 206–7, 209, 211
  Australian system of 12–13
  executive arm 13–14
  functional map of 20–1
  internet sites 229
  machinery of 206–8
  map of 17, 30
  network governance 30
  as policy 21–3, 26–8
  as politics 21, 26–8
  powers 79, 88
  routines 28–31
  and third sector organisations 18–19
  system of 210–12
Government Communications Unit (GCU) 175

habitat preservation 78
Hasluck, Sir Paul 30
Headey, Bruce 52
Hendriks, C. 102
Hood, C. 87, 88, 89, 94, 96
horizontal alignment 138–9, 143
Howard, John 15, 24, 25, 42, 148, 153, 161, 218
Howlett, M. & Ramesh, M. 87, 166
Hughes, Owen 12, 13

ill-structured problems 52–3
impact evaluations 187
implementation 40, 159–78
  cabinet implementation units 163–4
  checklists 177–8, 220–8
  choices 170–1
  communication failures 174
  conditions for successful 166–7
  conflicting directives 173
  conflicting objectives 172–3
  and evaluation 181
  inadequate administrative resources 173
  inappropriate agency 172
  incentive failures 173
  incomplete specification 169–72
  instruments 167–8, 169
  limited competence 173
  opinion polling 176–7
  and policy design 160
  policy learning and feedback loops 160–3
  political dimensions to 164–5
  strategy design 174–6
  ten conditions for perfect 160
  traps 168–74
inclusion (deliberative democracy) 103
incrementalism 57, 82–3
influence (deliberative democracy) 103
information 106, 107–8
information papers 152
integrated government 139
interest group meetings 109
internal issue drivers 47–8
international public policy resources 234–5
internet research tools 229–38
intractable problems 53–4
issue attention cycle 50
issue drivers 44–8
issue identification skills 55–6
issues, identifying 38, 50–2

Job Network 162–3, 167, 171
'joined-up government' 30, 105, 138, 139
jurisdictional limits 79, 207–8

Keating, Michael 41, 64, 125, 127, 148
Kingdon, J. 45, 51–2
knowledge-management 68, 161

Lasswell, Harold x, 6, 32
law and policy instruments 86, 89, 94–5

lead agency model 140
learning organisation 161, 215
legal framework and policy analysis 72, 79–80
legal internet sites 233–4
legislation submissions 151–2
Legislative Standards Act 1992 79, 81
liberal democracy 12
Lindblom, Charles 82, 83, 168, 178
line agencies 133, 135, 136, 142, 192, 208

Mabo v Queensland 46
management and the policy process 204–6
mandate 164–5, 186
matters without submission 152
media 19
Members of Parliament (Staff) Act 1984 17
memoranda 151
meta-evaluations 182
ministerial advisers 16–17
ministerial staff 209
ministerial statement 5
ministers
    briefing 152–4
    portfolio 208–9
money and policy instruments 86, 89, 91–2
moral capital 89–90
Muller, Denis 52

National Competition Policy (NCP) 75, 88
National Institute for Governance 138, 232
national peak bodies 108
Native Title Act 46
natural resource management 78
network governance
    and coordination 125
    definition 91
    and policy instruments 86, 89, 91
    rise of government by 30
news resources 234
non-decisions 54–5
non-government organisation (NGO) sector 18–19
NSW Waste Minimisation and Management Act 1995
    101–2

one-stop-shop model 140–1
opportunity cost 73–4
Organisation for Economic Cooperation and
    Development (OECD) 98, 106, 110, 112
outlay reduction 75

participation
    citizen 100, 116–17, 144
    and consultation 122–3
    social justice principles 77
partnership and consultation 106, 110–11
performance audit versus evaluation 182
performance indicator 188–9
policy
    advice 84, 216, 224
    advice performance 215–17
    advisers 195
    agenda 43–4, 45, 48–50
    alignment 138–42
    analysis 38, 57–85
    as authoritative choice 6–7
    capacity 217–19
    consultation 38–9, 97–123
    coordination 39, 124–43
    decision 39–40, 144–58
    definition 20
    design 160, 227–8
    development 161
    evidence-based 67–71
    framework 126
    government as 21–3, 26–8
    as hypothesis 7–8
    implementation 40, 159–78
    jurisprudence 80
    making, rational 83
    as objective 8–10
    professionals 46, 48, 72, 84, 86, 202
    routines 28–31
    submissions 151
policy agenda
    characteristics 49
    defined 43, 45
    defining problems 52–3
    identifying issues 50–2
    issue attention cycle 50
    issue drivers 44–8
    issue identification skills 55–6
    issue selection 48–50
    metaphor 44
    non-decisions 54–5
    wicked and intractable problems 53–4
policy analysis 38, 57–85
    agreement 82–3
    economic framework 72–7
    environmental framework 72, 78
    formulating the problem 61–2

Index

identify decision parameters 63–4
incrementalist approach 57, 82–3
legal framework 72, 79–80
objectives and goals 62–3, 83–5
political framework 72, 80–1
purpose of 58–9
and rational policy making 59–60
search for alternatives 64–5
sequence for 60–7
social framework 72, 77–8
solutions 65–7
toolkit 72–81
policy cycle 32–42
   alternatives 34–6
   Australian 37–40
   checklist 224–7
   and evaluation 180–2
   good process and good policy 41–2
   and institutions 40
   models 36–7
   routines 30–1
   timetable 203
policy instruments 38
   and advocacy 86, 89–90
   Australian 88–9
   choosing 95–6
   classifying 87–8
   definition 86
   and government action 86, 89, 92–4
   and law 86, 89, 94–5
   and money 86, 89, 91–2
   and network governance 86, 89, 91
   types 86
policy process 191–219
   accountability framework 211–12
   approach 35
   cabinet processes 212
   constraints 208–12
   law, the 211
   management 192, 204–6, 219
   organisational choices 212–13
   planning projects 200–2
   politicisation, professionalisation and democratisation 197–200
   procedural integrity 193–4
   and professionals 199
   resource constraints 212
   roles and ethics 194–6
   summary 222
   system 210
   timing 202–3
political framework and policy analysis 72, 80–1
political issue drivers 45–6
political players 194
politics and coordination 141–2
portfolio ministers 15
Pressman, J. 160, 172
Prime Minister 15–16, 21
private prisons 73–6
privatisation 76, 107
proactive evaluation 187
problems
   identifying 50–2
   ill-structured 52–3
   intractable 53–4
   and policy analysis 61–2
   structured 52–3
   well-structured 52–3
   wicked 53–4
professionals 199
program
   delivery 170–1
   design 227–8
   evaluation 180
   linkages model 140
public hearings 106, 109, 112
public information campaign 108
public inquiries 108, 111
public policy
   definition 5–6
   email lists 237
   institutions of 12–31
   internet research tools 229–38
   organising for 206–8
   principles for well-organised 213–15
   risk aversion 55
   versus private policy 7
public servants 16, 25
Putnam, Robert 113, 114, 162

'rational comprehensive model' 59–60, 82–3
rationality 59–60
reduced outlays 75
referenda 88, 107, 112–13, 144
reform 80
regulatory impact 75
rights (social justice principles) 77
risk-uncertainty management approach 34
Rittel, H.W.J. & Weber, M.W. 54
routines 28–31

Sabatier, P.A. & Jenkins-Smith, H.C. 33, 35, 167
Schultz, Julianne 47
service 80
Shand, D. & Arnberg, M. 106
Shergold, Peter 17, 133, 165, 176, 192
significant appointments submission 152
Simeon, Richard 34–5
Simon, Herbert 52
social capital and community engagement 113–16
social framework and policy analysis 72, 77–8
social infrastructure 77–8
social justice 77–8, 84, 127
statutory authorities 107, 125
Sturgess, Gary 93
submissions 146, 150–2, 157–8
Sundakov, A. & Yeabsley, J. 55
surveys 106, 107, 176
system of government 210–12
systems approach 34

Taylor, Jeremy 61
third sector organisations 18–19

town hall meetings 109
transcendent 99
transformative 99
treasury 134–5

value-adding approach 34
vertical alignment 138–9, 143
virtual government 93
virtual policy networks (VPNs) 117

Weiss, Carol 67
Weller, Patrick 15, 16, 24, 41, 145, 147, 156, 193
well-structured problems 52–3
white paper 5
whole of government 16, 40, 126, 129, 131, 132, 136, 138, 139, 143, 153, 199, 210
wicked problems 53–4
Wildavsky, Aaron 8, 57, 62, 160, 172